ETHICS
IN A WORLD
OF POWER
The Political Ideas of
FRIEDRICH
MEINECKE

ETHICS
IN A
WORLD OF
POWER

THE POLITICAL IDEAS OF

FRIEDRICH

MEINECKE

BY

RICHARD W. STERLING

PRINCETON, NEW JERSEY

PRINCETON UNIVERSITY PRESS

1958

PREFACE

THE problem with which this book attempts to deal is one which has become ever more poignant for an America that suddenly and not so very long ago found itself at the pinnacle of world power. The responsibilities of great power in a volatile world society have always had both a sobering and an exhilarating effect on thoughtful men. Since the day when the dynamics of international politics have had to be calculated in terms of the terrifying dimensions of nuclear weapons—a period coincidental with the emergence of the United States as the most powerful political force on earth—the sobering sensation is understandable enough. Indeed, there is real danger that the consciousness of heavy responsibility may chill us to the point of inaction for fear of the pitfalls that beset our path whichever way we move the forces at our command. Should such a situation come to pass we would resemble the psychotic individual for whom the choices which human beings must make have become too heavy a burden and whose personality is immobilized and shattered by fear of his own acts in an environment of which he sees only the menacing aspects.

To escape this dangerous effect of great responsibility requires a sense of exhilaration which comes from the knowledge that power brings opportunity as well as danger. In the long era before the atomic age came upon us those men who wielded power creatively and built great political and civilizing edifices were sustained by a feeling of high adventure as they calculated risk against gain. Today one is tempted to say that the admonition appropriate to their situation was the obverse of that suggested above—that the political men of previous ages needed to be warned that power brings danger as well as opportunity. We may tend to feel that their political strivings were characterized by a certain naïveté because their risks were at once less apparent and more manageable than the fearsome perils confronting us today.

Yet before we make these assumptions part of our credo it would be well to recall that throughout history human beings have known what it is to fear the loss of all they hold dear. This fear, and the degree of courage and resourcefulness with which it is met, has been an ever-recurrent theme in poetry and drama as well as in history and biography. Seen in the light of such a recollection, the problems of the atomic age are not fundamentally different from those men faced in the past. That is as true for the specific problem which concerns this book as for any other.

This problem, simply stated, raises the question of how to achieve wisdom in the conduct of foreign policy, with wisdom understood as bringing expediency and justice into a satisfactory relationship. It will be investigated by means of analyzing the ideas of a man whose reputation—insofar as he is known in the English-speaking world—derives from his position as the most distinguished German historian of this century.

Friedrich Meinecke was a political philosopher as well as a master of intellectual history. His studies of history and his experience of the crisis of modern society provided him with a political understanding that penetrated the issues of his time in a way which has direct relevance to the present phase of that crisis, both in its particulars and as a temporal manifestation of the timeless issues of politics. A generation ago, when Meinecke was at the height of his intellectual powers, too many of his fellow countrymen were incapable of apprehending the wisdom in his political counsel. Harassed by pride and insecurity, they stumbled from one disaster into another with infinitely more evil consequences. Eclipsed by the second disaster, Meinecke emerged after twelve years of Nazi barbarism with an intellectual and moral stature enhanced and refined by the fires which destroyed so many of lesser mind and character. In his old age he found a wider hearing as a political thinker from Germans whose greater perceptiveness was purchased at bitter cost.

PREFACE

As we shall see, Meinecke dealt with the problems of history and politics in terms of a basically dualistic philosophy which posited a series of polarities as the most satisfactory method of analyzing human affairs. It was the polarity of power and justice, and most specifically in the realm of international politics, which constituted the greatest challenge to Meinecke's mind and heart. Throughout his long years of creative scholarship he pondered the problem of reconciling the realities of an anarchic world society with the norm of moral conduct in the human community.

The effort which went into the writing of the present book was sustained by the belief that the fruits of Meinecke's contemplation provide insights of lasting value for those who seek to understand the processes of world politics. Beyond insight, there is inspiration to be found in the intellectual and moral development of a thinker who had the courage to deal truthfully with the supreme issues of politics and ethics. Meinecke displayed this courage at a time in the history of his own country when most of his contemporaries were either despairing or callous, and candor was not popular. Despite the disappointments and tragedies which such an environment was bound to produce and despite his own errors and weaknesses, of which he was often poignantly aware, Meinecke never tired of seeking that narrow meeting-ground where power and justice could join to support the good society. The goal itself was sufficient to exalt his spirit, and the progressive revelations of man's political nature and of ever new evidences of heroic achievement amidst failures and tragedies sustained the excitement of his search. It is the hope of the writer that the boldness as well as the humility which characterized Meinecke's examination of the problems of foreign policy will find resonance in this time of America's power and danger.

ACKNOWLEDGMENTS

I SHALL always be profoundly in the debt of Friedrich Meinecke whose political ideas are the subject of this book. His wisdom helped to clarify my thinking regarding many troubling problems that accompany thought and action, particularly in the realm of international politics. The friendship he offered me in the late years of his life is a continuing source of inspiration. I am also deeply grateful to his widow, Frau Antonie Meinecke. Her warmhearted aid in research problems is only one of many reasons for gratitude.

My teachers, Arnold Wolfers and Hajo Holborn, have given over the years the kind of insight and counsel which seems to me indispensable. Frederick Watkins' criticisms of the manuscript in its first form were of great benefit.

I am indebted to members of the Friedrich Meinecke Institute of the Free University of Berlin, in particular to Dr. Georg Kotowski, Dr. Peter Classen, and Miss Barbara Voelker, for making possible easy access to research materials. I am similarly indebted to members of the staff of the Prussian State Archives in Berlin.

The following publishers and persons have kindly permitted me to quote excerpts from copyrighted material:

F. A. Brockhaus Verlag, Wiesbaden, publishers of *Die Deutsche Katastrophe*.

J. G. Cotta'sche Buchhandlung Nachfolger, Stuttgart, publishers of *Das Leben des Generalfeldmarschalls Herman von Boyen* and *Die deutsche Erhebung von 1914*.

K. F. Koehler Verlag, Stuttgart, publishers of *Vom geschichtlichen Sinn und vom Sinn der Geschichte*, *Schaffender Spiegel*, and *Aphorismen und Skizzen zur Geschichte*.

B. G. Teubner Verlagsgesellschaft, Stuttgart, publishers of *Deutschland und der Weltkrieg*.

Frau Antonie Meinecke, as legal heir of Friedrich Meinecke, has generously granted me permission to quote from all of Meinecke's works not cited above.

Yale University, Dartmouth College and the Rockefeller Foundation have been generous with their aid at various times during the period of research and writing, and I should like to record my appreciation here.

I am grateful to Miss R. Miriam Brokaw of Princeton University Press for her thoughtful editorial guidance.

This book could not have been written without the assistance of my wife.

CONTENTS

ETHICS
IN A WORLD
OF POWER
The Political Ideas of
FRIEDRICH
MEINECKE

Friedrich Meinecke in 1949
Photograph by Fritz Eschen, Berlin

CHAPTER I

INTRODUCTION

SINCE it is the purpose of this book to explore the problem of moral conduct in foreign policy through the medium of an individual thinker, it will be appropriate to begin the undertaking with an assessment of his personality and the basic ideas and questions which guided his endeavors.

Friedrich Meinecke devoted his life to a quest for an ethical system which did not do violence to the world of reality as he saw it. This in itself is not so remarkable, since such a quest probably plays a role in the life of every man—at least to the extent that "the hero seeks justification for his behavior in his own mind."[1] What gives Meinecke's quest its remarkable quality is the combination of his personality and the times in which he lived.

His personality joined a profound and tireless intellect with a finely-strung conscience and a poignant sensitivity to the problem of justice. In one sense, it may be said that the attributes of character ought to weigh more heavily than the qualities of intellect in any assessment of his personality. In any case, kindliness, humility, and reverence for life—to use a phrase of Albert Schweitzer's—were constant companions of his intellect. They inspired it, disciplined it, and gave it direction. The directions were not always the right ones, but the mistakes were never ir-

---

[1] Cf. *Die Idee der Staatsraeson in der neueren Geschichte*, Munich and Berlin, 1924, p. 535 (hereafter cited as *Staatsraeson*). This phrase, which appears several times in Meinecke's writings, originates with Leopold von Ranke, the most eminent German historian of the nineteenth century. Meinecke was Ranke's foremost modern interpreter.

The book here referred to has recently been given its first English translation and was published under the title of *Machiavellism* by Yale University Press in the autumn of 1957. This volume contains a general introduction to Meinecke's works by Dr. W. Stark which is regrettably misleading and in many aspects indefensible.

retrievable, precisely because character and intellect joined to achieve the realization that all human points of view are imperfect and subject to revision.

If Meinecke had been so naïve as to suppose that he had arrived at his sense of human fallibility by means of purely intellectual processes, he might have become a spokesman for the ethical relativism which both fascinated and repelled him in the political doctrines of Machiavelli. But Meinecke was not so naïve. Indeed, critics might contend that his appreciation of the limitations of human reason was almost overwhelming. Whatever may be said in this regard, his belief that there are explanations beyond human ken plus his own observation and experience of authentic moral achievement sufficed to make his understanding of the relativity of human values an agent of resilience rather than of cynicism or despair. These were the sources from which he drew courage continuously to renew the quest for moral significance, and they made possible a growing freedom which gave him serenity in the midst of turmoil and which in retrospect can only be called triumphant.[2]

The measure of any triumph is in the nature of the obstacles overcome. Meinecke lived from 1862 to 1954 and so experienced nearly a century of German history.[3] Stress should be placed on the German side of this history, for Meinecke was

[2] The personal element in these reflections is based on the author's acquaintance and friendship with Meinecke during the years 1948-1951 in Berlin, a relationship which continued through the medium of an intermittent correspondence until the time of Meinecke's death in 1954.

[3] Meinecke was born in Salzwedel in the so-called Altmark region of Prussia on October 30, 1862, and died in Berlin on February 6, 1954. It is no exaggeration to assert that the period of his active experiencing of history is only a little shorter than Meinecke's physical ninety-one years. In his memoirs he recalls having written at the age of seven a blood-and-thunder war poem based on the Prussian victory over Austria at Koeniggraetz in 1866. Cf. the first volume of his memoirs, *Erlebtes, 1862-1901*, Leipzig, 1941, p. 33 (hereafter cited as *Erlebtes*). At the other end of his life-span, his mind remained keen until his death, shortly before which he was following with interest, but with no great expectations, the Four Power Conference of foreign ministers at Berlin in the winter of 1954.

intensely German. He was a German nationalist politically and philosophically; the German world of ideas was both the most tangible source of his ethical norms and the central object of his professional attention as an historian. That he was able to combine such parochial concerns with an authentic cosmopolitanism is one of those broader human paradoxes with which Meinecke so often dealt and to which we will give consideration later.

It is sufficient for present purposes to note that Meinecke's Germanness and his never-relinquished conviction that German culture had a unique and indispensable role to play in the larger world inevitably compelled him to live his long life in the German milieu with utmost intensity.[4] His commitment to values which he saw as specifically German made it a painful task when he felt it necessary to criticize pre-1914 Germany. The First World War was a very personal tragedy for Meinecke, both in terms of its outcome and of what it did to corrupt German political life. In the Weimar Republic he was lonely in his highly qualified hopes for democracy in Germany; he deliberately turned his back on his conservative and monarchist sentiments and associations in the conviction that the republic was Germany's best hope against both reaction and Bolshevist revolution. It was a deep disappointment to him that so few of his professional colleagues and of better-educated Germans in general shared this conviction. The disappointment turned to shame when the middle classes embraced National Socialism and so plunged Germany into the degradation of the Third Reich.

His uncompromising hostility to the Nazi regime and his unshaken faith that the better German values would yet prevail gave Meinecke an unmatched moral stature among Germans in the post-Hitler years. In this final period of his life he overcame the obstacles of great age to resume his work as teacher

---

[4] The diary notes from the fall and winter of 1918-1919 which Meinecke published in the second volume of his memoirs provide dramatic documentation of this intensity, as do many of the formal writings which often enough display the passion of his feelings. Cf. *Strassburg—Freiburg—Berlin 1901-1919: Erinnerungen*, Stuttgart, 1949, pp. 264-278 (hereafter cited as *Erinnerungen*).

and to give to a rootless and despondent youth a feeling of tradition and connection with a more remote and better heritage.

The political events which molded so much of Meinecke's character were equally important in giving direction to his intellectual development. The great political experience of his life was the First World War. Prior to this, the awkward displays of Wilhelminian power politics and Europe's uneasy and increasingly hostile reactions kept the problem of Germany's place in the world in the forefront of Meinecke's political thought in the prewar years. Moreover, the political-intellectual tradition of the German historian's craft at the time Meinecke entered it in the 1880's centered around the achievement of German unity and the warlike methods which Bismarck employed in the process. Complementing these concerns with foreign policy were the critical attitudes toward contemporary German life which Meinecke developed in the 1890's which pressed him to reflect on the bonds that hold a political community together. Such reflections, superimposed on his growing professional involvement in nineteenth-century German history, kindled his interest in the nation-state as a particular type of political organization.

As a consequence of these experiences and reflections, the problems of war, foreign policy, sovereignty, and nationalism became an integral part of his thought. Both the traditions of German political thought since 1800 and his own times led him to give first consideration to the nature of politics beyond the confines of the civil society. Insofar as he developed a theory of the state, it inevitably had to encompass the sphere of foreign policy.

Here the German political tradition and Meinecke as one of its representatives diverge significantly from the dominant schools of political theory in Western Europe—and most particularly in England and the United States—which have tended to deal with the proper organization of the state as an isolated unit and hence to throw little light on the interrelationship of internal and external politics. One need think only of Hobbes, who equated the world of states to the state of nature, and of

Hume, who relegated international relations to an eternal sphere of violence beyond the range of the "calm passions" that make harmonious society possible. Bentham, on the other hand, entertained assumptions concerning a natural similarity among all men. From these assumptions he derived the prospect of a world in which all political organizations would resemble one another, finding in political uniformity a prescription for world harmony. This prescription has had a more powerful impact on Anglo-American thinking in international politics than have the gloomier conclusions of Hume and Hobbes. But both approaches, however much their tendencies are at variance, have in common a reluctance to treat the international society politically, that is, to conceive of a set of political relationships which could offer some basis for order in the actual world of a multiplicity of widely divergent autonomous societies.

It is also relevant in this connection to mention the Marxist tradition. Its concentration on the class struggle has consistently prevented it from undertaking a serious analysis of the nature of international society and the dynamic forces therein which make for conflict or cooperation.

In contrast to the political doctrines which have essentially ignored the realm of inter-state relations, the dominant strain in German political thought has seen international issues as the essence of history and politics. This orientation has been due in large part to Germany's own concrete experience during a century and more of effort, first to achieve political unity and then to play the role of a great nation. A powerful case can be made for the proposition that German unification in 1815, 1848, 1870,—and again since 1945—has depended more upon the manipulation of forces beyond the borders of Germany than upon the processes of domestic politics. Certainly in the period from 1870 to 1945 during which Germany functioned as a nation-state, it was abundantly evident that its fate was intimately linked to the larger movements of world politics.

One consequence of the impact which international relations has exerted on German history was to help create a congenial atmosphere for the application of a conceptual tool in political analysis which is traditionally associated with the name of Leopold von Ranke. During the age of Metternichian restoration, early in his long career as the father of modern history, Ranke elaborated a view which anticipated and which was bound up with his whole development toward the idea that true history is world history. He believed that foreign policy has primacy over internal policy, that the state must tailor its domestic institutions to suit the needs of its external relations. Ranke's doctrine of the primacy of foreign policy offered novel and persuasive insights to those who reflected on the German political experience. Meinecke, as Ranke's devoted if increasingly critical disciple, took over this primary tenet and made it one of the basic axioms with which he operated in political and historical analysis.

A second consequence which flowed from German concentration on the international aspect of politics was to require of German political thought long and hard reflection on the use of violence. It is true that modern theories of the state based on Western European and American experience, even though they may pay little attention to the state's external circumstances, do not ignore the problem of force. Inevitably conditioned by their environment, however, their chief emphasis has tended to rest on the elaboration of peaceful techniques of political decision and dispensation of justice in an integrated civil society. Such a society presupposes a very considerable degree of concord and community, and Anglo-American thinkers in particular have very largely tended to build this presupposition into their theories without too searching an examination of its implications. The validity of such a presupposition depends upon a continuing agreement to be abstemious in the use of radical political tactics. Where this agreement persists, there will be a reasonably orderly and harmonious society. But in such surroundings the political theorist will always be subject to the temptation to neglect a thoroughgoing analysis of the more radical aspects of the political process.

In international politics, on the other hand, one must be sadly lacking in perceptivity to fall victim to this temptation. Here the sense of community has been nearly nonexistent for all practical purposes, and the frequent resort to the radical political methods of violence and deception has been all too apparent. The internal politics of integrated states have been well labeled "domestic" if we understand them to be very different from the "untamed" politics in the realm of foreign relations.

In any case, a credible theory of politics which subjects international politics to a careful scrutiny must perforce consider at greater length and in greater depth the role of force, of guile, of arbitrary action, of bad faith. Like all political theory, it must consider these phenomena in terms of both utility and justice. The ubiquity of such tactics suggests that they have been found useful. Even in the age of nuclear weapons and missiles they have not been abandoned. How useful they will be in any particular situation, therefore, is an authentic problem for the political theorist.

Beyond the question of their utility looms the issue of whether or not they may be justly used. The perennial idea of the just war, the recurring vindications of secret diplomacy, the uncertain nature of international alliances and friendships—all warn against an out-of-hand judgment that the radical political methods which have characterized so much of international relations can never be justified. Certainly it would be difficult for those who admire the political genius of Bismarck to render such a judgment. And whatever his criticisms of the Germany Bismarck created, and of Bismarck himself, Meinecke was an eminent Bismarckian.

From what has been said so far, it should be evident that Meinecke's political ideas can claim the particular attention of the student of international relations. What are the conditions of survival in international politics? Do they inevitably demand at least some decisions from the statesman which are in conflict with moral law in any or all of its diverse interpretations? Can the statesman be justified in imposing decisions by force if need be? In short, can one discover a tenable political ethic in the realm of international relations? These were the questions which Meinecke asked. His commitment to "realism"—if not to the corruptions of *Realpolitik*—and the keen sense of justice we noted earlier combined to make his answers important.

These remarks should suffice to define the scope of the present undertaking. It is in no sense a biography of Meinecke. Nor can it do more than sketch the wider range of Meinecke's concerns as background intimately related to the central issues here. These are in essence two: Meinecke's conceptions of the ideal kind of political organization in terms of realizing human values, and the methods which such an organization must employ in order to preserve its identity. These issues were both philosophically and historically interlocked in Meinecke's thinking. In the course of his intellectual development he first addressed himself to the problem of the relation of political and cultural values. Seeking the political form which would establish and maintain the most creative relationship between them and, consequently, between individual and society, he chose the nation-state as the ideal political community. Logic and emotion were joined in the resultant denial that political community on a worldwide basis could be a superior or even satisfactory alternative to the nation-state.

As Meinecke elaborated this position he was continually confronted with the problems and tensions created by the coexistence of disparate nations and states on the one hand and the larger society of mankind on the other. If he opted for the nation-state as the ultimate in political organization, he had to assume a world without political community. This resulted, in turn, in a rising interest in the kinds of political techniques appropriate to the self-preservation of his chosen ideal for political society in an essentially anarchic international environment. These were the techniques of diplomacy and war, and it was Meinecke's concern with them which led him to abandon his concentration on the nation-state as such and to move on to an examination of the more general ethical implications of his political postulates.

Long before 1914 Meinecke responded to the challenge of which Machiavelli was the classic symbol, but it was the experience of the First World War which made firm his decision to come directly to grips with the great issues of politics and morals. The present inquiry into Meinecke's thought will follow this pattern of development. The first chapters will seek to portray Meinecke's efforts toward a definition of the nation-state and to discuss the political and ethical values which led him to the position that a body politic based on nationality is superior to any other form of political organization. Chapters VII and VIII will show how the war of 1914-1918 contributed to a reappraisal of the earlier position, but they should also make clear that the crisis which the war provoked in Meinecke's mind and personality was by no means the sole cause of that reappraisal—it simply accelerated the process by which he was moving from the particularity of his concerns with his German milieu to the level of a general theory of the relationship of politics and ethics. It may be pointed out here that this changing focus of interest was both cause and effect of a change in Meinecke's over-all intellectual orientation and identifications— away from Treitschke and Droysen and the so-called national school of history which they represented and toward the essentially more internationalist position of Ranke and, indeed, of Jakob Burckhardt.[5]

[5] Since Meinecke's relationship to Burckhardt has attracted considerable attention, it may be useful to refer the reader at this point to Meinecke's review of Burckhardt's *Weltgeschichtliche Betrachtungen* in the *Historische Zeitschrift*, vol. 97, 1906, pp. 557ff. A reading of this early appraisal will show that Meinecke placed Burckhardt next to Ranke in the measure of his objectivity and of his freedom from the presuppositions and prejudices of his time. Although Meinecke expressed criticism of the Swiss historian, especially in regard to his attitudes toward politics in general and German political development in particular—he could not accept Burckhardt's dictum that "power is intrinsically evil"—he nonetheless urged German historians to take instruction from Burckhardt. If Meinecke saw weaknesses in Burckhardt's conceptions of history

The final chapters will concentrate on analyzing and evaluating Meinecke's contributions to an enduring set of generalizations about the nature of political ethics. While this will involve, in the first instance, an appraisal of his post-1918 works, it should not be overlooked that these later writings are intimately connected with the earlier works. Essential to the development of *Staatsraeson*, published in 1924, was Meinecke's pioneering study in the history of ideas which appeared in 1908 as *Weltbuergertum und Nationalstaat.*[6] This book, which estab-

and politics, he also saw strengths which he felt were lacking in the dominant German historical tradition. Above all, he eagerly joined forces with Burckhardt in scoffing at the assumption that any one cultural or political concept could be set up as an absolute standard by which others must be compared and judged.

Meinecke's essay on "Ranke und Burckhardt" (Berlin, 1948), one of the final products of his scholarly life, should be seen in the light of these reflections on Burckhardt some forty years earlier. A number of interpreters of the 1948 essay have apparently overlooked the earlier appraisal. As a consequence, they have tended to portray Meinecke as recognizing the significance of Burckhardt only late in life and then as having indicated a preference for the Burckhardt view of history over that of Ranke.

The political conclusions in these interpretations have generally suggested a belated conversion of Meinecke from a nationalistic to a cosmopolitan view of history or even from conservatism to liberalism. The latter deduction is particularly erroneous, though neither is acceptable. As has been suggested already, Ranke himself is better described as an internationalist rather than a nationalist. In any case, the 1948 essay actually finds Ranke and Burckhardt to be indispensable complements to one another, and in this sense does not differ significantly from Meinecke's views in 1906.

Certainly Meinecke paid greater tribute to Burckhardt in 1948 than he did in the era before the two world wars. But his basic concern in the later work was to bring into better balance his views on the two great historians and the political and historical approaches they represented rather than to replace one by the other.

("Ranke and Burckhardt" was published in English in Hans Kohn, *German History: Some New German Views*, Boston, 1954.)

[6] *Weltbuergertum und Nationalstaat: Studien zur Genesis des deutschen Nationalstaats*, Munich and Berlin, 1908 (hereafter cited as *Weltbuergertum*). In *Staatsraeson*, Meinecke explicitly affirmed that the problems with which he there deals "grew out of those treated in *Weltbuergertum und Nationalstaat.*" Cf. *Staatsraeson, op.cit.*, p. 27.

lished Meinecke as one of the great men of intellect in twentieth-century Germany, was in a sense a summation of his prewar political thinking. One must appraise it, however, in conjunction with other less comprehensive works which he produced in the 1890-1914 period in order to apprehend the full sweep and potential of his political ideas and properly to relate the earlier to the later Meinecke.

The many wartime writings, both journalistic and scholarly, have an obvious importance as indicators of Meinecke's reactions to the crisis which so profoundly altered the political and cultural face of Germany and Europe. They also trace the directions in which Meinecke was moving toward the new political and intellectual positions he was to assume in the postwar world. At the same time they help to document the fact that the new emphases and concerns which took on their lasting form after 1918 were more in the nature of outgrowths of the earlier approaches than highly antithetical to them.

Die Idee der Staatsraeson, appearing six years after the armistice of 1918, provides a logical culmination for a study of Meinecke as a political thinker. After its publication he began to turn away from political theory to the still more comprehensive problems of a philosophy of history. These he dealt with in what was perhaps his finest work, *Die Entstehung des Historismus*.[7]

It would not do, however, to risk leaving the impression that Meinecke's political thought ceases to be of interest after the appearance of *Staatsraeson*. On the contrary, it has already been suggested that Meinecke made his supreme political decision and achieved his profoundest political understanding during the Hitler years of enforced political silence. This final development was reflected in *Historismus*, in his postwar interpretation of the rise and significance of Nazism,[8] and in the stream of other

---

[7] Munich and Berlin, 1936 (hereafter cited as *Historismus*).

[8] *Die deutsche Katastrophe*, Wiesbaden, 1946 (hereafter cited as *Katastrophe*). This book was published in English under the title of *The German Catastrophe*, translated by Sidney B. Fay, Cambridge, Mass., 1950.

books and articles which flowed from Meinecke's prolific pen in the twenty-five-year period after the publication of *Staatsraeson*. But *Staatsraeson* remains his major effort at a systematic statement of his political ideas. As we shall see, it foreshadowed the subsequent insights he achieved which were registered in a more comprehensive context and above all in his own personal political behavior. These later years and writings will be considered in a final chapter to the extent that they supplement, alter, and in a sense transfigure the positions taken in *Staatsraeson*.[9]

If enough has been said to suggest the attraction which Meinecke has for the political scientist, it is necessary to keep in mind that Meinecke was first of all an historian. In the final analysis his concern for the whole of history, for the problems of historiography and of a theory of historical knowledge or "historical reason" was probably of greater moment to him than his interest in politics. Undoubtedly this order of preference contributed significantly both to the measure of objectivity Meinecke was able to achieve concerning Germany and to his own personal serenity in the tragic era in which he lived. But after this is said, it still remains true that his search for an acceptable ethic was his paramount objective in life. His own words in his capacity as an historian speak most eloquently here: "a concept of history without a firm ethical foundation becomes a plaything of the waves."[10] And both in history and in the events of his own lifetime he found the greatest challenge to his ethical sense in the realm of politics.

Any examination of an individual's political thought should establish contact not only with that individual but also with the

[9] Hence the later writings will not be drawn upon extensively but only to the degree that they aid in clarifying and completing the treatment of the central problems with which the present study is concerned.

[10] *Vom geschichtlichen Sinn und vom Sinn der Geschichte*, Leipzig, 1939, p. 20 (hereafter cited as *Vom Geschichtlichen Sinn*). This book is a collection of essays written between 1924 and 1938. The present quotation is taken from "Geschichte und Gegenwart," an article first published, significantly enough, in 1933.

culture and times of which he is a part. The intensity of Meinecke's identification with Germany as a political unit and as a unique culture has already been noted. Hence the problems he faced and his approach to them must be seen in terms that are in part, at least, alien to the English-speaking world.

It was not only the physical events fashioning the period of German history through which Meinecke lived that gave his environment its distinctive features. Meinecke was part of a German intellectual tradition reaching far back into history and differentiated from the rest of European culture, particularly during the later years of the Enlightenment. The period between Kant and Hegel was the classic age of German arts and letters. Its characteristic quality derived from its challenge to the assumption that the history and destiny of man could be explained as a process of ever-growing rationality. If Hegel still posited such a process, he had radically changed its content to the point where rationality and irrationality were meshed and fused into a dynamic unity.

The ideas of Herder, Schiller, Goethe, and Wilhelm von Humboldt brought into question not merely the validity of the rationalistic theories of the Enlightenment but also their desirability. Were not the irrational regions of man's being an indispensable source of his personality and creative power? Philosophy and education based on the principle of eliminating irrationality threatened to rob the human being of his essential nature. Moreover, such a principle bore within it the norm of uniformity—there were many irrationalities but only one timeless and universal reason. Was it not precisely the diverse and manifold nature of the world which gave it so much beauty and fascination?

These were the questions which led to the Romanticism of the early nineteenth century. They established an atmosphere peculiarly congenial to the growing number of historians whose stock in trade was first the recording and then the analysis of myriad concrete societies, events, and personages. Like the anthropologists of a later day, they provided vast quantities of evidence of the endless variety of human experience. This evidence could be used to topple one long-established generalization after another about human behavior. Indeed, in the historian's craft which reached its nineteenth-century apogee in Germany and in the person of Ranke there was an evident hostility to the idea that human experience could be reduced to a series of systematic generalizations. Armed with the rich legacy of its classic poets and thinkers and with the continuing achievement of its scholars, German thought did battle with the still dominant rationalism of the West and with the new Western philosophy of positivism.

Among the most vigorous German enemies of positivism was Meinecke's teacher, Johann Gustav Droysen. Of all the influences on Meinecke during his university years in the early 1880's the historian Droysen made the deepest impression. Along with Ranke and Wilhelm Dilthey, Droysen contributed decisively to the directions which Meinecke took in his intellectual development. These men were, in fact, all part of a milieu and a tradition that produced the brilliant constellation of German social scientists and humanists as the twentieth century began—Freud and his school in psychology; Weber and Mannheim in sociology; Troeltsch in religion; Meinecke, Hintze, and Delbrueck in history; Rickert, Simmel, and Jaspers in philosophy. If many of these thinkers now began to embrace the idea of systematized knowledge and to come to terms with positivism, they insisted upon both the recognition and the positive value of the irrational factor in human life. In this sense they remained true to their Romantic forebears.

Treitschke, to whom Meinecke was deeply attracted as a personality more than as a thinker, was Hegel's heir as a symbol of the dominant political concerns in the German intellectual tradition. The nineteenth century began with defeat and disaster for the German body politic. Liberation from the Napoleonic yoke was followed by a long period of weakness and stagnation. Then came the efforts to unite the Germans in one state, culminating in the military and political successes of Bismarck. These facts made Treitschke's sermons on the importance of power tremendously persuasive. Memory of former impotence and pride in the power which succeeded it combined to create an atmosphere in which there was general agreement on the necessity for a strong state.

This salient political characteristic of the milieu in which Meinecke and his contemporaries matured both contradicted and blended with the Romantic tradition. It was in contradiction to Romanticism's stress on diversity and individuality because the state, and particularly one with pronounced military and bureaucratic characteristics, was the agent *par excellence* of uniformity and rational organization. But the Romantics had emphasized the uniqueness of cultures as well as of individual human beings. The contrast between a quasi-authoritarian Germany and the Western European democracies excited admiration as a good in itself among those predisposed to value diversity at any level.

In world politics rules and generalizations of international law did not greatly impress historically-minded intellectuals whose training taught them to seek out the specific interests behind the abstract language of legal relationships. Here the properties of universality, stability, and permanence characterizing the idea of law were challenged by the historical concepts of individuality, dynamics, and change. Germany was emerging into a world of power and empires where other nations with long headstarts now tended to play the role of agents of law and order. A vigorous and aggressive foreign policy backed by a strong and orderly state and a certain cynicism regarding the pretensions of international legalism seemed to meet the requirements of the German situation. Pride in cultural and material achievements suggested that the world would be the richer for a more intensive and extensive acquaintance with the German way of life.

Thus Germany's points of stress with Western Europe were at once political and cultural. Along with his contemporaries, Meinecke was deeply involved in the resulting conflict. His judgments, until the critical phase of the First World War, were on the whole representative of his fellow intellectuals in the aristocratic-bourgeois German world. Only when that world began to disintegrate did he become a deviant. He then traveled a road only a few were willing to take as he probed for the roots of German disaster in Germany's own cultural heritage.

In order to examine the political concepts of his culture Meinecke had to carry out his inquiry in the larger context of European civilization. Despite an emphasis on the qualities of diversity, he had always insisted on the underlying unities which also fashioned that context. Now he was at pains to find means to reconcile the conflicts to which the diversities had powerfully contributed without, however, forsaking his inmost convictions concerning the individuality of culture. Meinecke's endeavor both to define more precisely his own cultural heritage and to relate and reconcile it with the larger environment of Western civilization gives his thought particular significance today for a Germany which can no longer proceed in isolation. And for the non-German student, Meinecke provides a peculiarly sensitive guide into the German world of ideas.

So far only the briefest reference has been made to dates and other external mileposts of Meinecke's career. While the purpose here is not to undertake a biography, it is appropriate that such facts now be sketched in somewhat more detail.

After the early years of childhood, Meinecke moved with his family from the town of his birth to Berlin. The move took place in 1871, so that Meinecke's later years of childhood and of adolescence were spent in the mushrooming capital of Bismarck's newly-united Germany. Family convictions had already molded him into a loyal Prussian. His school and university years succeeded in intensifying his fervor. As Meinecke recalled in an essay written at the outbreak of World War I, "For a great part of the generation growing to adulthood in the 1880's, there was only one possible party: the party of Bismarck."[11] As was fre-

[11] *Die deutsche Erhebung von 1914*, Stuttgart and Berlin, 1914, p. 21 (hereafter cited as *Erhebung 1914*). This book is a collection of essays

quently his wont, Meinecke used this moment of war enthusiasm not to cast a glow over his early partisanship for Bismarck but to remark that he had been far too uncritical of Bismarckian policies. Another later self-characterization is appropriate to record here: "for long years . . . I remained social- and conservative-minded with full faith in the selflessness of the social policies of the Conservative Party."[12]

This unquestioning acceptance of the robust realities of a prosperous, powerful, and conservative Germany did not carry over into Meinecke's feelings for his Prussian background, however. He spent his second university year in Bonn, and this first venture into the Rhineland in 1883 caused him to subject his Prussian traditions to a more critical appraisal. He described his reaction to his experience in Bonn as "the first incident in a process which extended through my whole life. It was not an estrangement but rather a loosening of the bonds of my inner relationship with the whole of my North German-Prussian homeland. I have always been loyal to it, and I honor and love it as my native soil, but I became critical of that which struck me as coarseness and want of cultivation."[13] In many ways the feeling of divided loyalties in respect to Prussia and the values which western Germany represented constitutes a parallel to the dual sense of allegiance to the nation-state and the larger community of mankind which was the central problem of *Weltbuergertum und Nationalstaat.*

Meinecke returned to Berlin to finish his doctorate in history. He presented his dissertation in 1886[14] and after a short period as tutor in a private home he began his fourteen years of service in the Prussian State Archives. Toward the close of this period he published his first book, a two-volume biography of General

---

which Meinecke wrote on the eve of the war and in the first months after its outbreak.

[12] *Erlebtes, op.cit.*, p. 80.

[13] *Ibid.*, pp. 95-96.

[14] *Das Stralendorffsche Gutachten und der Juelicher Erbfolgerstreit,* Berlin-Potsdam, 1886.

Hermann von Boyen, who had achieved eminence in the Prussian Reform movement and who was chiefly responsible for the introduction of universal military service in Prussia.[15] During this same period Meinecke became closely associated with the *Historische Zeitschrift*,[16] the leading German scholarly journal in the field of history. In 1896 he assumed full responsibility as publisher, and he continued in this position for nearly forty years until the Nazi regime forced him to resign in 1935.[17]

The decade during which Meinecke worked on his biography of Boyen was a period in which his political attitudes were very much in flux. Despite his admiration for Bismarck, he was critical of Bismarck's resistance to internal reform and was therefore inclined to defend the new Kaiser's decision to drop Bismarck in 1890. During that eventful year Meinecke first read Wilhelm von Humboldt's essay in which the autonomy of the individual was set over against the state and limits were prescribed beyond which the state ought not to go.[18] Humboldt's ideas made a deep impression, and while Meinecke continued to feel that the powerful state and the free individual could and did live in reasonably harmonious unison in Germany his concern over the "new course" of Kaiser Wilhelm grew. At the same time, the partisan atmosphere which accompanied the founding of the German Empire in 1870-1871 was becoming a historical memory. Meinecke and other young historians felt free to indulge in a more critical appraisal of Prussian-German history.[19]

More and more antagonized by the erratic personality of Wilhelm II, Meinecke gradually developed a strong distaste for the foreign and domestic policies of the new regime. He names 1895 as "the year in which I began to slip into an oppositionist frame of mind."[20] He turned his back on the Conservative Party when it failed to stand by its program of social reforms.

---

[15] *Das Leben des Generalfeldmarschalls Hermann von Boyen* (two volumes), Stuttgart, 1895-1899 (hereafter cited as *Boyen*).

[16] References to sources in the *Historische Zeitschrift* will be identified by the abbreviation *HZ*.

[17] *Erlebtes, op.cit.*, p. 182.

[18] *Ibid.*, p. 173. [19] *Ibid.*, p. 185. [20] *Ibid.*, p. 206.

Since he considered the National Liberals of that time deficient in both ideas and integrity, he was unable to find a political home there. In this situation Friedrich Naumann's social liberalism attracted Meinecke's attention. It was his hope that Naumann would succeed in the formation of a great new party of moderates whose function it would be to bring about a reconciliation between the socialist workers and the bourgeois-aristocratic state.[21] This reconciliation remained Meinecke's supreme objective in all that he undertook in regard to German domestic politics.

Meinecke noted in his memoirs that his intellectual pursuits were also having an impact on his political attitudes. The story that Meinecke had to tell in the second volume of his Boyen biography—the conservative resistance to the reforms which Boyen and the other liberal reformers sought to introduce in Prussian military and political life—aroused his anger. Boyen's liberalism, his concern for enlightened social legislation, and his efforts to humanize the Prussian military system were drawn in sharp contrast to the reactionary policies of an "ossified nobility."[22] Meinecke's long preoccupation with Boyen brought him into intimate contact with the whole era of early nineteenth-century German history and of the Prussian Reform. It was this period of the flowering of German literature and philosophy and of liberal statesmanship in Prussia which was to become Meinecke's "spiritual home."[23] This affinity for the times and ideas of the Prussian reformers and the classic poets provided Meinecke with an intellectual and moral platform from which to appraise and criticize his own times and the impress which Bismarck's regime left on them.

New horizons and perspectives opened before Meinecke when he accepted a call in 1901 to join the faculty of the University of Strassburg. This was the beginning of a thirteen-year stay in what was then southwestern Germany, first in Alsace and then from 1906 to 1914 in Baden at the University of Freiburg. The

[21] *Ibid.*, pp. 206-209, and *Erinnerungen, op.cit.*, p. 123.
[22] *Boyen* II, *op.cit.*, pp. 389, 594 and *passim*.
[23] *Erlebtes, op.cit.*, p. 135.

liberal traditions and French influences in this region contributed further to the process by which Meinecke was divesting himself of Prussian parochialism. At the same time he was carrying on further research in the era of the Prussian Reform. In 1906 he published his study of Stein and his fellow reformers.[24] *Weltbuergertum und Nationalstaat*, which appeared a year later, was also devoted in large part to the men and ideas of the Reform period. Liberal and humanitarian principles—above all, the ideal of personal liberty—thus became an integral part of his thinking.

It would be a mistake, however, to portray Meinecke's political development as a simple process of moving from the camp of the conservatives into that of the liberals. The truth is that throughout his life he remained torn between the outlooks which these two camps represented. His recollections of his mood in the early 1890's were characteristic: "I felt myself to be both revolutionary and conservative."[25] His description of himself and his wartime political intimates as "conservative reformers" is equally characteristic.[26] Meinecke's ambivalence toward the actual political parties of his day was a concrete expression of the abstract problem that was to dominate so much of his thought: the liberty of the individual versus the necessities of state.

Meinecke was called to the University of Berlin in 1914 to occupy the chair of modern history held by Ranke and Treitschke before him. Here he taught until 1932, when he retired to devote himself to research and writing. After the Second World War he responded to the call of his profession by once again offering seminars to limited numbers of students. When the Soviet authorities began to transform the University of Berlin into little more than a training institute for communist functionaries, Meinecke resigned in protest and accepted the post of first rector of the Free University of Berlin, which was founded

[24] *Das Zeitalter der deutschen Erhebung*, Bielefeld, 1906 (hereafter cited as *Erhebung*).

[25] *Erlebtes, op.cit.*, p. 173.

[26] *Erinnerungen, op.cit.*, p. 283.

in 1948. Located in the American-occupied sector of the city, this university has helped to rebuild the traditions of free learning which disappeared from the old university first under the Nazis and then under the communist regime.

Thus Meinecke spent the final forty years of his life in Berlin.[27] The first four were the terrible years of World War I, and Meinecke's presence in the German capital both deepened his involvement in the mighty issues at stake and brought him the opportunity of still closer contact with German political life. In addition to his activities as patriotic publicist and articulate supporter of moderation in war aims and of reform in domestic politics, he began to be called on as consultant to important figures in the German government, including Bethmann-Hollweg and Kuehlmann.

We have already noted that after the events of 1918 Meinecke gave of his time and talents to the task of establishing and strengthening the Weimar Republic. He joined the German Democratic Party, the most liberal of the bourgeois, nondenominational parties, and he identified himself with that bloc of Democrats, Catholics, and Socialists which comprised the so-called Weimar coalition. But in view of earlier remarks it is worthy of mention that Meinecke would have been ready to consider joining a conservative party which stood with and not against the Republic. He made it clear that one of the continuing attractions which conservative thought held for him was its tradition of a sense of responsibility for the state, and particularly for the power of the state in the realm of foreign affairs.[28]

---

[27] With the exception of a fifteen months' period beginning with the spring of 1945, when the danger from bombings and imminent Russian capture of Berlin persuaded him to seek refuge with his family in the Bavarian countryside. He returned to occupied Berlin in July 1946.

[28] "Republik, Buergertum und Jugend," pp. 8, 19-20, in *Die Paulskirche*, 1925. He noted, however, that the contemporary German conservatives, precisely because of their bitter hostility to the Weimar Republic, had forsaken this tradition and were in fact undermining the integrity of the state both in internal and external politics. Hence he remained loyal to the German Democratic Party and to its successor in the early 1930's, the *Deutsche Staatspartei*.

Philosophical as well as political considerations led Meinecke to place heavy emphasis on the necessities and prerogatives of state. This will become apparent as we now turn to a preliminary examination of the basic ideas which he brought to or developed as a result of his work in history and politics.

It was a fundamental proposition in Meinecke's thought that both history and political theory must avoid abstractions and focus on concrete individuals and institutions in order to gain insight into the meaning of human affairs. This is one of the most important reasons why he found the empiricism of Machiavelli congenial. Machiavelli, he contended, was the first of the moderns to articulate a great political doctrine which sought to describe and defend not the best state but the state "as it really was."[29] Machiavelli's formulation applied alike to politics and historical research, for success in both fields demanded that the practitioner's conclusions be governed by empiric evidence and not by abstract ideas about the nature of man and his cosmos.

The phrase "as it really was" establishes a connection not only between Machiavelli and Meinecke but between Machiavelli and Ranke and hence with the whole historical tradition which Meinecke represented. Ranke's *"wie es eigentlich gewesen"* became the great motto for empiricism in history in the same way that Machiavelli's realism became a symbol of empiricism in politics. Ranke's ideal was to present the events and eras of history without adornment and let them speak for themselves. The historian would only distort their significance if he attempted to judge their values in the light of his own era or his own personal preferences. Should he make such a judgment, he was in effect absolutizing his own time and person. Ranke took the opposite course, at least in terms of a consciously formulated principle, when in another famous phrase he announced his desire to approach history by "erasing my own personality."

The aim of Machiavelli and Ranke was to seek out the concrete reality. Machiavelli accomplished this by focussing his at-

[29] *Staatsraeson, op.cit.*, pp. 23-24 and 47-49.

tention on individual states and rulers. Ranke also did this, but he went one step further and utilized the practice itself as the foundation of another theoretical proposition: General truths can be approached through the examination of individualities. But however many universal or typical features a particular individuality may display, they perforce appear in combination with unique qualities. Hence what is true for one individuality is only indirectly true for another. The truth of each individuality is to this extent unique and inimitable, so that generalizing from a myriad of individual truths to a universal truth becomes an overwhelmingly difficult task. This was the background of Ranke's position—which otherwise might be regarded as only a platitude—that it was not possible for men to know the whole truth of their existence, that eternal truths and universal reality were visible only where alloyed with the individual and the temporary.

This is simply another way of saying that men's minds can master only relative and not absolute truths. It was the essence of Meinecke's thinking that one should accept this human situation and make the most of it. One should probe the individual realities because of their intrinsic worth as relative truths and because they represented the only feasible means of establishing contact, even if only imperfect and incomplete, with absolute truths and values.

It was in this spirit that Meinecke asserted in the first of his major works that modern thought "removes the ideal of [an undifferentiated] humanity . . . from its workshop in order that the brilliance of the ideal may not blind the eye to reality. It does not reject the ideal, but it relegates it to other and more rarefied spheres. Modern history conceives its task as one of exactitude, comprehensiveness and objectivity in portraying the actual diversity of individual historical human beings."[80] In the same spirit thirty years later Meinecke began his final great work with the proposition that "The essence of historicism con-

[80] *Weltbuergertum, op.cit.,* pp. 52-53.

sists in replacing a generalizing with an individualizing approach to historical forces in human life."[31] In these words Meinecke made explicit his continuing belief that the more important proposition is not "all men are the same" but "all men are different."

For the historian, this approach meant that he must record reality in its individual and thus limited sense. For the statesman, because he is not only a recorder of experience but also an actor, there was a further implication. He must find his work and his justification in his own concrete state and not in some ideal of a universal polity. Two very practical considerations bolstered Meinecke's position here. The statesman was likely to be ineffectual unless he shared the peculiar qualities of the individual society in which he found himself. A man alien to his people could not hope to elicit from them the kind of responses that are essential to any political achievement. If this was the formula for political success, then any successful statesman would necessarily be limited in his political identifications and any ideals which he might entertain of a universal polity would in practice be more like a world empire than a world republic.

The equation of a universal political community to universal conquest—this was an *idee fixe* in all of Meinecke's political thinking. The theoretical principle behind this conviction was that the diversity of human societies ruled out their incorporation into a single political system except by force. The great practical experience which fortified the conviction was Napoleon. For Meinecke's preoccupation with the early nineteenth century not only provided him with a specific perspective in which to view his own times; it also brought him into intimate historical contact with Napoleon, who then became the symbol of the inevitable corruption of universalist ideals in practice.

Napoleon also had another function in Meinecke's thought; he was the symbol of German weakness. At the time of Ger-

---

[31] *Historismus, op.cit.,* p. 2.

many's greatest achievements in the realms of art and intellect, Napoleon burst into the land of "poets and thinkers" and threatened to destroy the individuality along with the independence of German culture. Political organization and force were the only possible answers. Meinecke's reverence for the men of the Prussian Reform was due to their success in providing the answers, at least to the extent necessary to end the immediate threat of Napoleon. His reverence for Bismarck stemmed from his belief that Bismarck had given Germany an enduring strength with which to repel any repetition of the Napoleonic danger. In many ways Bismarck and Napoleon functioned as antitheses in Meinecke's thought.

If man was bound both as a thinker and an actor to the individual and the concrete, he was *ipso facto* fated to operate in a world of subjectivities; he could not hope to achieve objective reality. As one of these subjectivities, he himself was a prisoner of his consciousness. Ranke felt this when he wanted to suppress his own selfhood. But here Meinecke parted with Ranke and showed his affinity for the philosophy of Wilhelm Dilthey.[32] To Dilthey it was axiomatic that one could not penetrate beyond the subjective limits of consciousness. One could only enlarge their radius by exhaustive study of the self as a prelude to establishing an empathic relationship with external objects. One must not seek to erase his own personality but to refine and use it as an indispensable instrument of comprehension.

Here again was an acceptance of the limitations of subjective

[32] Meinecke recalled that Dilthey's influence on his contemporaries came only late in his life, for only since the 1890's did that "intellectual revolution take place which led away from the prosaic atmosphere of empiricism, utilitarianism and positivism and toward a new metaphysical idealism." Contending that Dilthey combined the best of idealism and positivism, Meinecke named him "the venerated leader of a generation which carried forward the social sciences (*Geisteswissenschaften*) no longer in philological but in philosophical terms. . . ." (Review of Dilthey's *Leben Schleiermachers* and of the correspondence between Dilthey and Graf Yorck von Wartenburg in *HZ* 130, 1924, pp. 458-459.)

human beings and the will to make the most of what such limitations allowed. Meinecke expressed this will in many ways but perhaps never more succinctly than in one of the last of his writings: "The historian . . . must reflect what has gone before not mechanically but creatively. He must fuse subjective and objective in such a way that the historical image he constructs is an honest and faithful reproduction of the past—insofar as it can be grasped—but which is permeated withal by the creative individuality of the scholar."[33] These words spoke not only of Dilthey but also of Thucydides.

But whatever their distinguished ancestry, the words confirmed the existence of a paradox at the center of the historian's method and at the heart of the statesman's code. Born into a world of infinite individuality and fated never to transcend his own subjectivity, how can the historian or the statesman—how can man—find that certainty for judgment and action which he seems to require for his own peace of mind? Will he not inevitably fall prey to a graceless relativism which destroys all sense of a hierarchy of values and in the chaos thus created permits the baser values to drive out the nobler? This was indeed Meinecke's great fear concerning the effects of the historicism of which he was an eminent advocate. Its core concepts of individuality, subjectivity, and the relativity of human values

[33] *Schaffender Spiegel*, Stuttgart, 1948, p. 7. These words were written as an introduction to this book which is a collection of reprints of earlier essays. We find the same thought expressed much earlier: "a method directed only to the discovery of the factual cannot achieve a deeper understanding of political events but can only describe their surface. The political situation in which the participants acted must be reexperienced." The historian thus uses his own capacity for experience as a means to understanding an external event. This capacity may be employed legitimately only when governed by two imperatives; it must not conflict with available sources and it must have credibility—"that is, it must correspond to the otherwise known attitudes and purposes of the actor as well as to the political situation and the forces which compose it—their pressures on the actor and the possibilities and opportunities they offer him." Review of Hugo Preller's *Salisbury und die tuerkische Frage im Jahre 1895*, Stuttgart, 1930, in *HZ* 142, 1930, p. 588. Cf. also *Vom geschichtlichen Sinn, op.cit.*, pp. 24-25.

could all too easily be seized upon by the ruthless to justify conduct uninhibited by any moral or rational restraints. It could also soften up the victims of the ruthless by suggesting that there were no authentic standards to which one could repair in defense of liberty and decency.

This was the "corrosive poison" which historicism harbored and which Meinecke identified as its chief problematic.[34] One might go further and call it the central problem of the main stream of German ideas since Kant made the assumption of a logically insurmountable barrier between subject and object. In any case, it was clearly central to the thought of all those whom Meinecke claimed as intellectual ancestors—Hegel, Goethe, Schiller, Schleiermacher, Humboldt, and Ranke. And it was certainly the great problem of those who were nearer in time to Meinecke or who were his contemporaries.

In a sense all that follows these introductory observations will testify to Meinecke's growing consciousness of the relativistic consequences of the recognition of human subjectivity. In the course of his intellectual and moral development Meinecke attacked the problem by elaborating an ever more explicitly dualistic philosophy of life. One can follow this process by noting his constantly increasing use of antipodal concepts as he moved from the nation-state problem in *Weltbuergertum* to the more abstract issues of politics and morals in *Staatsraeson* and then to the still more abstract questions surrounding the subjective-objective enigma in man and history in *Historismus*. Here it is pertinent to observe that this dualism was in evidence in Meinecke's earliest writings and that it provides an underlying and unbroken continuity in his thinking which even some of his friendly critics are prone to overlook.[85]

[34] *Vom geschichtlichen Sinn, op.cit.*, pp. 13-14.

[85] Cf. Walther Hofer, *Geschichtsauffassung und Weltanschauung*, Munich, 1950, pp. 25-37, and Ludwig Dehio, *Friedrich Meinecke: Der Historiker in der Krise*, Berlin, 1953, pp. 12-13.

For documentation on this point, see Meinecke's two articles in an emphatically dualistic vein which he wrote at the age of twenty-five under the title of "Willensfreiheit und Geschichtswissenschaft" and published

If Meinecke insisted on a dualistic approach to history and politics, it was because he feared that any monistic system is, in the final analysis, forced to do what Hegel did—to equate the real with the ideal. Such an equation did not solve the problem of a relativization of values but only intensified it. At the other extreme, however, the dualism which separated subject and object, real and ideal, was the very root of relativism.

In his long years of thinking about the world of politics Meinecke explored the area between the extremes of monism and dualism. In the light of the reality of power and of the necessity of its use in social life, could the statesman argue that power was the more important reality when he used it in violation of moral norms generally held to be binding? Could he go even further and assert that conduct so sanctioned was in harmony with the objective reality of an ultimate identity of power necessities and moral values toward which mankind was striving? Could he assume a process whereby each subjective individual act was but part of an objective and irresistible dialectic which necessarily expressed itself in antitheses and hence could not be defined as right or wrong but only as "real"? These questions were treated affirmatively in Hegel's monistic "realism"—in this sense one can say that it is misleading to speak of Hegelian "idealism."

In his early years, despite his criticisms of Hegel, Meinecke was attracted as well as repelled by such a monistic system. But during his lifetime the antithetical qualities of political and moral conduct were demonstrated on a scale so awesome that he could not be content with the consolation that justice and freedom are trampled on by power strivings only in order that the divine spirit in mankind might more perfectly express itself in some

---

in the *Vossische Zeitung* (Sunday Supplement), November 27 and December 4, 1887.

Philip Wolfson rightly criticizes attempts at a rigid periodization of Meinecke's thought and stresses a basic continuity. ("Friedrich Meinecke, 1862-1954," *Journal of the History of Ideas*, vol. 17, No. 4, October, 956, pp. 520-521.)

ultimate manifestation. Thus he professed, with increasing emphasis during the first World War and thereafter, the dualistic position that men are forced to serve two masters. In politics this meant that the statesman could not justify his acts in terms of some higher calculus of power realities but that he was fated to be continually torn by the injunction to be powerful and the injunction to be good.[36] Where was he to take his stand in the all too frequent concrete situations where the two injunctions were in conflict? This was the crucial question posed by a system of thought which asserted that political man must be judged by two standards. Was there not just as much room for political license and crime in the confusions produced by such a double standard?

During the whole course of his explorations of monism and dualism Meinecke was unable to come free of the paradox created by human subjectivity. He became ever more convinced that the dualistic approach was a more realistic and safer method to probe the paradox because it intensified men's sensitivity to the antinomies of human life. But in order to obtain guidance for commitment and action Meinecke had to augment his intellectual structure with tenets prescribed by feeling and faith. Since he regarded the intellect as only one of the instruments of human understanding Meinecke felt no embarrassment in calling upon all the resources of his personality when he took his stand.

[36] Meinecke's criticisms of Hegel, which were explicit and implicit from his earliest years of scholarship and which will be discussed in later chapters, should provide ample refutation of interpretations which portray him as a crypto-Hegelian. Dr. Stark falls into this error of interpretation in his introduction to Meinecke's work in *Machiavellism, op.cit.*, pp. xvi, xxi, xlv, and *passim*. Stark's error is compounded by the reviewer of *Machiavellism* in *The Times Literary Supplement*, December 6, 1957, pp. 729-730.

CHAPTER II

THE NATION-STATE:
THE IDEAL POLITICAL COMMUNITY

MEINECKE's quest for a political ethic perforce meant that he was seeking not simply a personal ethical standard but one to which an entire society could adhere. In his search for such a standard, the concept of the individual nature of men and societies moved him to resist philosophies which imposed an abstract ethical doctrine on this multiformity. Instead he attempted to derive an ethic from the study of the nature of the individuality itself in order that it might not violate that nature. Such an ethic, it was clear, would tend to be as unique as the individual for which it set a standard. Meinecke was willing to deal with the consequences of this tendency, but in order to avoid superficial value-judgments and to achieve "the highest possible degree of empiricism, these heterogeneous phenomena must be treated in the first instance as ends in themselves."[1]

It was in the world of relative realities and relative norms that Meinecke felt the answers lay to his questions concerning personal and political ethics. This belief confirmed Meinecke's place in the dominant tradition of nineteenth-century German thought which posited insurmountable barriers between men's intellects and objective reality. In politics this position encouraged an attack on the idea of a universal natural law as the macrocosm and foundation of all societies. Meinecke both carried on and transcended this tradition when he presented the alternative of the nation-state as the true macrocosm. "Man needs community," he wrote, "and . . . of all the great communities in which he can find a place, there is surely none which appeals so directly to the whole man, which reflects so faith-

<hr />

[1] *Weltbuergertum, op.cit.,* p. 53.

fully his natural-spiritual being as does the nation. . . . There is no other community with so authentic a claim to the title of 'man writ large.' "[2]

Meinecke contested the natural-law theory of the state and embraced the nation-state for both theoretical and practical reasons. Thinkers in the natural law tradition tended to assume that all political societies were created by the rational decisions of human beings who desired to create order out of chaos.[3] They were inclined to overlook the reality that factors making for association have always been present, quite apart from a rational desire for order. Geography, propinquity, family ties, common needs of self-preservation and reproduction, common fears—all these are irrational or non-rational forces and serve as illustrations of the role of chance and of the unconscious in the evolution of a society. Thus Meinecke could not accept a natural-law theory which equated social order with rationality and disorder with irrationality. At every step in the political process he saw fortuity and unreason intimately joined to reason, with the result that irrational and nonrational forces were inherent components of every human society.

The presence of factors beyond the compass of rational or conscious will dispels not only the concept of society as a rational organization; the idea of the universal similarity of societies is also undermined. The differing soils, topographies, and climates in which men live are only the most obvious of the variations in man's external environment. The intercourse between spontaneous individuals and physical environments which vary over the earth's surface stands at the beginning of a process of apparently limitless differentiation in the development of societies. The original uniqueness of a particular juxtaposition of human beings and physical environment is overlaid with a constantly expanding series of unique conflicts with and adaptations to the environment. Since climate, soil, and even topography are subject to change, men experience only a certain degree of con-

[2] *Ibid.*, p. 9.
[3] *Erhebung, op.cit.*, p. 41.

stancy in physical environment, and a change in any of the physical factors can bring about a whole new sequence of conflict and adaptation. Man's mobility adds still further potentialities for differentiation. He may change his location and thus respond to a new environment in new ways, with his previous patterns of action now functioning as a substructure. Finally, through the whole dynamic process of environmental relationships run the even more volatile patterns of human relationships. The differing capacities of individual human beings and the contingencies which bring them together reveal the full dimensions of history as an almost inexhaustive process of change, differentiation, and individuality.

In the face of this "abyss of individuality"[4] any attempt to establish a universal theory of the state and universal norms of government on the basis of the natural-law idea seemed to Meinecke to be destined to futility. Moreover, he was acutely aware of the shortcomings of natural-law propositions when applied to the sphere of international relations. If, as natural law contended, all men were the same and their societies all basically similar in rational structure and purpose, it might be expected that they would have developed a more harmonious set of relationships between societies than one constantly torn apart by violence and war. Any argument that increasingly intensive intercourse among peoples automatically makes or will make for more orderly adjustment is refuted by the recurring phenomenon of quarreling neighbors and alliances between widely separated powers. Nor is there any guarantee of cooperation between societies which have developed similar governmental forms. There has seldom been a conflict, for example, in which one set of allies was composed solely of democracies while the opposing side was made up only of tyrannies.

Some or all of these difficulties, Meinecke felt, were responsible for the tendency of the natural-law tradition to shy away from intensive examination of the problem of international re-

---

[4] *Weltbuergertum, op.cit.,* p. 63. Meinecke makes frequent use of this expression throughout his writings.

lations. It usually constructed theories of civil society in a vacuum and removed the issues of international politics to the realm of chance and aberration. The basic reason was that the natural-law thinkers "lacked a full understanding that beneath and above the world of conscious action still stronger historical forces were operating which swept individual human beings into their orbits."[5] Nonrational and irrational as well as rational factors were always at work absorbing individual human beings into particular and differentiated societies. International conflict and cooperation did not depend on mere chance or the degree of familiarity between similar individuals in similar but separate groups. The same physical environment and social contact which produced similarities and cohesion in a particular group of men accentuated and institutionalized the differences as among groups. Inter-group conflict could not be dismissed as an inexplicable aberration from the rule of human sociability but must be seen as contention between individual societies with differentiated needs and purposes.

Indeed, Meinecke accepted the central thesis of the sociability of human nature far more as a problem than as an axiom. He tended to believe that men's social proclivities were not in themselves strong enough to create societies without the aid of historical and environmental forces transcending the individual. Meinecke was closer to Hobbes' pessimistic portrayal of "natural man" than to the more optimistic notions of Locke. Without the super-individual forces binding men together, the persistent impulses toward self-assertion of the individual might render any social organization an impossibility.

Meinecke regarded the nation as the strongest of these super-individual forces because so many of its characteristics coincided with the nonrational as well as the rational factors making for community. "A common domicile, common ancestry (or rather, since there are no racially pure nations in the anthropological sense, common or similar miscegenation), a common language,

5 *Erhebung, op.cit.,* p. 41.

common spiritual life, membership in a confederacy or federation of several similar states—all these can be important and definitive criteria of nationhood."[6] But Meinecke was not rigid in his definition: "this is not to say that every nation must have them all in order to be a nation." He saw only two qualifications as essential: "a natural matrix of blood relationship" as a prerequisite to assimilation and "a community of intellect and spirit which has developed in history, together with a more or less clear awareness of the existence of this community."[7]

Once these assumptions concerning the nation-state were made explicit in Meinecke's *Weltbuergertum und Nationalstaat*, it became clear that this first major exposition of his political thought was intended to celebrate the political triumph of the nation-state in Germany.[8] It followed, then, that men and ideas would be judged in terms of whether they helped or hindered the achievement of this triumph. But at this point an element of ambiguity enters. *Weltbuergertum* spanned nearly a century of German history, including both the era of the Prussian Reform and the beginnings of Bismarck's regime. Both the liberal reformers and the conservative Bismarck sought German unity, but the kind of united Germany each had in mind was very different. In the light of this difference of approach it was a very much more subtle and elusive task than would appear from superficial examination to decide which men and which ideas had contributed most to the German nation-state. This was particularly true in regard to that ideal concept of the nation-state which comprised a "community of intellect and spirit" as well as an association brought about by irrational and non-rational factors.

Here the era of the Prussian Reform as Meinecke's "spiritual home" exercised a powerful influence in his analysis. The men of the Reform were the more ardent seekers of a community of spirit and intellect; nonetheless, Meinecke identified the conservative tradition as the greater contributor, for it gave to Ger-

---

[6] Weltbuergertum, *op.cit.*, p. 1.   [7] *Ibid.*, pp. 1-2.   [8] *Ibid.*, p. 331.

many "the three great liberators of the state . . . Hegel, Ranke and Bismarck."[9] The great reformers—Stein, Humboldt, Gneisenau, Boyen, and the others—had also dreamed of and striven for German unity as well as German liberalism. But Meinecke's final judgment, much as he honored them, was that they lacked the ability to adjust to the trends of history. Their liberal and democratic reforms and ideas sparked the rejuvenation of the Prussian state in its successful efforts to throw off the Napoleonic yoke. They were stopped in their tracks by the pressure of domestic and international realities in the post-Napoleonic era. The reformers had expected too much of human nature. They had assumed a political consciousness among the people which had yet to develop and whose manifestation during the Wars of Liberation was only a first stirring galvanized by the struggle against Napoleon.

Particularly in regard to the problem of German unity did Meinecke find the reformers wanting in a sense of reality. All of them were ardent advocates of a German nation. But Meinecke's judgment that Stein's "national ideal bore more of an ethical than a political coloration"[10] illumines the problematics of the reformers' approach to the issue of political unification. Stein's concentration on the nation as a means to develop a civic morality prevented him from probing more deeply into the political ramifications of his objectives. Thus at the Congress of Vienna Stein concocted proposals for an international guarantee of a national German state, trusting that the ethos of a European community would prevent the guarantor powers from abusing their status.[11] Earlier, when all the reformers had been driven from office and Prussia was allied with Napoleon in his thrust against Moscow, Stein had favored a British-controlled state in Northwest Germany as part of a future British-Austrian-Russian guarantee of German freedom.[12] Independent of such guarantees, Stein worked out still other proposals during the Congress of Vienna for a strong German federation. He was at times willing to see

[9] *Ibid.*, p. 278.   [10] *Erhebung, op.cit.*, p. 230.
[11] *Ibid.*   [12] *Ibid.*, pp. 202-204.

the Prussian state disappear if national unity required it. At other times he assumed the continued existence of Prussia and tried to reconcile the conflicting claims of Austria and Prussia by conceding the formal authority of the imperial crown to Austria while giving Prussia a status which would not in fact be subordinate.[13]

Meinecke saw Stein's schemes as "impossible and utopian efforts to unite what could not be united"[14]—"a politically viable constitution for Germany could not be fabricated with such ideals."[15] All that came of Stein's proposals was the establishment of a federal structure which was totally without power because Prussia had to yield to the desires of Austria and the particularistic medium-sized German states for the loosest kind of confederation.[16] "Only the Prussian sword could end the confusion" of Prussian, Austrian, and German national interests, and for this Prussia felt itself too weak.[17] Thus defining the problem that was to dominate the next half-century of German politics, Meinecke united the issues of 1815 with those of 1848-1870 and cast Bismarck's wars against Austria and France in the perspective of causal necessity.

In 1815 and the years thereafter the objectives of Prussia and Austria as autonomous Great Powers joined with the particularism of the smaller German states to stem the movement toward national unity. But Meinecke stressed his point that these were by no means the sole obstacles to the realization of a German nation. The unity movement itself suffered from a "lack of maturity and realism. There were still too many apolitical or supra-political ideas." Unification projects of the great reformers contained "too much of their personal ideals whose abundance was their strength and whose over-abundance was their weakness."[18]

The superabundance of personal ideals was due in very large part to the prominent role of intellectuals in the Prussian Reform. Hitherto most of the great German philosophers and poets

[13] *Ibid.*, p. 231.   [14] *Ibid.*   [15] *Ibid.*, p. 230.
[16] *Ibid.*, pp. 231-232.   [17] *Ibid.*, p. 231.   [18] *Ibid.*, p. 232.

had been indifferent or even hostile to the state. They were individualists and cosmopolitans whose primary concern was for the individual as a creative being in an all-embracing world of spiritual values unaffected by political considerations. "The actual state . . . the real society—what did these mean to men who recognized only the fate of the world as stronger than their own spirits? The intermediate powers were disregarded. One felt oneself too strong and too exalted . . . to accept the limitations of real life."[19] The thinkers and the writers unwittingly enjoyed the protection of a relatively tolerant Prussia whose neutral position in the decade following 1795 served Germany as a dike against the rampage of revolutionary France.[20] Only when the dike had been broken by Napoleon's military victory over Prussia at Jena did the interdependence of individuals and political institutions become clearer.[21] Then Wilhelm von Humboldt and Fichte led the procession of intellectuals who turned to the defeated Prussian state as the best hope for a rebirth of the individualist and cosmopolitan values which they regarded as the peculiar contribution of the German nation and which they felt were doomed to be crushed under Napoleonic tyranny.

Meinecke made Humboldt's entry into the service of the Prussian state symbolic of the whole movement. It was more than a simple reaction against a foreign invader. Humboldt's objective was to "infuse the idea into reality and to mold life in accordance with this fusion." Humboldt became a statesman because he recognized that "life in the service of the totality offers new and enhanced opportunities for the development and . . . effectiveness of the individual."[22] Under the shadow of Napoleon, the "totality" was no longer humanity at large but the concrete German-Prussian state. One of the intermediate powers which had previously been ignored by the intellectuals now became the center of their cosmos. Nationality, history, geography, and their own humanitarian ideals excluded their participation

[19] *Ibid.*, p. 43. [20] *Ibid.*, pp. 39-40. [21] *Ibid.*, p. 63.
[22] *Ibid.*, p. 103.

in or acceptance of Napoleon's universal monarchy. They were forced to recognize for the first time that even the world of spiritual values is not without political boundaries.

To Meinecke, "the attraction which the Prussian state exercised over the German spirit and the rebuilding of the state by that spirit must be regarded as the first great step by which the ideal descended into reality . . . the first of the great concrete achievements of nineteenth-century Germany."[23] To act in real life one must abandon the concept of the unencumbered individual in an undifferentiated world of the spirit. There must be a recognition that the individual is bound by historical circumstance to a concrete political and social environment which is historically different from other past or contemporary environments. Men cannot escape, Meinecke argued, from the ever-present demand of their milieus for practical action to solve practical problems.

The great practical problem was to rid Germany of Napoleon, and to secure it against a repetition of foreign invasion. The practical answer was a reinvigoration of the Prussian state. And, as we have seen, Meinecke felt that the answer which the reformers and their contemporaries among the intellectuals attempted to provide could not serve as the basis for an enduring political system. Their hopes for German unity were burdened with fantasy, and their plans for domestic reform did not assess political obstacles realistically. Time and circumstance were not in their favor, but neither did they have the political feel which might have given them a greater mastery over the political and social forces with which they had to deal.

[23] *Ibid.*, p. 63. It is noteworthy that Meinecke used the metaphor of "descent" in this judgment. It is one of many evidences throughout *Erhebung* and other early works that Meinecke felt that the displacement of cosmopolitan by state and national concerns involved losses as well as gains. (See Chapter VI below.) As such, it is at variance with Hans Kohn's assertion that in Meinecke's "younger years he praised the German 'ascent' from the cosmopolitanism of a Kant or Goethe to the nation-state of Ranke and Bismarck." Cf. Hans Kohn, *German History: Some New German Views*, Boston, 1954, p. 24.

Now Meinecke's thesis that Hegel, Ranke, and Bismarck were the liberators of the German state begins to take on content. He saw these men as the three great individuals who had done most to come to grips with the rational-irrational nature of the state and the individuality of the concrete society. They beyond all others had identified and acted in concert with the particular historical forces making for political community in Germany. Theirs were the supreme contributions toward a growing consciousness that a self-reliant German nation-state was both necessary and right.

Hegel posited a necessary congruence between nation and state.[24] In so doing he went beyond the nationalists of the Prussian Reform. They, too, wanted to make the nation a political entity. But, as Stein's projects revealed, their nationalism was so abstract that they were willing to sacrifice the most essential considerations of political viability in their quest for the nation. To Meinecke this inability to shape the desirable content into a durable form was the signal weakness of the reformers. Hegel's formula overcame this weakness because it implied a reciprocal relationship between the nation and the state. Congruence meant that the idea of the nation could not ignore the realities of the state any more than the state could ignore the aspirations of the nation.[25]

Political unity of a nation was meaningless unless it was based on the principle of autonomy.[26] Unless the nation could defend its existence in the given environment by means of its own resources and organization it could not call itself political. Stein's international guarantees would not create or defend a nation-state. National sovereignty was the indispensable foundation for political nationhood. Hence the nation was bound to the realities of politics and to all the super-individual forces which shaped the evolution of a society. The political nation was a concrete growth, not an abstraction, and the limits of its growth were identical with the limits to its sovereignty. In effect, Hegel was

[24] *Ibid.*, p. 281.   [25] *Ibid.*, pp. 280-281.   [26] *Ibid.*, pp. 281-282.

saying that if one wants a political organization one must come to terms with politics, and Meinecke felt that this advice was the needed corrective to the national ideas of the reformers.

Hegel's contribution to the German nation-state was not exhausted in pragmatic counsel. His philosophical system was comprehensive enough to encompass the mighty tensions of rational and irrational forces which go into the making of a state and to deduce that every human institution was a compound of " 'passions, interests, [rational] objectives, aptitudes, virtues and vices, force, injustice, and external contingency.' "[27] If morality existed in human institutions, then morality existed in the concrete compound reality and not in a priori abstraction. Here was the political aspect of Hegel's identification of the "real" with the "right." Both the political nation and the moral law were concrete and not abstract. The nation-state must assure its own existence and demonstrate its own morality. Hegel's philosophy thus broke the twin monopolies of political truth and moral dignity to which natural law had traditionally laid claim. For all practical purposes, Hegel transferred these monopolies to the nation-state.

Ranke's use of the historian's empiric methods documented the Hegelian thesis. He examined the empirical natural forces and human relationships which led to the development of differentiated political societies and demonstrated that the history of the great states of Europe and the growth of the national idea could be understood only in terms of the interplay of rational and irrational forces.[28] He took careful soundings to detect the political shoals upon which the will to nationhood could founder. Ranke's observation that the political community was the product of " 'the nature of things and of chance, of genius and of luck' " closely corresponded to Hegel's assertion of the heterogeneous character of human institutions. Like Hegel, too, Ranke saw the state as an autonomous entity embodying an individual expression of the moral spirit.

[27] *Ibid.*, pp. 282-283.   [28] *Ibid.*, p. 298.

Ranke did not follow Hegel in equating the "real" to the "right." He thus avoided the Hegelian conclusion that the total character of the actual state could be justified as the worldly expression of the moral spirit. Ranke pictured the state as the majestic earthly arena in which men's "moral energy" was confronted at the highest level with amoral and immoral forces.[29] Hence the state could not be equated with morality but only with the supreme opportunity for the secular expression of morality. Ranke posited morality as a commandment to the state and not a description of its nature.

If morality was the norm and not the nature of the state, then the state must meet certain qualifications and standards. It must be the " 'spiritual fatherland' of the individual"; it must represent the " 'spirit of the community.' " And in order to meet these qualifications, the state must rest on national consciousness: "if the state is permeated with nationality it means that the state is filled with moral strength."[30]

Hence Ranke saw the nation as a beneficial force in the life of states, offering and demanding new opportunities for moral achievement within the sphere of politics. He also saw the potency of the national idea as a power factor, as a broader and deeper foundation for the development of great autonomous political societies. Meinecke emphasized Ranke's fascination for the spectacle of mighty power agglomerations, but he insisted that this fascination was subordinate to Ranke's moral imperative. His conclusion was that Ranke had avoided both the worship of power and the worship of an abstract and unrealistic morality and had established "the proper relationship between the ideal and the world of experience."[31]

Ranke's power politics centered on a cluster of moral precepts, and power had the same reciprocal relationship with ethics as did nation with state. The interrelationship of power and ethic was a source of strength to both and an admonition to each. Ranke saw every human being and every individual society in

[29] *Ibid.*, pp. 298-299.   [30] *Ibid.*, p. 299 (Meinecke's paraphrase).
[31] *Ibid.*, p. 302.

terms of this interrelationship in which the dynamic interaction of ethics and power considerations led to the development of moral personality. This view of the relation of power and morality was profoundly different from that of Hegel. At the same time, it is obvious that in conceding to the power factor an essential role in the process of moral expression Ranke also effected its legitimation.

Ranke rejoiced in the idea of nationality as a new means to both power and morality, and Meinecke felt that in so doing he joined the individualist ideals of the reformers and the realism of the power-politicians. "What attracted Ranke to the new political community was not the simple fact that it united masses of people but [the idea that] this community [was the matrix] of a specific spiritual personality. Individuality, then, was the motto of both Ranke and Humboldt. The only difference was that the concept of personality now reached out to encompass the great collective personalities. The pioneering discoveries in the realm of the individual that the German mind had undertaken . . . began to include the individuality of all those phenomena which united individuals into masses. When Ranke now said of nations and states that 'true harmony will emerge in differentiation and self-determination' it was an echo of the basic assumptions of Humboldt and of classical individualism."[32]

With these words Meinecke illuminated the background of the paradoxical oscillation of German thought between the glorification of the unfettered individual and the exaltation of the state with the individual's consequent subordination. Here state and individual were not conceived as antagonistic opposites, the one representing the uniform and the other the unique. Instead, both were individualities, with the state, or any other community for that matter, viewed as a personality of larger dimensions and more complex content. Since any viable personality demands a considerable degree of organization and integration of its components, the very existence of the state personality depended upon a hold on its constituents that went

[32] *Ibid.*, pp. 300-301.

beyond merely their desire or convenience. In this way the state was endowed with the quality of a commanding super-personality. Here was the root of that characteristic assumption of German political thinking that the whole is greater than the sum of its parts. In the very process of extending the concept of individualism to all forms of life the objectives of German "classical individualism" tended to be subordinated to the collective.

For a thinker like Meinecke who recognized the dangerous as well as the fruitful implications of this chain of ideas, it was important that the collective personalities be attuned as finely as possible to the individual human beings who comprised them. All Meinecke's observations on the nation-state seemed to him to bolster its claim to be the best guarantor of such a harmony. The bonds of nationality were strong enough to assure the integrity and cohesiveness of the state personality. At the same time they corresponded so closely with the specifics of the society-oriented qualities of man's nature that the nation-state's claim to authority could evoke a spontaneous response from its citizens. And in the element of spontaneity resided the moral nature of the community between citizen and state.

Ranke's interpretation of the nation as an agent for the realization of moral values in the state was thus seen by Meinecke as having established the philosophical basis of the state as a moral community without flaunting the realities of the state's function as a power organization. Ranke asserted that each state must build a moral community in its own way and that power was essential to the building. Hence there could be no universal commandment against the use of power, nor could there be a universal standard for political organization. The different states must develop their own form of "moral energy" for " 'each people was a different expression of God's idea of humanity.' "[33] Here was a joining of practical means and moral ends which set Ranke clearly apart from those who worshipped power for power's sake.

[33] *Ibid.*, p. 292.

Ranke nonetheless gave practical aid and comfort to the power politicians. The whole impact of his writings tended to dispel the ubiquitous concept of Europe as the true political community. Specifically, he defined the Napoleonic era of united European action against a common foe as a passing phase, destined to be superseded by a reversion to what he regarded as the authentic moral-political community of the individual nation and state.[34] With this dictum he undercut many of the ideological restraints on state egoism which had been built up by the theory of European solidarity among the conservative monarchies and so prepared the philosophical basis for the policies of Bismarck.

Moreover, while Ranke adhered to the idea of the nation as primarily a cultural entity, he did not draw the conclusion that the nation-state could result only from a spontaneous combustion in the cultural group. He avoided the doctrinaire position of both liberals and conservatives who tended to think of the nation in apolitical terms. The liberal supporters of a united Germany propagated the idea of the cultural nation as a means to refute all arguments defending the political considerations of the existing German states. The conservatives, on the other hand, emphasized the cultural aspects of the nation but attempted to deprive them of political content in order to protect the existing states. Ranke, in contrast, proclaimed the utility of planned political action by an individual German state conscious of its own interests as a means to bring political nationality to a culturally homogeneous people.[35] He therewith removed all philosophical barriers from the path by which Germany actually achieved unity—via the political dynamism of the Prussian state.

By means of empiric observation, Ranke undermined both the universalist-natural law ideas which dominated revolutionary liberalism and the conservative ideology which regarded the nation as a nonpolitical entity. Bismarck toppled them by

[34] *Ibid.*, p. 306. [35] *Ibid.*, pp. 298, 299, 303, 305.

means of empiric action. He rejected the admonitions of his conservative associates that the supreme principle of state policy should be the ethical command to fight revolutionary tendencies and insisted that the supreme principle was always derived from the immediate interests of the state itself. Here was the radical application of the Hegelian and Rankian positions that state actions had their own inherent morality; Bismarck could and did ignore ethical-political doctrines which transcended or were alien to his own Prussian state. He could not be wrenched away from his preoccupation with the interests of Prussia even when the political-ethical doctrine took the form of a united nation. He used Germany as the larger field for the exercise of Prussian policies, and he accepted the idea of national unification only as he became convinced that it corresponded with Prussian interests.[36]

Bismarck's ties to aristocratic and military-minded Prussia led him to create the only kind of German state in which Prussia would consent to play a role—one in which Prussia achieved the position of a hegemonial power. Indifference to democratic aspirations enabled him to fashion a successful plan for German unity acceptable to the entrenched interests of the conservative dynasties in the smaller German states. His unsentimental attitude toward force freed him from any compunction against solving the conflict with Austria and France by war. Bismarck unified Germany with the Prussian sword, and he interpreted the unification as a triumph of Prussian policy rather than as a vindication of the ideal of a political nationality. As we have seen, Meinecke considered force as the only solution to the problem of German unity. And Prussian predominance, he felt, was the *sine qua non* of Prussian participation in a German national state. Thus he saw Bismarck working successfully to direct the historical trends of his time toward the unification of Germany, and he regarded Bismarck's techniques as the only techniques by which these trends could be shaped into an enduring political community.

[36] *Ibid.*, pp. 317, 319-320, 322-324, 326.

We have also seen, however, that Meinecke could not be content with mere political technique and that the form which Bismarck gave to Germany would be intolerable to him without a content transcending Bismarck's power objectives. The philosophical realism in Hegel and Ranke and the activist realism of Bismarck were indispensable to the achievement of a sovereign Germany. But political thought and deed were of little moment to Meinecke unless they furthered cultural and moral ends. If the nation was the true macrocosm of "man's natural-spiritual being," it was not simply a community of power. It was also a community of spiritual values. As a macrocosm, the nation could not be a one-sided expression of man's need for power and order. It must be the vehicle for the expression of the total personality of the individual. In short, the nation must also function as the basis for individual freedom.

Individual freedom was the credo of the German reformers and intellectuals at the turn of the nineteenth century. The idea of freedom was the bond which united both those who entered the service of the state and those, like Goethe, who continued to hold aloof from political action. Napoleon was the immediate antagonist for most, but all had understanding and even admiration for many of the motivations and ideals of the French revolutionaries. All were critical of the traditional political institutions of Germany and more particularly of the Prussia of Frederick the Great. They regarded Frederick's state as a power apparatus with no further concern for its subjects than as instruments for its own ends.[37] Instead of seeking to unite the individual with the state by identifying his interest with the state's interest, the dominant policy in eighteenth-century Prussia assumed that the great masses were incapable of developing a political consciousness. Hence the statesman's task was seen as one of utilizing an indifferent populace as raw material in the making of policies with which the populace had no real concern.[38] However enlightened Frederick's policies, he remained

---

[37] *Erhebung, op.cit.*, pp. 14, 50, 93-94, 95.
[38] *Ibid.*, p. 51.

a despot, and his government was consequently based more on force than consent.

The guiding idea of the reformers was to reverse the balance between force and consent. The mighty spectacle of a militant nationalism springing from the French Revolution roused the reformers to an effort to tap the same roots of spontaneity in the German people which had transformed a decadent France into a nation of seemingly boundless energy. Meinecke spoke for all the reformers when he depicted Boyen as desiring to replace "mere external force, egotism, and special interests with justice, spontaneity, sense of honor, love of fatherland and of one's fellow men."[39] The state could no longer be thought of in terms of a simple power mechanism in which the rulers manipulated for their own ends the subjects over whom they ruled. Humboldt, Fichte, and Arndt took up the Kantian imperative and demanded that every individual human being be treated as an end in himself.[40] While Stein did not share the philosophical individualism of the intellectuals, his emphasis on the need for community also focussed attention on the concrete requirements of the individual and placed a premium on consent as the cornerstone of a political society.[41]

The reformers were convinced that the idea of common nationality would provide the mortar by which the more democratic system of government could be held together. This conviction sprang largely from a growing consciousness of the unifying force of language and common traditions—a consciousness which was developed in major part by the renaissance of German arts and letters since about 1770. Most of the great individual figures of this renaissance joined the idea of individual freedom to a concern for Germany as a cultural entity.[42] While those who went into the service of the Prussian state did so in response to the threat from Napoleon, their aims ranged far beyond the immediate challenge of the Napoleonic system.[43]

[39] *Ibid.*, p. 123.   [40] *Ibid.*, pp. 40, 59, 181.   [41] *Ibid.*, p. 94.
[42] *Ibid.*, pp. 65, 84, 93, 95, 110.
[43] *Ibid.*, pp. 10-11, 89.

French imperialism was only the latest in a series of events over the centuries which had subjected Germany to centrifugal tensions. The new consciousness of a German cultural entity fortified the hostility to Napoleon's efforts to recast Europe in his own image, and it provided the impetus to put an end to the recurring dangers of fragmentization to which Germany had been subjected.

Hence the reformers went a step beyond intellectual appreciation of German culture and dedicated themselves to policies which strove toward the achievement of national political unity as the guarantor of a German cultural community. Beyond all the individual reforms by which they effected a redistribution of power among the various social and economic groups in Prussia, they sought to rebuild political strength by appealing to a German national consciousness transcending special class interests.[44] At the time, these nationalist convictions constituted a harmonious complement to the ideal of individual rights.

Meinecke applauded the reformers for their efforts on behalf of a government by consent, and he agreed with them that the nation was the foundation of consensus. Thus his insistence on the nation as the proper basis for political organization was intimately related to his concern for the freedom of the individual in a society congenial to his free development. Sharing with the reformers the ideal of the free individual and the free nation, Meinecke was led to generalize that nationalism was the key both to personal liberty and to community. He saw the national idea as the modern answer to the old question of the sources of state authority. If the state is to become something more than a mere agglomeration of power, "its foundations must be dug deeper and must rest on the sentiments of the nation."[45]

[44] *Boyen* I, *op.cit.*, pp. 163-164, 377-378.
[45] *Erhebung, op.cit.*, p. 10. It should be noted that Meinecke did not question the political viability or philosophical desirability of such multinational states as Switzerland or Austria-Hungary. It has already been pointed out that he was not rigid in defining the properties of nationality.

Here the ideas of the liberal idealists and the conservative realists converged. To Meinecke it was Ranke beyond all others who took the threads of liberal and conservative thought and wove them into a harmonious pattern. He felt that Ranke had eliminated or at least reduced the friction created by the diverse considerations and ideals revolving around the symbol of the nation and that Ranke's political concepts established the philosophical basis for the development of the nation as a community of power and a community of moral values.

Ranke's understanding of the individual interests and power drives of states placed him in opposition to the idealists of the Prussian Reform and to the liberal idealists among his own contemporaries who sought German unity at Frankfurt in 1848 and 1849. The men who made the Frankfurt Constitution "wanted to use Prussia as a means to a German nation, but at Prussia's expense. Ranke also saw Prussia as the key to German unity but wanted to preserve the historical individuality of the Prussian state."[46] Like Stein, the liberals of 1848 did not value Prussia as an institution. Hence they also tended to ignore or do violence to Prussian interests in their efforts to realize a united Germany.[47] They worked against, rather than

---

Actually, he differentiated between several kinds of nations. He regarded pre-1870 Germany as a "cultural nation" since it shared many common traditions but was not politically united. Switzerland was a "political nation" with very diverse cultural elements. In general, Meinecke thought that most nations represented individual combinations of political and cultural phenomena which gave the "nation" a sense of group identity. Meinecke asserted that nations are basically founded on volition in varying degrees of consciousness. With the qualification that the object of volition can vary and must be defined in each instance, Meinecke accepted the dictum of Renan that *"L'existence d'une nation est un plébiscite de tous les jours." Weltbuergertum, op.cit.,* pp. 3-5.

[46] *Weltbuergertum, op.cit.,* p. 460.

[47] *Preussen und Deutschland im 19. und 20. Jahrhundert,* Munich and Berlin, 1918, pp. 5, 8, 10. This book is a collection of prewar and wartime essays and lectures. The reference here is to the lecture "Preussen und Deutschland im 19. Jahrhundert" given on April 19, 1906. The book will hereafter be cited as *Preussen und Deutschland.*

with, the major forces of their time. Ranke, in contrast, worked with these forces by "uniting calm historical contemplation to cool political calculation."[48] But his concept of the state as a collective individual with a moral personality which could be realized only by community participation in the life of that state reflected the spirit of the reformers and set him apart from those like Bismarck who tended toward the mere manipulation of the masses in the interest of the rulers.

In the light of all that has been said, however, it is clear that none of the three men whom Meinecke regarded as liberators, not even Ranke, was an active partisan of the nation-state in the form in which Meinecke conceived it. Hegel's philosophical system was too much geared to the rationalization and justification of the social and political structure of a profoundly conservative Prussia to show the way to a state in which each individual had a right to participate in political activity. Bismarck saw and used the idea of a German nation as an object and instrument of political tactics and strategy. Ranke's concrete commitment was to the existing Prussian state as the true political nation rather than the as yet unrealized German nation-state.[49]

Meinecke clearly went beyond the "liberators." He asserted that the value of the state could be justified only if it were conceived as "an ideal, super-individual corporate personality" and that such a conception could be achieved only when "the community sentiments and energies of the individual citizens permeated the state and transformed it into the nation-state."[50] Meinecke's words were close to those of Ranke, but whereas Ranke praised the Prussian state and the idea of community, Meinecke was committed to the German nation and the idea of the individual in the community.

[48] *Weltbuergertum, op.cit.,* pp. 457-458. Meinecke acknowledges somewhat obliquely that Ranke's own status as a Prussian subject was also a factor in his political judgments.

[49] *Ibid.,* pp. 296, 306, 307.

[50] *Ibid.,* pp. 10, 11.

Whatever the differences in Meinecke's own approach to the nation, the men he called liberators had contributed powerfully to the rise of the German nation-state. They had established political realities and thought patterns which created the foundation for Meinecke's view of the nation-state as the supreme idea uniting all members of a given society in a common political undertaking in which each member had a right to participate. Meinecke's nationalism was essentially a liberal one, and if the men to whom he paid tribute could not be located in the liberal tradition, he felt nonetheless strongly that they had created the only conditions under which a free society could flourish. What the "liberators" lacked in liberal conscience Meinecke supplied by invoking the spirit of the statesmen and intellectuals of the early 1800's. In this way he rounded out the picture of the nation-state as the ideal political community.

CHAPTER III

COSMOPOLITANISM AS A POLITICAL ILLUSION

THE ultimate service of the nation-state's "liberators," Meinecke felt, should be measured in the light of the obstacles which they had to overcome both in theory and practice. It was all very well to long for an ideal society in which all men were free to develop themselves in harmonious cooperation with their fellows—this much the men of the Prussian Reform had done. It was quite another matter to "infuse the idea into reality."

Those men in nineteenth-century Germany who thought about and acted for the more perfect society wanted to create this society in Germany. Their success or failure was consequently dependent on the measure of their ability to diagnose and act upon the historical situation in which Germans found themselves. This meant that they had to assess correctly the strengths and weaknesses of the traditional political and social institutions in Germany. They also had to calculate and work with the forces and ideas making for change in these institutions. And the geographical position of Germany and the history of disunity and exploitation by the great powers of Europe made foreign policy of paramount importance in the reckoning.

Once the diagnosis was made, the men who sought the nation-state had to advance their ideas and policies in the face of bitter opposition based on entrenched interests and ingrained prejudices. Above all, they had to liberate themselves from an ideology which Meinecke regarded as the most formidable of all the road-blocks to German political unity. This was the ideology of political cosmopolitanism.

The central theme in *Weltbuergertum und Nationalstaat* was the emergence in Germany of the idea of the autonomous nation-state from the cosmopolitan doctrines of both rationalism and romanticism.[1] Meinecke saw the struggle of ideas which culminated in the French Revolution and the Napoleonic era as one wherein both contenders rationalized and justified their specific political interests by invoking cosmopolitan symbols and universalistic theories. The French Revolutionaries claimed to be acting in the name of universal reason and of the rights of man. They used the cosmopolitan content of their ideology to "exhort all peoples to accept a uniform governmental structure and curried favor by appeals to the desire of individuals for equality and freedom."[2] Revolutionary cosmopolitanism consequently tended to undermine the autonomy and the historic individuality of the political systems of all European states and drove the most powerful of these states to band together in a common cause which inevitably developed its own cosmopolitan aspects.

The very fact that there was a common cause among the European states fighting the Revolution and Napoleon generated a compulsion to define the nature and rights of a European community transcending the individual states. Each state was engaged in a struggle for its own survival, but as more and more fell prey to Napoleon, a pattern emerged in which the survival of the particular state began to be overshadowed by the issue of the survival of the traditional European political system as a whole. In this situation "the concept of European community and the self-interest of states and nations harmonized with one another. Indeed, to a certain extent they were identical."[3]

The imperative of common action by Europe's powers was not the only source of the growing cosmopolitan character of the contest with Napoleon. The ruling groups in many of the states had to reassess and recast their internal political structure in the light of the dynamism generated in France by the joining of the concepts of democracy and nationalism. In theory the French Revolution proclaimed the right of political action by all men by virtue of their being men. The great practical ef-

[1] *Weltbuergertum, op.cit.,* pp. 1, 263, and *passim.*
[2] *Ibid.,* p. 303.   [3] *Ibid.,* p. 304. See also p. 163.

fect of this theory was to summon new sources of energy for the French state by granting political rights and initiative to all Frenchmen by virtue of their status as French citizens. The revolutionary French state succeeded in identifying the great masses of its populace with its objectives as a power organization. The opponents of the Revolution had to follow the French lead if they were to match the enormous increase in political vitality and military power which this identification had made possible. The new French democratic nationalism claimed to be the prototype for all nationalisms, and the defenders of the older order themselves had to strike the spark of nationalism and to portray the Revolution as an imperialist usurper of the national idea.

In a sense, then, there was agreement on both sides of the contest that two of the great issues involved were the true nature and norms of the European political community and the true nature of the national idea. Here the conflicting states were caught up in a struggle which tended to sublimate their specific interests in universal values.

This trend was reinforced in those countries where the ruling groups saw opportunity and advantage in policies designed to permit the development of a political consciousness among the masses. When Napoleonic imperialism began to shatter and remold the life of Europe in its own image and to its own interest, it was comprehensible that those opposing Napoleon sought to seize the initiative away from the apostles of the Revolution by countering with their own ideas on the nature and rights of man. The people were in fact summoned to participate in a common undertaking with their leaders. In order to persuade the populace to abandon its traditional apathy toward the power struggles of the rulers, the rulers had to demonstrate that the masses had a real stake in the contest. In the case of Prussia, we have already noted Meinecke's recognition that those in power borrowed many of the ideas of the French Revolution and were inspired by the idea of the timeless and universal rights of man as much as by the hope for specific military and political advantages flowing from a more articulate populace.[4] Hence "the spiritual forces [of nationality] which the states evoked, particularly in Germany, were themselves shot through with universalist concepts."[5] To the universal issues of the nature of the European community and of the idea of nationality there was now added the issue of the nature and rights of man as such.

Meinecke saw still another element involved in the development of the cosmopolitan aspect of Europe's struggle—"the special interest groups which regained power with the advent of the restoration."[6] These groups were the landed nobility whose descent from power could be traced to the rise of the absolute monarchy long before 1789. They "proclaimed their opposition to absolutism in any guise, be it the monarchical absolutism of the *ancien régime* or the democratic absolutism of the revolutionary era. . . . They fought the autonomous state in every form. . . . They would not and could not completely shun the national movement. But they sought to render it innocuous by the elaboration of a conservative concept of the nation-state which glorified the aristocratic class-state as the authentic product of the folk-spirit and of the nation as a cultural phenomenon. It is very understandable that at the same time they held fast to universalistic concepts of a European community of legitimist Christian powers. . . . It was precisely the idea of such a community which inhibited the power-drives of individual states and nations so dangerous to the traditionally static life of the feudal society. . . . The idea of community took on positive content in the postulation of supreme moral and legal commandments which claimed precedence over all power interests of states and nations. These commandments received a religious consecration in that they were invoked as divine law and revelation."[7]

With these illustrations Meinecke sought to demonstrate that the universalism of the French Revolution had given birth to a whole host of universalistic ideas and finally to the opposing

---

[4] See Chapter II, above. [5] *Weltbuergertum, op.cit.*, p. 304.
[6] *Ibid.*   [7] *Ibid.*, pp. 304-305.

universalism of the Holy Alliance. Revolution and counter-revolution cut under and through the political structures of the old secular monarchies and the new secular nations. Religious and ethical ideals thus asserted a leading role in the struggle and served often enough to mask the political interests of those involved.

Meinecke did not intend to deny that the injection of cosmopolitan and universal ideas in the life of states served a positive purpose in the resolution of Europe's crisis during the quarter century of revolution and Napoleonic imperialism. But, consistent with his commitment to the nation-state, he contended that the positive purpose became negative in the longer run development of nineteenth-century Europe and more particularly of nineteenth-century Germany. Thus the proclamation of the rights of man by the French revolutionaries became the spiritual basis for the French attempt to "despoil and subject other states and peoples to the yoke of its universal rule."[8] The borrowing of universalist democratic ideas from France tended to deflect the borrowing state from its objectives as a power organization. The idea of an international fraternity of democrats was bound to deny the state's "absolute claim to self-determination."[9] The existence of a common cause among the states fighting Napoleon created the vision of a European solidarity which was to become a mirage and a dangerous chimera in the post-Napoleonic world.[10] Finally, the reactionary forces of the aristocracy which reasserted their power with the advent of the restoration traded on their own brand of religious-legitimist universalism to protect their own interests and to "restrict the autonomy of the state personality."[11]

Meinecke's basic theoretical discontent, which runs through all of his discussion of universalistic concepts and ethical ab-

---

[8] *Ibid.*, p. 303.   [9] *Ibid.*, p. 304.

[10] *Ibid.* The alliance against Napoleon "brought a certain degree of harmony . . . between the concept of the European community and the self-assertion of states and nations. . . . But beyond this degree . . . the boon could become a curse."

[11] *Ibid.*, p. 305.

solutes in their various forms, was that these concepts and absolutes tended to distort and polarize political life into a series of rigid and antagonistic opposites. The absolute and universal nature of French revolutionary philosophy impelled its critics toward a counter-absolute and a counter-universal, even where those critics did not wish to condemn the Revolution *in toto*. The arrogance of Napoleon's quest for a universal monarchy produced the opposing arrogance of those who were determined to restore and perpetuate a reactionary *status quo ante*. The proclamation of the ideal rights of man as absolutely superior to the practical rules of statecraft and politics tended to increase misunderstanding and hostility between governments and peoples. The assumptions about the universal community of men in general and the European community in particular contributed not to a marriage but to a divorce of the ideal and the real in politics.

Above all, the polarization process forced rigid and narrow concepts of right and wrong on those who formulated policy. In both domestic and international politics the maneuverability of the statesman was threatened with an ideological strait jacket which classified some policies as wholly righteous and others as wholly wicked. Moreover, the tendency of groups in power to praise anything favoring their interests as good and anything hindering them as evil received a potent stimulus. A façade of absolute moral values created the ideal conditions for a ruthless opportunism, and the forces supporting the Holy Alliance exploited these conditions to the full.

The tragedy was that the idealists constantly gave the opportunists their cue. The progress of the French Revolution is an obvious case in point. But the drama was repeated in Germany and throughout the continent when Napoleon succeeded in dividing Europe into two camps, each calling itself good and the other evil. Again and again Meinecke discerns his heroes of the Prussian Reform bringing political interests under absolute ethical principles. There was much truth in Gneisenau's observation that "the world is divided into those who voluntar-

ily or involuntarily fight for or against Bonaparte's majesty.' "
But he went on to assert that "In this situation it seems to be
a matter more of principles than of countries.' " "Now," Meinecke added, "the conflict became one between world tyranny
and world liberty . . . and the freedom of nations and states was
subordinated to the idea of the freedom of the world."[12] Meinecke agreed with Stein's biographer that Stein saw the Congress of Vienna "not as a struggle for power but as a contest
between good and evil.' "[13] "Gneisenau, Stein and Arndt . . .
divided Europe into the sphere of freedom and the sphere of
slavery and utilized this distinction as the principle from which
to judge the special [interests] of Prussia and the other German
states."[14]

Meinecke did not decry the ideals of the reformers as such;
rather he felt that they represented the extremes of essentially
desirable attitudes and that, like all extremes, they tended to distort and obscure the very objective which the idealists sought.
These were the assumptions upon which Meinecke developed his
theory of the basic antagonism between cosmopolitanism and the
idea of the state. The cosmopolitans were operating with precepts which ignored or disguised the true nature of politics and
in so doing inevitably tended to regard the needs of the state as
either unimportant or evil. Meinecke defined cosmopolitanism
and universalism as a body of "ideas with ethical or religious
content."[15] By definition, then, they were normative and universalistic concepts which transcended the interests of individual
states. Meinecke quarreled not with transcendent norms as
such but with arguments which absolutized these norms and
attempted to subject the state to them with no regard for its
political interest. Those who so argued, Meinecke reasoned,
were enemies of the state. "The [conservative] Romantics and

[12] *Ibid.*, p. 176, and *Erhebung, op.cit.*, pp. 202-203.
[13] *Weltbuergertum, op.cit.*, p. 190. The quotation is from Max Lehmann's biography of Stein (vol. III, p. 447).
[14] *Ibid.*, p. 177.
[15] *Ibid.*, p. 91.

the apostles of the Enlightenment had a common enemy in what they regarded as the unethical state of the *ancien régime.* Their real enemy was the power-state as such. . . ."[16]

Hostility to the power-state certainly did not mean hostility to power in the abstract. Meinecke's fundamental conviction that all men and all human associations seek power as well as moral and cultural values dismissed any contention that the state's detractors might be the true advocates of ethical purity. He felt that only hypocrisy or self-deception could result from propositions which branded the state as evil and portrayed the opponents of state power as good. If the revolutionary nationalists and the conservative romantics attacked the state, it was because the state constituted a barrier to their own power goals or because they had no clear understanding of the state's significance. More often than not, cynicism and illusion were secret partners.

The unfolding drama of the French Revolution was the classic example of the process in which a naïve anti-statism and vaunting of human rights prepared the way for a deification of the state and the extremes of imperialism. The men of 1789 demanded surcease from the Machiavellianism of the absolute monarchy which exploited the people and dragged them into conflict with neighboring peoples to satisfy the ambitions of the monarch. They promised that the era of the democratic nation would end the selfish practices of war and exploitation. Meinecke let Herder speak for the hopes of the artless: " 'Cabinets may deceive one another; political machines may clash until one or both are destroyed. But fatherlands do not draw the sword; they live together in peace and support one another in the manner of a family. A bloody struggle between fatherland and fatherland is the worst barbarism the human mind could produce.' " As the father of cultural nationalism, Herder "shared the illusion of many friends of the Revolution, . . . conceiving cosmopolitanism and the nation-state . . . as two forces in an intimate relationship of mutual conditioning and support."[17]

[16] *Ibid.*   [17] *Ibid.*, p. 32.

It was precisely this coupling of nationalism and cosmopolitanism which lent enormous strength to the militants of the Revolution. Here was the root of the myth that the wars of France were wars to liberate other peoples from their decadent and exploitative regimes. The early friends of the Revolution all over Europe were those who resented the oppression and inertia of the traditional monarchies, and in their resentment they nourished the myth. The dynamism of the revolutionaries and Napoleon's rule " 'met least resistance where the spirit was ready,' where the social ideas of the Revolution . . . and the cosmopolitan aspects of the Enlightenment had already taken root. . . . Particularly in Germany . . . [the myth] weakened the national will to resist."[18]

Like all myths, the cosmopolitan nationalism of the French Revolution was concocted of both truths and falsehoods. But as the French democracy burgeoned into empire, the inherent contradictions of its ideology began to overwhelm the elements of truth, and the myth became unambiguously false. Meinecke did not deny that Napoleon brought good as well as bad to the conquered states of Europe and that he cleared away much dead wood and released energy and imagination where before there had been only rigidity and inertia. "But he also threatened everything that was still viable. He endangered every semblance of external and internal independence, and so caused the nobler spirits in Germany to rise against him. . . . If Prussia had sinned in treating the great mass of its subjects as means to its own ends, Napoleon now manipulated whole states and peoples as mere instruments. . . . He exploited the ideals of 1789 and at the same time killed the nerve of freedom which had given them life."[19]

Hence Meinecke saw the Revolution as a drama in which the prophets who set out to slay the state in the name of humanity ended by themselves becoming the apostles of the super-state.

[18] *Ibid.*, p. 327. The phrase in single quotes is from Ranke.
[19] *Erhebung, op.cit.*, p. 64.

But if he contended that hypocrisy and imperialism were the inexorable destinations toward which the radical anti-statists traveled, he identified them as points of departure for the conservative restoration. In this he was consistent with the chain of ideas constituting his criticism of the conservative heritage which emerged with the second volume of his biography of Boyen.

The Prussian conservatives of the restoration were determined to restore the old predominance of the aristocracy, and their greatest enemy was the vigorous state.[20] The greater the power of the central authority, the weaker the role of the landed nobility. This was as true for the monarchy of Frederick as for the rejuvenated Prussia of the reformers. Indeed, Meinecke regarded the reformers as "truer sons of Frederick the Great than the Junker officers and court aristocrats who permitted the idea of Prussian greatness and power to wither away because . . . it could only be realized by the attenuation of their political and social preponderance."[21] The conservatives fought the proposals for universal military service because of the financial burdens it would impose and because of the social mobility it would introduce. They feared the " 'arming of a nation [would] organize and encourage resistance and rebellion.' " And they complained that an armed Prussian people could arouse the suspicions of other states and that the liberal proposals for the Prussian military establishment were in " 'glaring contrast to the mild and loving religion of Christ animating the Holy Alliance.' "[22]

Hence Meinecke saw the restoration conservatives out to strip the state of its power not because of any sense of outrage over downtrodden human rights but in order to reassert and protect

---

[20] *Boyen* II, *op.cit.*, p. 310.

[21] *Ibid.*, p. 315.

[22] *Ibid.*, pp. 310-312. The quotations are from memoranda by an unknown author found in the papers of Prince Wittgenstein. Wittgenstein was Prussian Minister for Police in 1815. Meinecke describes him as the "most influential leader of the court party" and reasons that Wittgenstein used these memoranda as a handy arsenal of arguments.

their own selfish interests. In Germany the Holy Alliance served the double function of supporting the conservatives in rolling back the gains in economic and political freedom which the reformers had achieved and of putting a damper on the aggressiveness of a Prussian foreign policy which, during the period of reform, had been moving toward the establishment of a united German nation. "The issues were an aristocratic regime at home and weakness abroad versus the spirit of a liberal citizenry at home and the vigorous development of an optimum power position in foreign affairs."[23] Thus Meinecke saw the Holy Alliance and its conservative supporters fighting social reform and national movements under the guise of a religiousethical universalism. The imperialism and contempt for human rights with which it operated matched the brutality and ruthlessness of Napoleon's universal monarchy.

Cosmopolitan and universalistic ideas in politics were capable of producing not only arrogance and imperialism; they could also result in self-deception and weakness. We have already seen that Meinecke condemned the reformers for entertaining illusions about a European solidarity and for believing that a united Germany could be achieved by appealing to that solidarity rather than by creating the conditions of political strength.[24] In his criticism of Stein, Meinecke did not charge that Stein was faithless to the national idea when he proposed that Russia and England should be brought into German affairs. Stein sincerely thought that such a policy would aid the cause of the nation. Meinecke's criticism rested on the proposition that Stein was caught in the toils of the cosmopolitan idea "that we have now transcended and recognized as an alien universalist ideology. . . . It was an ideology which failed to recognize the basic forces of egoism in politics and over-estimated the common interests of Europe."[25]

Here again the naïveté of the reformers and the heritage of

[23] *Ibid.*, p. 312.
[24] See Chapter II, above.
[25] *Weltbuergertum, op.cit.,* pp. 186-187.

cosmopolitanism could play into the hands of the restoration reactionaries. The humanitarian ideals of the German intellectuals in the 1790's which viewed nations in general and Germany in particular as exclusively cultural and spiritual associations were later joined by the ideal of a European community. Both functioned as barriers to political realism. One must understand this constellation of ideas, Meinecke felt, in order to explain the contradictory goals of those who in one breath called for German national autonomy and in the next argued for a European guarantee of a German constitution. The first eleven of the German Articles of Confederation were in fact incorporated into the treaties of the Congress of Vienna. "If there was no guarantee of the German constitution in the strict sense, [this procedure] certainly conferred upon the European signatory powers a dangerous claim to such a guarantee and to the right of intervention."[26] This result, Meinecke pointed out, corresponded exactly to the policies of Metternich "who, naturally, was thinking of nothing else than the interests of Austria."[27]

In an atmosphere which gave German politics more a European than a national character, it was not surprising that the liberals should emphasize the European function of a German nation. Thus Stein's view of France as Germany's "eternal enemy" was linked to his division of Europe into a zone of freedom and a zone without freedom. He envisioned the abiding and supreme mission of German foreign policy as one of holding France and unfreedom at bay.[28] Although Humboldt rejected the rigidity of Stein's conception and demanded that Germany be in a position to defend herself against any enemy,[29] he too accepted the idea of an international guarantee of the German Confederation and tended to gloss over the frictions inherent in the relationship between Austria and Prussia.[30] And if Humboldt was realistically unwilling to tie Germany to a permanent anti-French coalition, he later formulated what Meinecke regarded as the epitome of negative policy—"a rejection

[26] *Ibid.*, pp. 206-207.   [27] *Ibid.*, pp. 207-208.   [28] *Ibid.*, p. 192.
[29] *Ibid.*, pp. 192-193.   [30] *Ibid.*, pp. 196-197, 198-199.

of any kind of vigorous policy based on Germany's own political interests and a restriction of activity in foreign affairs to the safeguarding of tranquillity."[31]

Meinecke used the observations of the Goettingen historian Heeren as an illustration of the logical consequences of the political ideas emerging in post-Napoleonic Germany: "The German Confederation . . . is in most intimate accord with the general and special interests of Europe [as a whole]. Hence the foreign powers cannot be indifferent to the structure of 'Europe's central state.' If this state were a great monarchy with a firmly-knit political unity and armed with all the natural forces of state which Germany possesses, what possibility would exist for a secure and tranquil status? How long would such a state be able to resist the temptation to assert its predominance in Europe? . . . The allied powers have now been wise enough to recognize that a state organization must be created which will be offensively weak but defensively strong—a 'peace-state of Europe.' "[32]

Writing these words before two world wars had shaken twentieth-century Europe to pieces, Meinecke was not moved to inquire whether Heeren might have been gifted with powers of prophecy. Instead, he treated Heeren's views as the ultimate in political folly. The German nation was to be pressed into the service of alien interests. "This central peace-state of Europe is conceived as the perfect logical counterpart to the universal monarchy; it too has universal functions—only the connotations are reversed. 'It must be the defender of the principle of legitimate ownership, because without this principle its own security would be gone.' Hence it would certainly be no over-extension of its function to intercede for the protection of this legitimate ownership and for the legitimate dynasties of Europe. . . . One sees again how strongly the political atmosphere of these years

[31] *Ibid.*, pp. 201-202.

[32] *Ibid.*, pp. 208-209. Meinecke paraphrases and quotes from Heeren's *Der deutsche Bund in seinem Verhaeltnis zu dem europaeischen Staatensystem*, published in 1817.

was impregnated with universalistic elements—the same years which give to the European nations . . . a feeling of independence."[33]

The difficulty was, Meinecke felt, that the new sense of national identity and freedom had not yet reached the maturity of full self-understanding. The intellectuals and reformers liberated the nation from the traditional state only to urge it to conform with preconceived notions of what all nations should be. In a world of the brotherhood of nations, each nation must subordinate its own interests to the idea of brotherhood. It was assumed that the new world of nations would be an era without selfishness and that the sovereign personality of the nation could be defended in terms of the spirit without reference to considerations of power. The community of nations, and not the nation itself, would be the wielder of power.

It was an easy step from the liberal ideas of the solidarity of nations to Heeren's solidarity of property owners and legitimate monarchies. Indeed, Heeren himself had gone through the transition in which an original emphasis on the supremacy of the nation gave way to the supremacy of property.[34] Another short step led to the reactionary position of the Holy Alliance supporters who desired to suppress all social reform and national strivings in the name of "tranquillity." The continuum that united and rationalized all these positions was the heritage of cosmopolitan thought which consistently implied the surrender of the power of political decision from the individual will-center to a universal community. There was, of course, no

[33] *Ibid.* p. 209. It is worthy of note that in the perspective of 1931, when Europe was burdened with economic depression and political crisis and the shadow of National Socialism was lengthening over Germany, Meinecke took an opposite view of Germany as a "peace state." Meinecke wrote that the German Confederation of 1815 contributed little to national life. "Still, it contained one positive idea which is easier to appreciate today than at the time when Germans were suffering under its defects. It was conceived as a confederation of peace, as a European peace guarantee. . . ." ("Zum 18. Januar, 1931," *Blaetter der Staatspartei*, Berlin, vol. 1, no. 1, January 5, 1931, p. 2.)

[34] *Ibid.*

dearth of power-wielders who utilized this rationale to shore up their own interests and to conceal the actual abodes of power.

Hence the universal idea which had been a major source of French power became the root of German weakness. ". . . the Germans felt themselves to be a universal world nation. But whereas other nations proceed from this proposition to infer a claim to world mastery, at that time in Germany the inference was drawn of a kind of world servitude. . . . This world servitude, this neutralization of the national force in Germany by means of [a collaboration between] the German Confederation and the European Great Powers surrounding it as benign patrons became one of the basic postulates of European history in the following decades. One can get a foretaste in Heeren's writings of the ideas surrounding legitimist intervention policies and the Congresses of Troppau, Laibach, and Verona."[35]

With this observation Meinecke established the link between the cosmopolitan ideas of the liberals and the conservatives in the era of the restoration. Until the rise of Bismarck he saw Germany foundering in a quagmire of universalistic illusions. The doctrines of both liberals and conservatives inhibited political insight and political initiative and prevented the development of a coherent policy, particularly in Prussia, leading toward what he considered the necessary objective of a German nation-state.

Meinecke saw the idea of a fraternity of European monarchs hanging like a pall over the reign of Frederick William IV, obscuring the Prussian king's understanding both of the ideal of a German unity and of the selfish interests which fed on the weakness of Prussian foreign policy.[36] Frederick William and the men around him denied that egotism was the basis of the state, insisting that the state must subordinate its own desires to the needs of a European community. "They bound [the state] to supreme moral commandments and thus limited its power objectives, its liberty of movement, and even its freedom of choice in alliances."[37]

---

[35] *Ibid.*, p. 210. [36] *Ibid.*, p. 326.
[37] *Ibid.*, p. 320. To buttress his argument, Meinecke cited (p. 320,

Meinecke labeled the regime of Frederick William IV as that which "made a practical effort to follow the ideas of political romanticism."[38] Frederick William did not believe that Prussia could formulate a policy resting on its own interests but was bound to a scrupulous observance of the European *status quo*. Meinecke used the king's moral condemnation of proposals to reconquer Alsace as the prime example of a policy of weakness and abnegation. "Here the interests, power requirements, and the [idea of] self-determination not only of the nation but also of the individual state were restricted and eternally bound to higher norms of law. Once again we see the old denial or at least diminution of the right of states to conduct autonomous policies. . . ."[39]

Meinecke's reproach was not that the conquest of Alsace during Frederick William's reign was politically necessary or would have been morally justified. His complaint concerned the rigid system of ethical taboos which prohibited a realistic consideration of policy alternatives on their merits. Moreover, this system of taboos no longer rested directly on the early restoration assumption of a universal league of states, so that there was no tangible principle of mutual responsibility of states for the upholding of ethical norms in international relations. The idea of the European community had worn thin in the decades following the Vienna Congress, and the fact that the individual states were following their own interests was not lost even on the Prussian romantics.

Despite the evidence, however, the Prussian king and his advisers merely excoriated it and expressed outrage at the " 'heathen' national pride of . . . Frenchmen of whatever party," insisting that the Prussian state must never succumb to this kind

---

footnote 2) Ranke's *French History* (vol. I, p. 117): "It was impossible to develop a more flexible approach to foreign affairs, derived from the needs of one's own special situation, as long as concern for the more comprehensive system of peoples and states to which one belonged was permitted to determine action."

[38] *Ibid.*, p. 259.   [39] *Ibid.*

of national or state egotism. "Now the primacy of law over power and of the universal world order of states over the interests of individual states was hammered into the conscience of statesmen as a doctrinaire norm. . . . Leopold von Gerlach proclaimed an exact correspondence between the relations among sovereigns and the legal relationships between the sovereign and his subjects. For both, there are no norms of law 'which are not in accord with morality and Christianity, indeed, which are not identical with them. . . . These legal relationships are no different from moral and Christian relationships, no different from all other human relationships. In short, they must be regulated in accordance with God's will.' "[40]

Fulminations against the sins of other states were accompanied by a political quietism and consequent lack of positive goals in regard to the Prussian state. This was the essence of Meinecke's criticism of pre-Bismarck Prussia. "In the power struggles among the states, Germany and German princes were expected to refrain from employing certain weapons of which their neighbors made use without the slightest scruple."[41] The Prussian romantics entertained "objectives which were alien to the state. In so doing they altered the techniques by which the state maintained its existence. Further, they revamped the whole of political thought and the whole range of conceptions of what was politically possible and capable of achievement and so created a source of political errors, mistakes, miscarriages, and humiliations."[42] Universalist doctrine "dominated the thinking of the leading personalities in the time of Frederick William IV to such an extent that it exercised an ominous pressure on practical politics and on the power position of the state. Ultimately it became a poison which the body had to eject if it was to be restored to its natural function. The doctor who removed the poison was Bismarck."[43]

Although Meinecke regarded cosmopolitanism and universalism as poisons which stunted and distorted the political de-

[40] *Ibid.*, p. 260.   [41] *Ibid.*, p. 261.   [42] *Ibid.*, pp. 320-321.
[43] *Ibid.*, p. 326.

velopment of Germany, he did not consider their lethal effects to be simply the product of their infusion into specifically German affairs. On the contrary, he felt that cosmopolitanism was basically alien to all tangible aspects of international relations. Again and again he demonstrated that the cosmopolitan idea of supposedly universal validity was in fact of very limited validity and sought to show that distortion and disaster could be the only results of any attempt to translate cosmopolitanism into concrete political action. The universals of the Revolution were in practice the specifics of French nationalism. The universal monarchy of Napoleon was in practice the reflection of Napoleon's own hypertrophied ego. The struggle which Stein and Gneisenau saw as one of world freedom versus world slavery was in fact one of specific interests which stood to gain or lose by the Napoleonic system. The Christian universalism of the Holy Alliance was actually a doctrine which absolutized and thus falsified the relative interests of the European aristocracy. The absolute pretensions of the Holy Alliance evoked in turn the counter-absolute of the European bourgeoisie. "Europe was again divided into two armed camps each claiming universality: the solidarity of the legitimate regimes on the one hand and the solidarity of the nations aspiring to freedom and self-determination on the other."[44]

"As long as this situation pertained, the individual nation-state uniting people and government was an impossibility."[45] This was the crux of Meinecke's criticism of the cosmopolitan idea. It provided no basis for practical and purposeful political association between the rulers and the ruled. It produced instead anarchy, revolution, and the tyranny of imperialism because it ignored the individual peculiarities of states and the historic development of societies in which group integration was always achieved by means of group differentiation. It sought to unite men with concepts which could not unite them because, Meinecke felt, only the bonds of propinquity, common experience

[44] *Ibid.*, p. 211.   [45] *Ibid.*

and traditions, a basic racial or cultural similarity and a community of values developed over long years of history could provide the coherence which a stable political order demanded. Every attempt to create a political system which flouted the laws of the individual growth of societies was doomed to failure or distortion.

The crowning irony was not simply that the cosmopolitan ideal had certain practical defects but rather that cosmopolitanism was in itself an individual and thus limited perspective which could never lay claim in fact to the universality of its pretensions. The cosmopolitanism of the eighteenth and early nineteenth centuries in Europe was a specifically European view of the world and a European value-system. It had no room for the primitive or exotic cultures which also represented humanity. Without reference to the extra-European world neither the revolutionaries nor the reactionaries of the restoration had any authority to speak with the voice of mankind. In these terms, cosmopolitanism harbored within itself a fatal error even before it was further distorted by interested partisans who used it for their own specific ends.

Hence the choice between the nation-state and the ideal of a universal community of mankind was in fact not the real choice which men must make. There was no option here between an individual and thus relative value on the one hand and a universal and thus absolute value on the other. The real choice was between two individual and relative values. Meinecke chose the nation-state because he regarded it as the concrete value. The nation-state must be nurtured and protected since a concrete alternative in terms of a universal political organization did not exist. The world community offered opportunities for speculation about values. The nation-state offered opportunities for the creation and preservation of values actually affecting man's concrete material and spiritual being.

Given the decision for the nation-state, it was necessary to clear the air of illusions about the existence of a concrete political community transcending the state. This was precisely what

Frederick William IV as the latest personification of cosmopolitanism could not do. His reference points and criteria for political action always transcended his own state. As a result he was powerless to conduct a vigorous and successful foreign policy. It was this issue which divided the Christian conservative Ranke from the Christian conservatism which dominated Frederick William's counsels.

Ranke rejected the ideas of the liberal democrats in the 1840's, but he had also held himself aloof from the court advisers of the 1830's. His distrust of abstract doctrine immunized him to the ideal of the universal political community as well as to the proposition that a national democracy would leave behind the earthier aspects of politics. If Ranke had a doctrine, it was a belief in the persistence of the individual state and the insubstantiality of political goals which sought to scrap the state. Ranke saw the "era of the Revolutionary Wars . . . as a kind of intermezzo of European-universalistic politics in which the development of the life of states was temporarily deflected from the normal pattern based on the autonomy of the individual state personalities. . . . Ranke's approach rejected the universalism of both the liberal doctrine and the legitimist ideology. He had no intention of conceding that Europe could be permanently divided into two armed camps of good and evil. He knew that the historical period in which this dualistic concept arose also breathed new life into the great powers and state personalities of the *ancien régime*. The future belonged not to the universal principle but to the autonomy of the regenerated nation-state. Here, before his eyes, the whole nebulous network of universalistic conceptions in which his generation grew up was torn asunder. The historian became a prophet who gained a profound insight into coming events."[46]

If Ranke had reintroduced reality into political thought, Bismarck had reintroduced it into political action. "He, [Bismarck] like Ranke, saw the era of revolution and restoration as . . . an intermezzo. . . . He reasoned that if there was a principle [of the

[46] *Ibid.* pp. 306-307.

eternal struggle of revolution and anti-revolution, the one bad and the other good] which served as the basis of all politics, it would hardly have escaped the Christian and conservative politicians already relatively plentiful prior to 1789. 'I cannot see that a statesman living before the French Revolution, however well-developed his Christian conscience might have been, would come up with the idea that his total political effort in both domestic and foreign policy must be subordinated to the principle of combatting revolution and that the relations of his country with other states must be appraised solely in the light of this criterion.' "[47]

Ranke and Bismarck thus set aside the idea of the universal community and its concomitant absolute principles and norms of action. Theirs were the decisive voices which secured ascendancy for a counter-proposition: realistic and successful policy could be formulated only if the statesman first looked to the situation and needs of his own state and then considered how these needs could best be realized in terms of the specific position his state occupied in the arena of international politics. Ranke and Bismarck preferred to deal in specifics, in facts, and in power. They regarded generalities about abstract ethical principles as compound sources of error in the formulation of policy. They insisted that the state derives its norms of action primarily from itself and viewed any doctrine forbidding the state to consult its own interests as either self-deception or hypocrisy. In so doing they established a pattern of thought in Germany which expressed itself in German diplomacy as a predilection for "calling a spade a spade" and which in the popular vocabulary came to be known as *Realpolitik*.

[47] *Ibid.*, p. 324. The Bismarck quotation is from a letter from Bismarck to Leopold von Gerlach, May 30, 1857.

CHAPTER IV

STATE AND NATION IN INTERNATIONAL POLITICS

STATE egotism was the fundamental presupposition of the *Realpolitik* which Ranke preached and Bismarck practiced. As we have seen, Ranke coupled the premise of egotism to the idea of a moral purpose which the state ego must fulfill. Bismarck was less concerned with such philosophical qualifications. He was inclined to leave moot the question of state morality and to proceed with the business at hand of serving and expanding the state's power. Almost as soon as Bismarck began to achieve political prominence during the years 1848-1850 he made evident his disagreement with his conservative friends who tended to regard the preservation of the European *status quo* as a sacred trust.[1] To some of them, he proclaimed as his ideal the aggressive policies of Frederick the Great.[2]

In Bismarck's speech of December 3, 1850, Meinecke found the decisive words which governed Bismarck's thinking about the state and which separated him from the other counselors of the king. It was here that "he articulated the great and simple truth which dissipated all the mists of political romanticism: 'The only healthy basis for a great state . . . is state egotism. . . . It is unworthy of a great state to contend for something which does not correspond to its own interests.' "[3]

These words of vigorous and self-confident egotism were in radical contradiction to the political ideas of Frederick William. The psychology of the Prussian king's weakness in foreign policy and of his hesitant and vacillating attitude which helped to frustrate the efforts for German unity in 1848-1850 is summed up

[1] *Weltbuergertum, op.cit.*, pp. 315-316.
[2] *Ibid.*, p. 319. See also pp. 325 and 35-37.
[3] *Ibid.*, pp. 319-320.

in a credo which was the precise opposite of Bismarck's: " 'I recognize the establishment of a true [political] community as a just demand on the part of the [German] nation and as a mission corresponding to the true interests of Prussia. But transcending this and all else is the divine commandment that I may not put my hand to that which is not mine. . . . I cannot express the high value which I place on the unification of the nation. . . . But my duties as a Christian king constitute a still higher value. The two are as far apart as heaven and earth. These are not empty professions. They are commandments. Here is my stand. I cannot do otherwise.' "[4]

The contrast between Bismarck and Frederick William leads to the heart of the problem. Bismarck asserted that the state must be guided exclusively by its own necessities and may take that which it must have. He demanded that the statesman think exclusively in political categories. Frederick William maintained that the state must be guided by the moral law and may not take that which does not rightfully belong to it. In this sense, he required the statesman to think in ethical-legal categories.

Meinecke felt history had amply demonstrated that Bismarck's policies had led to strength and accomplishment while Frederick William's principles had led to weakness and failure. As a scholar, Meinecke could not help appreciating that Bismarck applied his ideas and achieved practical successful results. Nor could he deny his own heritage, since he believed himself and his contemporaries to be the beneficiaries of Bismarck's works. As a result he made Bismarck the activist hero of *Weltbuerger-*

[4] *Ibid.*, p. 275. The quotation from Frederick William appears in Radowitz's *Neuen Gespraechen* (volume I, p. 206) which Radowitz published in 1851 as "an epilogue to the events of 1848-1850." Hence the quotation may not be the actual words of Frederick William but Radowitz's rendition of them. Radowitz was an influential counselor to the Prussian king and was Foreign Minister for a brief period in 1850. He broke with Frederick William when the king yielded to Austrian pressure and abandoned Prussian efforts to assume leadership in the German Confederation. The agreement of Olmuetz in 1850 registered the Prussian retreat and came to be regarded as a symbol of the weakness of Prussian policy under the regime of Frederick William IV.

tum und Nationalstaat, and he accepted the premise of state ego-tism as the fundamental law of politics.

In particular, Meinecke believed that Bismarck's policies, despite their primary concern with the welfare of the Prussian state, were authentic reflections of the idea of the nation-state "because he had to seek the principles governing his actions in the vital internal and external interests of a people united in political community."[5] "His politics are derived from the heart of the moving forces themselves, their essence is individuality, process, and immanence. . . . They vibrate from moment to mo-ment, since they are determined by 'all the nuances of con-tingency, probability and intent.' "[6] In these words Meinecke portrayed Bismarck as the supreme exponent of the autonomous political society which created its own political values, objectives, and methods.

Again Meinecke used the clash of contrast to illustrate the still wider significance of Bismarck's political concepts—here with Bismarck's arch-conservative friend Leopold von Gerlach. Gerlach's rigid insistence on the anti-revolutionary principle as the supreme norm of policy led him to warn Bismarck of the dangers threatening a state which consulted only its own inter-ests. He sought to show that Prussia's welfare had always been advanced where it adhered to a consistent policy of aligning itself with those who fought revolution. He reasoned that a state which did not ground its policy on the bedrock of principle would forfeit its prestige and position among the other powers: " 'He alone is reliable who acts upon certain basic principles and not according to fluctuating conceptions of his interests.' " Meinecke did not deny that Gerlach's ideas could create the ap-pearance of a certain integrity of purpose which "in times of

---

[5] *Ibid.,* p. 320. Here again Meinecke is being consistent with his very flexible definition of a nation. A nation could exist without being politi-cally unified. Moreover, a nation-state could exist without bringing all members of a culture or language group within a political framework, as demonstrated by the relationship between Germany and Austria. (Cf. pp. 11-15.)

[6] *Ibid.,* p. 323. The phrase in single quotes is Bismarck's.

tranquillity could secure to the state a modicum of repute. . . . But at the same time it meant uniformity, rigidity, inability to achieve purposeful adaptation to changing circumstances, suppression of the vital forces of nature and of historical development. He sought the laws of movement not in the moving forces themselves but in that universal, transcendental and absolute relationship into which his faith projected them."[7]

Both Gerlach and Bismarck were determinists, Meinecke admitted, for if Gerlach sought to make an ethical concept the sole determinant of policy, Bismarck's policy was determined by the needs of the state. "But [Bismarck's] kind of determinism belongs to the authentic process of self-determination. The self can only grow and develop and assert itself in struggle and contradiction with the external world. Hence Bismarck's view of the interrelations of states is by no means lacking in forces making for consistency and permanence. These forces are 'the inherent and natural interests of the individual states.' They are clearly not so subject to flux as Gerlach supposed. Indeed, they are more durable than the principles which Gerlach saw as fixed and immutable. Through every change of governmental forms the abiding interests of the state persistently assert themselves. They claim their due whether the state has joined the camp of revolution or anti-revolution. . . . Bismarck gave his friend only the essentials in order to justify his principle of self-determination which required that 'every door be kept open, all action be contingent.' "[8]

Thus Meinecke's argument that states must depend on themselves and not on abstract principles or assumptions about international solidarity in order to achieve security culminated in the example of Bismarck. States were the protagonists on the field of international relations and they must look to themselves if they were to play their roles skillfully. For both Bismarck

[7] *Ibid.*, pp. 322-323.
[8] *Ibid.*, pp. 323-324. The quotations from Bismarck and Gerlach are taken from letters which they exchanged in May 1857.

and Meinecke, this was a matter of correct tactics and strategy in the world of political necessity.

But as always, Meinecke looked beyond Bismarck. He could not be content with mere skill in the game of politics, for he would not concede that the game itself was sufficient justification for the rules imposed by necessity. He insisted that the game be imbued with a spirit which related the politically necessary to the morally desirable. In order to achieve this union of the expedient and the good, it was necessary that the participants in the political game of self-preservation be worth preserving. The basic division between Meinecke and Bismarck was that Bismarck automatically assumed the worthiness of the causes he stood for.[9] Meinecke rejected any such automatic assumptions, and particularly as they applied to the Germany which he both loved and criticized.

Hence Meinecke could not be content to make Bismarck the sole hero of his drama in *Weltbuergertum*. If Bismarck was the activist hero, Ranke was the philosophical and moral one. Ranke and Bismarck were both exponents of *Realpolitik*, but Ranke questioned the purpose of the game in a manner which was

[9] Meinecke's characterizations of Bismarck throughout *Weltbuergertum* are generally pointed in this direction. His review of Bismarck's memoirs in 1899 was more specific. Although Meinecke was full of praise for Bismarck and the memoirs and termed Bismarck "Germany's greatest statesman," he described Bismarck's class-consciousness as "naïve." Bismarck "followed his inborn Prussian-monarchist feelings and his solid instinct for authority." He never displayed any understanding for the authentic idealism of the liberal opposition. He accorded recognition to "the world of ideas of the German middle class . . . only insofar as it created political values capable of realization." Indeed, as Bismarck progressed from one height to another, all factions became merely forces which must be manipulated for the benefit of the state. This was true of his attitude toward the conservatives, his own social class, and the German labor movement. "He is a royalist not from theoretical conviction but because the Prussian monarchy is the healthiest and most vital force in his cosmos." "He does not contend with inner doubts nor indulge in struggles with himself. He serves objective forces—the simplest and most natural there are. . . ." Review of Bismarck's *Gedanken und Erinnerungen, HZ*, vol. 82, 1899, pp. 282, 290, 291-292, 293.

alien to Bismarck. Ranke's answer was that the state's "power and its right to personality are not gifts for random use, not even to enable it simply to preserve its own existence. 'But the condition of [the state's] existence is that it create a new avenue of expression for the human spirit, that it articulate this spirit in unique form and reveal it ever anew. That is its mission from God.' "[10]

In *Weltbuergertum und Nationalstaat*, Meinecke accepted Ranke's answer as his own. Ranke and Bismarck transcended the old dualism of both liberals and conservatives which had assumed that the state ego and the moral ideal were always in contradiction and that the former must bow to the latter. But whereas Bismarck rejected the dualistic concept as an unnecessary and inconvenient hindrance to pragmatic political achievement, Ranke rejected it on philosophical grounds and effected at least a partial merger between self-interest and ethical imperatives by giving the state itself a moral purpose.

So doing, Ranke actually represented a continuation of the two great traditions of the idealist reformers and the romantic conservatives, both of which denied that the state was simply a free agent with no obligations beyond its own self-concerns. The difficulty with these traditions, Meinecke argued, was that the constraints which both liberals and conservatives sought to place on the state were so alien to its nature and to all political reality that the strong would brush them aside and the weak would be hoodwinked. Here Ranke introduced the essential modification. Ranke, too, saw states subject to a universal commandment. "But this commandment does not do violence to the individual and immanent development of states. . . . Ranke did not drive the metaphysical from history but placed it where it belongs: at the glimmering boundaries of experience. Similarly, he did not expunge the universal [idea] from the life of great states but located it where it no longer inhibited their free evolution."[11]

---

[10] *Weltbuergertum, op.cit.*, p. 301. The Ranke quotation is taken from Ranke's *Frankreich und Deutschland*, p. 73.

[11] *Ibid.*

The state, then, exercised power at its own discretion. Its proper criteria for action were its own concrete interests on the one hand and Ranke's universal ethical commandment on the other. But if this commandment could be discerned only at the very edges of experience, it was likely to provide a highly uncertain balance to the weight of political interest. There was clearly need for a more concrete point of ethical reference if the statesman was to follow in practice policies which were more than merely expedient.

Ranke himself had interpreted his universal commandment so as to give it a more concrete content. When he said that "each people is a different expression of God's idea of humanity" and that "nationality imbues the state with moral strength," it followed that service by the state to the nation was clearly a moral achievement. Certainly, as Meinecke contended, Ranke's political philosophy "incorporated elements from the classic and romantic movements—the idea of the cultural nation, of the spirit of the people (*Volksgeist*), of a unique spiritual nationality [capable of] creating new spiritual individualities."[12]

Yet Ranke refused both in thought and action to equate the concrete manifestation of a universal norm of politics with the nation as such. As we have seen, he did not share the liberal enthusiasm for the nation-state as it was expressed in the era of Prussian Reform and in the efforts to achieve national unity during the Frankfurt Conventions of 1848-1850.[13] His fundamental conviction, in common with the conservatives, was that the German spirit was most truly expressed in the then existing system of sovereign individual states and that the vigor and individuality of these states was the best service to the nation. Above all, he regarded "the state as by nature a far more cohesive entity than the nation."[14] Hence, like Bismarck, he favored the interests of the Prussian state over those of the German nation. The concrete emanation of the universal command-

---

[12] *Ibid.*, p. 305.
[13] See Chapter II, above.
[14] *Weltbuergertum, op.cit.*, p. 296.

ment was identified with the vigorous political will-center as such, quite independent of the question whether the community it represented was a national community.

Meinecke criticized Ranke for "very seriously underestimating the forces in Germany which were pressing toward a more systematic political unification of the cultural nation."[15] He did not go beyond this pragmatic censure in *Weltbuergertum und Nationalstaat*, and only in later works did he expand his critique. But it is clear that from the start Meinecke found Ranke's interpretation of the universal commandment still too abstract and ambiguous for a practical political ethic. He could not be wholly satisfied with a system of ideas which tended to see mere political vigor as a justification for egotistic conduct.

Once again, Meinecke turned to the values of early nineteenth-century Germany to complete the picture of state and nation to his own satisfaction. He had drawn on the ideas of Stein, Boyen, and Humboldt to portray state and nation as the bringers of freedom to the individual. Now he turned to the philosophy of Fichte in order to identify the political nation as the supreme concrete justification and rationale for state egotism in international politics.

Under the impact of Napoleon's triumph over Prussia, Fichte exhorted the German nation and its leaders to embrace the teachings of Machiavelli. The erstwhile cosmopolitan and detractor of the state now called for a maximization of state power in order to break Napoleon's grip on Germany. He now asserted the absolute right of the state to defend itself and to use whatever weapons necessity commands.[16] But, like Ranke, Fichte probed for a deeper meaning to the imperative of political survival. "He sought to find reason in a process of apparently egotistic forces and to reconcile it with his highest ideals of humanity."[17] More clearly than Ranke and more nearly like Meinecke, Fichte identified the nation as the giver of light in the political struggle. He did this by removing the idea of divine sanction

[15] *Ibid.*, p. 307.   [16] *Ibid.*, pp. 102-103.   [17] *Ibid.*, p. 104.

from the camps of both revolution and counter-revolution and locating it in the nation itself: " '. . . every nation strives to expand the unique good which it represents to the limits of possibility and to encompass within itself, insofar as it can, the whole of humanity. This is in accordance with a God-given impulse in man, causing that interrelationship of creative tensions upon which the community of peoples rests.' "[18]

Meinecke called Fichte's formulation "among the most significant and profound words of his time; it reconciled the essentials of the old power struggles of states and the new nationalism of peoples with the cosmopolitan and universalistic ideals of the contemporary German spirit."[19] Fichte had taken the "decisive step in that he recognized the power drive of states as a natural and beneficial life-impulse and so accorded it a place in a moral philosophical system. The teachings of Machiavelli and the counter-arguments of the anti-Machiavellians were partially transcended and partially elevated to a higher level and there reconciled with one another."[20] Fichte was able to make this contribution to political thought, Meinecke asserted "only because the concept of the nation now joined the concepts of the state and of humanity to put the state in a new light. If the state was not simply the will of the prince, if it was not driven solely by a cold interest in its own self-preservation but was borne by a vital national community and if this community was of value to humanity precisely because of its individuality, then the power-drive of the state gained nobility and morality."[21]

Here Meinecke fully revealed the decisive role which the nation played in his thinking about the politics of states. The nation was the concrete criterion by which the statesman could be guided and the state judged. So long as the state served the nation, it was worth preserving, and the struggle for power and survival was imbued with a moral significance transcending and justifying the techniques appropriate to political contest.

Meinecke had already identified the nation as the ideal po-

---

[18] *Ibid.*   [19] *Ibid.*   [20] *Ibid.*, p. 105.   [21] *Ibid.*

litical community because it best corresponded to the rational and nonrational dynamics which make for group association and identification. By virtue of this correspondence the nation was the best foundation for the organizing of harmonious human relationships and hence for a community in which the human being would achieve the highest possible degree of self-expression as an individual personality and as a member of society. Now the ideal nature of the nation as the giver of internal freedom was paralleled by the ideal nature of the nation as a participant in international politics. The external power relationships of nation-states, including the impulses toward expansion and self-aggrandizement, could be justified in Fichte's terms as natural strivings of morally creative communities to increase the area and effectiveness of their moral achievements. The conflicts arising among political nations were thus part of that process of "creative tension" which was the basic characteristic of the world community.

The last philosophical barrier to the complete autonomy of the nation-state was now removed. Since the nation was the natural guarantor of internal political freedom, it must be co-extensive with the sovereign state. Since the nation was an agent of human freedom, its own security and the advancement of its interests were moral values which the state was duty-bound to serve. Since the nation was the optimum concrete social expression of the universal commandment of moral community, it could not be transcended. And since the nation, like the individual personality, could develop moral stature only in the process of conflict and adjustment with the external world, collisions between nations were part of a natural and moral process of growth. By virtue of its service to freedom and by virtue of the fragmentized and differentiated world in which it existed, the nation must be free in its external relations and must brook no interference with its sovereign self.

Meinecke thus affirmed the sovereignty and autonomy of the nation-state, but he did not construe national sovereignty as a claim to unlimited freedom of action. On the contrary, he believed that the idea of the sovereign political nation provided the most realistic and practical restraints on the arbitrary exercise of power. Internally, the national concept guaranteed the right of political participation to all the members of the national community and thus put a premium on voluntary social cooperation rather than on arbitrary exercise of force. Externally, the nation faced a multitude of other nations whose sovereign virtues and rights were as good as its own. Hence the logic of Meinecke's argument was that while nations might be free to clash with one another in the pursuit of their individual and sometimes inimical ends, they might not impose their wills on one another to the extent that the vanquished in a particular contest would cease to exist as an independent entity.

Finally, if the individual nations were expressions of and subject to the universal commandment to realize moral values in a moral community, every nation had in fact a universal function to promote the moral dignity of man. It was in this sense that Meinecke established a positive connection between the universalist assumptions and cosmopolitanism of the eighteenth century and the emergent nationalism which followed in their wake. Although *Weltbuergertum und Nationalstaat* celebrated the triumph of the nation-state over the cosmopolitan idea, cosmopolitanism "originally was not simply a poison; it was also an antitoxin."[22] The same rationalists, revolutionaries, and reformers whose idealism and universalistic assumptions about the nature of human society distorted or vitiated their political accomplishments had provided the major impetus toward the development of a new sense of political responsibility on the part of both the rulers and the ruled. The years of revolution and revolutionary wars created a ferment that sapped the foundations of the traditional monarchies in which the rulers had exercised their power with no sense of accountability to their subjects.

The revolutionaries and reformers preached the rights of man.

[22] *Ibid.*, p. 326.

The logic of events indicated that the nation was the vehicle for the practical realization of these rights. Thus "the invasion of the state by universal and by national ideas occurred simultaneously and in intimate mutuality."[23] Historically, the cosmopolitan idea had played the indispensable role of catalyst in the rejuvenation of the state and in the fostering of the nation-state.[24] Philosophically, the cosmopolitan concept of the state as a community for the protection and promotion of the rights of man had an enduring validity; it was an abstract reflection of the same universal commandment of moral community whose concrete manifestation was the nation. In this light, the apparent contradictions in the admixture of cosmopolitanism and nationalism are resolved in a deep-rooted consistency which united the dominant ideas of eighteenth- and nineteenth-century Europe and animated the men who participated in the formulation and elaboration of these ideas. Fichte's dictum that "the state is the means to the higher purpose of the fulfillment of pure humanity in the nation"[25] and Ranke's words that " 'each people is a different expression of God's idea of humanity' "[26] symbolized the profounder unity of concepts which on the surface were highly antagonistic. Symbolic, too, was the fact that Revolutionary France, "springing from the womb of the eighteenth century, which was saturated with ideas of universality and cosmopolitanism, . . . was the first great nation-state of Europe."[27]

Thus Meinecke viewed the concepts of nation and humanity in the same kind of perspective in which he viewed the relationship of real and ideal—in a polarity of opposites. Each was indispensable to the other, for the existence of each was possible only in the "creative tension" generated by its opposition to the other. Meinecke saw the universal needs and values of human-

[23] *Ibid.*, p. 327.

[24] *Ibid.*, pp. 327 and 331.

[25] *Erhebung, op.cit.*, p. 84.

[26] Meinecke notes the close correspondence between Fichte's and Ranke's ideas and the influence which Fichte had on Ranke. Cf. *Weltbuergertum, op.cit.*, pp. 105 and 298-299, note 2.

[27] *Weltbuergertum, op.cit.*, p. 19.

ity and the individual needs and values of the nation always confronting and conditioning one another. When he wrote that "[history's] truest function is both national and universal,"[28] it was a generalization which beheld the interaction of the two sets of values as defining the supreme dimensions of historical thought and investigation.

Hence each set of values had its own legitimacy. Neither could claim absolute validity, and the historian or statesman would err if he proceeded on the assumption that one or the other was the exclusive source of political understanding or moral insight. Meinecke's affirmation of the nation was not a superficial glorification of the national idea versus the idea of humanity. Rather it was the result of an investigation of the national and universal components which went into the building of the modern nation-state.[29] It was a judgment that the nation was essential to a cohesive body politic in the modern world. But it was also a judgment that state and nation must serve the universal function of human dignity. ". . . If the modern nation-state is to remain capable of self-renewal it must harbor within itself a vein of universal life and must be constantly justified before the judgment seat of the highest ideals of men."[30]

Meinecke contested the simplistic nationalist idea that the

[28] *Ibid.*, p. vi. (Foreword to the second edition, May 21, 1911.)

[29] "It is the common belief that the awakening of the idea of nationality and the nation-state was preceded in Germany as elsewhere by an age of cosmopolitan thought. If our investigation should serve only to validate that opinion, we should merely be entering doors already opened. But that common belief confronts cosmopolitanism with national sentiment as though each was a mode of thought exclusive of the other, as though both were always in conflict and had no further relationship than one of mutual displacement. Such a conception cannot satisfy the historical sense which is trained to think in terms of broader relationships and to seek the core of continuity in every intellectual development. Thus it is one of our major tasks to demonstrate the true relationship between national and universal ideals in the rise of modern German thinking about the nation state." *Ibid.*, pp. 19, 20.

[30] *Ibid.*, p. 59.

era of cosmopolitanism was wholly harmful or superfluous. "Nothing is superfluous which establishes the inner spiritual continuity of two great epochs. . . . Nothing is superfluous which gives wing to the historic deed in moments of great decision."[31] Here again, Meinecke turned to the Prussian reformers to illustrate his point. "Could Stein have persuaded the Czar at the end of 1812 to pursue the war beyond Russia's borders had he not been the European statesman . . . who could go beyond state and national interests to deal . . . in universal ideas transcending the state?"[32]

Indeed, in deprecating the cautious policies of Frederick William III toward Napoleon, Meinecke indicated that the long-run balance of political truth lay with those who placed the ideals of humanity higher than the state. "Measured by ordinary standards, the intent of the king to eke out the existence of his weakened country would have been a healthy and realistic policy. . . . But Napoleon was an anomalous force. . . ." and Prussia's continued survival or destruction depended on his arbitrary will so long as it either vacillated or did nothing. "This was the weak point in the policy of the king and the strong point . . . of the reformers" who wanted to throw all caution to the winds and have Prussia fight alone if necessary to free Germany and Europe from slavery. Meinecke conceded that the king's caution might have been the factor which saved Prussia from final disaster. But he asserted that Prussia's ultimate contribution to the defeat of Napoleon in 1813 and 1814 could never have been possible without the spirit and presence of the radical reformers who thought in terms of "world freedom and world slavery."[33]

There is a paradox worthy of further investigation in the fact that the men who did most to infuse the Prussian state with a new dynamic were those who were most ready to sacrifice the state. Meinecke observed that "Stein and his supporters were not dismayed by the possibility that Prussia's challenge

[31] *Ibid.*, p. 327.   [32] *Ibid.*   [33] *Erhebung, op.cit.*, pp. 197-203.

[to Napoleon] might result in its destruction."[84] And he summed up the feelings of the reformers with Boyen's words " 'As men of honor let us face the storm so that the coming generations will not completely despair of the values of our time.' For him too, the most Prussian of all his compeers, there were higher values than the eking out of the state's existence at any price. Here spoke the 'epoch' and the 'man'."[85] Meinecke was unstinting in his admiration for the men of the Prussian Reform who transcended the state and, so doing, rejuvenated it, but he did not probe deeply into their paradoxical ambivalence toward the state. And he was nonetheless firm in his belief that the "antitoxin" of universalism which they injected into political life inevitably became a "poison."

It was this conviction that underlay his general tendency to treat nationalism as the positive idea and cosmopolitanism as the negative. So long as Meinecke accepted Bismarck's state, this treatment was inevitable. His depreciation of the cosmopolitan idea stemmed not only from his belief that it could not be realized in terms of a practical political community but also from his German patriotism and from all the political preferences and choices associated with it. The judgments arising from both insight and bias combined and harmonized with Meinecke's affinity for the idea of the individual and his abhorrence of the conformism which universalist concepts implied.

Finally, his insistence on empirical techniques of investigation as the proper method of the historian further intensified the emphasis on the nation. Meinecke argued that the factors making for the growth of a community "can be ascertained not by some universal theorem but only by an investigation of the concrete particulars."[86] Hence specific and observable po-

[84] *Ibid.*, p. 193. Cf. also *Boyen* I, *op.cit.*, p. 161.
[85] *Erhebung, op.cit.*, p. 200.
[86] "If general laws are operative in this process, they are not accessible to our experience. It is true that here and there one can believe that he has seized upon a fragment giving evidence, if not of general laws, at least of general tendencies, and that he has observed similar basic characteristics and developmental stages in all or many nations. A more in-

litical interests commanded greater attention than more nebulous ideas about the nature of man and humanity as such. And, like any good historian, Meinecke went to great efforts to uncover the specific interests which these ideas often enough succeed in disguising.[37]

Thus intellect and emotion joined to make Meinecke primarily an heir of the conservative nationalist tradition. Burke and de Maistre too had used the historical method to counter the revolutionary concept of the universal rights of man with the concept of the specific rights of Englishmen and Frenchmen. In *Weltbuergertum und Nationalstaat* Meinecke defended the specific rights of Germans to pursue in their own way the organization of a political nation.

With all his emphasis on the validity of nationalism, Meinecke's basic purpose was to reconcile the dominance of the nation-state in his political thinking with the retention of the essence of the cosmopolitan idea. He sought to show that the autonomy of the state and nation was both natural and right and at the same time asserted that state and nation have obligations to a universal norm transcending themselves. In his development of this dialectic between liberty and obligation, Meinecke's awareness of the constant presence of the two conflicting concepts undoubtedly determined his increasing use of the word "autonomous" and his more and more consistent avoidance of the word "independent" when discussing state and nation. For "autonomous" still implied an interrelationship

---

tensive examination, however, reveals that each nation has a completely unique and individual aspect. While the social sciences in general may seek to ferret out as much as possible of the general and typical components of nations, the authentic historian will be more concerned to observe the unique aspects of the individual nation with a maximum of accuracy and discrimination." *Weltbuergertum, op.cit.*, p. 2.

[37] Indeed, Meinecke felt that history must continue to make state and nation its chief concern in order "to avoid succumbing to a vague dilettantism" which was the likely product of too great a concern with the idea of universal history. Cf. *Geleitwort zum 100. Bande der Historischen Zeitschrift, HZ*, vol. 100, 1908, p. 6.

among individual political or cultural entities which "independent" did not.

At the same time, the comprehensive freedom of action which he accorded to the autonomous entities demanded that the interrelationship between them be defined so abstractly as to become almost enigmatic. Here is where the convergence of Meinecke's ideas with Ranke's is most apparent. Though Meinecke insisted on identifying the nation as the concrete expression of Ranke's (and Hegel's) universal commandment (or world spirit)[38] in order to have a more practical criterion by which to judge the internal actions of states, he was content to adhere to the rest of Ranke's system of ideas. Thus he left the universal relationship among states and nations at the "glimmering boundaries of experience."[39]

With Ranke, then, Meinecke could say that "the origin . . . and purpose [of states] are embedded in the universal, but their actual life is only a living out of themselves. It is true that the study of history which contemplates and reflects [this phenomenon] is necessarily universal in so far as anything human cannot be alien to it. But the objects of historical observation, the individual states, can be understood only if they are granted the unconditional right to act solely in accordance with their own nature and profit. Here we find a marvelously constructed antithesis: the actions of states are generated not by universal but by egotistic motivations. But their connotations are universal and the perspective from which they are observed must also be universal."[40]

[38] *Weltbuergertum, op.cit.,* p. 292.

[39] Transcending politics and dealing with the idea of history itself, Meinecke, like Ranke, repeated the process in which he derived the idea of autonomy from the dialectic between liberty and obligation: "In order to give back to historical life its full autonomy it was not necessary to eliminate the universal principles which had hitherto constrained it. It was simply a matter of drawing other and better boundaries between history and universals and to extend the universal idea so wide and so high that history could lead a full and uncramped life under its arc." *Ibid.,* p. 286.

[40] *Ibid.,* pp. 301-302. The Rankian ideas which Meinecke interprets

This basic antithesis which Meinecke affirmed in *Weltbuer-gertum und Nationalstaat* in order to give the state the greatest possible freedom of action constituted the central problem of all his thinking about the state. Since he was deeply aware of the ease with which the state dynamic could brush aside so nebulous a conception of its universal obligations, he invoked the idea of the cultural nation in order to establish more concrete restraints on the arbitrariness of political sovereignty. He saw the nation in a sense mediating between the idea of the state and the idea of universal humanity, admonishing the former that it had transcendent obligations and the latter that the political and cultural community was individual and unique and not universal and uniform.

In this framework of ideas Meinecke could embrace both nationalism and cosmopolitanism, both the realists and the idealists. His nationalism was both political and ethical, and his nation was both a community of power and a community of spiritual values. Hence the nation-state was the ideal political community and the true macrocosm.[41]

Meinecke's insistence on the freedom of the individual po-litical-moral entity of the nation and his consequent disembodi-ment of the universal commandment to which the entities were subject symbolized his own quest for freedom and his abhor-rence of tyranny. His identification of the nation-state as the citadel of liberty is an understandable conclusion from his prem-ises as to where the danger of tyranny lay. As he considered the history of Europe since the time of the French Revolution, he saw the phenomenon of tyranny revealed again and again in terms of supra-national philosophies and movements. The French Revolutionaries, the Napoleonic monarchy, and the Holy Alliance were all manifestations of the tyranny of men who claimed to be the true agents of humanity or the true serv-

here are from *Ueber die Verwandschaft und den Unterschied der His-torie und der Politik* (*Saemtliche Werke*, vol. 24, p. 291).
[41] See Chapter II, above.

ants of God's will when in fact they were usually serving only themselves. In each case these tyrannies sooner or later denied the idea of the national community because of their basically cosmopolitan assumptions.

Their cosmos varied both geographically and spiritually according to their purposes and the political task at hand. As long as the French Revolutionaries were mainly occupied with the seizure and consolidation of power at home, their cosmos was in fact the French nation itself. When they began to push outward and topple the hostile governments surrounding them, the cosmos became Europe. Underlying and reinforcing this pragmatic expansion of horizons was the initial revolutionary postulate of the rights of man which recognized no geographical boundaries whatever. Thus, over the revolutionary nation and revolutionized Europe there always hovered the image of the world and all mankind organized in a universal society of reason.

The dynamic of the Holy Alliance was the product of an analogous conjunction of practical political objectives and philosophic assumptions. Behind the cosmos of the European community of legitimate monarchies lay the cosmos of the Christian universe. The interlocking practical objectives were the maintenance of European tranquility and the restoration and perpetuation of an aristocratic social system. But the justifying myth transcended Europe and visioned all humanity organized in a universal society of faith.

The universalistic assumptions of both revolution and reaction inevitably made the idea of the sovereign power-state their ultimate enemy—hence Meinecke's assertion that both were equally antagonistic to the absolute state of the traditional monarchies and to the national idea which injected new life into these monarchies.[42] The existence of a plurality of autonomous political-cultural entities was in irreconcilable conflict with political doctrines which claimed absolute validity for the whole

---

[42] See Chapter III, above.

of man's material and spiritual cosmos. For Meinecke, the conflict between the sovereign nation and the idea of the world community was profounder than that between revolution and reaction. To support his thesis, Meinecke pointed to the experience of nineteenth-century Europe in which the sovereign state successfully asserted itself and in which both revolution and reaction retreated before the rising force of nationalism.

Accepting the classical identification of tyranny with revolution and reaction, Meinecke thus saw the nation as the strongest bulwark against these two evils. The positive achievements of the national idea in the liberalization of nineteenth-century European society dove-tailed with Meinecke's theoretical propositions about the nature of human association and served as a powerful reinforcement to his conclusion that the nation was the ideal political community. Hence in *Weltbuergertum und Nationalstaat* he portrayed the national idea as the champion of the liberty of the individual state and of the individual human being as well.[43]

If the nation-state was the citadel of liberty it was because it protected the individuality of men and societies against the pretensions of philosophers and politicians who sought to make the world and all mankind conform to their own assumptions and desires. Given this view of the function of the nation-state, it is evident that Meinecke's embrace of nationalism was at least in part due to his fear of imperialism. He did not deny the validity of the cosmopolitan ideal in the abstract; he resisted it only in the concrete. His argument for nationalism was to a

[43] The intellectual debt to Burke is here most obvious. Meinecke explicitly acknowledged this debt by praising Burke as a deep political thinker who preached "the higher purposefulness of much that had previously passed for weakness or irrationality and [saw] the grain of wisdom in the shell of prejudice. He taught respect and even love for the natural and half-wild growth which is imbedded visibly and invisibly both in the private life of the individual human being and in society and the state." Meinecke cites with approval Burke's famous dictum on the state as a historic contract which may not be " 'dissolved at the fancy of the parties.' " *Weltbuergertum, op.cit.*, pp. 137, 138.

large degree an argument for political modesty: there are practical limits to political organization in a world of infinitely variegated individuals and societies. No man and no political philosophy can hope to comprehend this vast realm of individuality in a single system of government. The nation-state is both realistic and moral, for it sets natural limits on political ambition and establishes attainable objectives for political action. The world state is both unrealistic and immoral, for it posits unattainable goals and provides no limits whatever on political ambition. Thus, in practice, the cosmopolitan idea always becomes the imperial idea.

Meinecke saw an inherent imperialism at work not only in the universal pretensions of the revolution and the restoration but also in the cosmopolitan philosophers of the German cultural renascence which he otherwise revered. Humboldt, Schiller, Novalis, Schlegel, and Fichte had all shared the concept of "the exalted universal mission of the German people."[44] If they viewed this mission as an essentially unpolitical one in which the Germans abjured power conflicts with other states in order to devote themselves to the cultural values of humanity, the seeds of imperialism were nonetheless present. The very assumption of a universal mission was the basic fallacy, for, once accepted, there were no compelling arguments to prevent the cultural pretension from becoming political. Thus Adam Mueller, the contemporary of the great philosophers and poets, could draw the inference that the universal mission was the Germanization of Europe.[45] For Mueller, Germany became the political agent of European freedom in the same way that the French revolutionaries and Napoleon had arrogated that function to France.

[44] *Ibid.*, p. 155.

[45] *Ibid.* " 'The great federal system of European peoples which the future will surely bring will fly German colors; for everything great, basic and eternal in all European institutions is, after all, German.' " The quotation from Mueller is found in his *Vorlesungen ueber deutsche Wissenschaft und Literatur*, p. 54.

Meinecke felt that imperialism was the inevitable and logical consequence of any theory which conferred universal virtues upon a specific and hence limited human society. This was true of the French Revolution and it was true of German philosophers who regarded Germany as "humanity's nation" (*Menschheits-nation*). And despite his affinity for the individual, it was true of Hegel too. Hegel "did not contend . . . that the German nation was the universal nation of humanity for all time, but . . . [that] every epoch of world history brings forth a world-historical people as the carrier of the particular stage of development of the universal spirit. [In such a capacity] this people acquires an absolute right against which the spirit of other peoples is without right. Indeed, the world-historical people . . . [acquires the right] to world domination." "The logical consequence of Hegel's construction was a violation of the rights of every historical individuality and the transformation of each into a mere unconscious instrument and function of the world spirit."[46]

Meinecke asserted that the empiric historian must deny such a philosophy. "Certainly the historian does not place equal value on all nations, but he does recognize in every advanced nation a unique and irreplaceable value, because every historical individuality which has developed a rich internal life is irreplaceable."[47] Meinecke pointed out that this was the issue over which Ranke broke with Hegel. It was also the issue which made Meinecke Hegel's critic, for Meinecke's deepest intellectual bond with Ranke was expressed in the concept with which Ranke countered Hegel's idea of the epochs of world history: " 'every epoch has a direct relationship to God. Its value resides not in its effects but in its own existence, in its own self.' "[48] What was true for the "self" of the epoch, Mein-

[46] *Ibid.*, pp. 283-284. Meinecke is paraphrasing from Hegel's *Philosophie des Rechtes* (paragraph 347, vol. 8, p. 433) and *Enzyklopaedie* (paragraph 550).

[47] *Ibid.*, p. 284.

[48] *Ibid.*, pp. 284-285. The Ranke quotation is from his *Ueber die Epochen der neueren Geschichte*, pp. 5 and 7.

ecke contended, "was also true for the 'self' of the state and the nation."[49]

The intensity of Meinecke's efforts to establish the autonomous nation as an insurmountable barrier to imperialism was a measure of his fear and hatred of the imperial idea. In his criticism of the concept of "humanity's nation" in *Weltbuergertum und Nationalstaat* there was already a recognition that the national idea could develop an imperialism of its own. But only with the advent of the First World War did Meinecke begin to investigate in a profounder sense the political and moral ambiguities of nationalism. Then the impact of German defeat, the rise of Hitler, and the Second World War combined to bring Meinecke to the tragic realization that no political organization is immune to tyranny and that the equation of liberty with nationality could not always be defended.

Whatever the difficulties and inconsistencies which Meinecke's original coupling of nationality and liberty cost him, the value of liberty was for him always the more important element in the equation. *Weltbuergertum und Nationalstaat* posited an identity between the national patriot and the free man. Meinecke's subsequent growth as a political thinker was attended by a shattering of this union and a search for a new identity. If the search was not completely successful, it nonetheless allowed Meinecke to transcend the storms of which his own nation became the center and to achieve political insights which revealed a more profound relationship between the ideal and the real in the conduct of states than he had at first assumed.

In the years before 1914, however, Meinecke did not see that in his defense of the nation-state he was in effect conferring upon it the same kind of absolute value for which he denounced the cosmopolitan idea. The national idea provided him with a relatively concrete goal toward which the state must strive in fulfilling its function as a community of power and of spiritual values. But its very concreteness tended to leave relations between states in a condition of anarchy. The concentration of

[49] *Ibid.*, p. 285.

real power and moral values in the nation-state outbalanced the abstract ideal of the universal commandment as it applied to international relations. In such a system the concrete needs of the autonomous state would always have precedence over the transcendent admonitions which could be ascertained only at "the glimmering boundaries of experience." To all intents and purposes, the will of the nation was absolute. If there was a general commandment that each nation had rights as good as any other, it was left to the individual nation to interpret this commandment. Hence there was the constant prospect that the strongest nation would provide the definitive interpretation with the resulting implication that there was no other law in international relations than the law of force.

For all Meinecke's efforts to retain the cosmopolitan idea within his political system, the ideas with which he constructed *Weltbuergertum und Nationalstaat* did in fact lead to a view of international relations in which force was the final arbiter. All the great German thinkers who served as spokesmen for the autonomous state and nation—Fichte, Hegel, and Ranke—assumed that the outermost limits of effective human law and justice coincided with the boundaries of the state.

Fichte had asserted that the prince was "bound by justice and law in relation to his people, but that in relations with other states 'there is neither law nor right beyond the right of the stronger.' "[50] In his relations with other states the responsibilities of the prince " 'raised him above the commandments of individual morality into a higher moral order whose material content is expressed in the words: *salus et decus populi suprema lex esto.*' "[51] Thus the state was a law unto itself, and Meinecke explicitly affirmed Fichte's view when he said that Fichte had defined one of the leading characteristics of statehood: the state's "right and duty energetically and ruthlessly to pursue its own

[50] *Ibid.*, pp. 105-106.

[51] *Ibid.*, p. 106. The passages in single quotes are Fichte's and are taken from Fichte's *Nachgelassene Werke*, vol. 3, p. 426.

self-preservation and to determine for itself what served that self-preservation."[52]

Fichte and Hegel saw the state serving a purpose transcending itself: in Fichte's case, "humanity," in Hegel's case, "the "world-spirit." But for all practical purposes, both let the state itself determine the service it would perform, and their state was thus far more the giver of laws than the receiver. "In the relations of states," said Hegel, "there is no magistrate who mediates and decides what the law is. There are only sovereignties confronting one another. . . . How could there be permanent agreement among states when in each there is a sovereign will?"[53] Meinecke believed that Hegel's words "finally gave even to war . . . an unconditional and definitive recognition and a place in a philosophical system which was unequalled in its efforts to perceive the rational meaning of the world. Hence the Kantian conception of eternal peace in a league of states was to Hegel nothing more than a dream."[54]

Hegel saw a family-like relation among the states of Europe which softened the harshness of the struggle for power. "But this ameliorating influence . . . did not mean that the [principle of] autonomous power politics on the part of the individual state personalities should be subjected to any restraints." Here again Meinecke made explicit his commitment to the emancipated state: "Hegel's thoughts about the relationships of states expressed an authentic empiric sense, a keen political-historical understanding."[55]

Ranke did not follow Fichte in setting the prince above the law. And we have already seen that he refused to accept the Hegelian equation of the real to the right.[56] Thus he denied that any specific state could be identified with the world-spirit or the moral law and saw instead a plurality of contending rights and expressions of the moral law, none of which was absolute.

[52] *Ibid.*

[53] *Ibid.*, pp. 281-282. Meinecke paraphrases Hegel's *Philosophie des Rechts* paragraph 333. (*Werke*, vol. 8, p. 427.)

[54] *Ibid.*   [55] *Ibid.*, p. 282.   [56] See Chapter II, above.

But neither could Ranke find an earthly magistrate to reconcile the different expressions of the moral law. The state could refer only to itself, for although "the ultimate origins and ends of its personality extend into depths and heights where universal forces are at work, . . . in the brilliant light of its daily life it follows universal ideas only insofar as they correspond to its own inmost needs."[57]

Thus state egotism was at the heart of all the ideas which Meinecke portrayed as the truth about politics. These were also the ideas which he believed had liberated his own nation-state of Germany from the doldrums of political quiescence and the threat of cultural annihilation. It was Bismarck who put these ideas into practice. Meinecke felt that Bismarck had given a mighty empirical demonstration that the state ego could regulate itself. Bismarck's knowledge of the egotistic dynamics of politics enabled him to steer a course which avoided the extremes of affront or capitulation. He knew that the German ego was only one among many and that it must find its place in a world of egos and that it could not hope to absorb the world any more than it should allow the world to absorb it. Bismarck thus demonstrated, Meinecke felt, that once the basic truth of state egotism had been grasped, it could serve to make the statesman not only vigorous and successful, but also moderate, wise, and even humble.

Meinecke required that the state serve itself wisely, and in his world of infinite individuality and complexity, wisdom meant moderation. He also required the state to serve the nation, since the nation was the cultural and moral community justifying the egotistic forces which determined the conduct of states. Beyond that, the nation-state was free to impose its will on its neighbors if it had good cause and the requisite strength. Indeed, it would be unnatural if it did not seek to do so in a world where power was a necessity and in which power was always a fluid and relative possession. Moreover, "the fate of the true nation-state is

[57] *Weltbuergertum, op.cit.*, p. 305.

not peace and repose but struggle, friction, and anxiety."[58] Like Hegel, Meinecke saw Kant's eternal peace as only a dream.

As he looked back over nearly a hundred years of European history since the Congress of Vienna, Meinecke could not find that any irreparable catastrophes had occurred. On the contrary, the burgeoning of a multiplicity of powerful autonomous nation-states had been attended by a vast increase in the material welfare of the individual human being. New concrete political freedoms were achieved, and there was a sense of identity between the rulers and the ruled which could be directly traced to the idea of national solidarity. Contrasting these developments with the monarchies of the *ancien régime* and with the imperialism of the French Revolution and the Holy Alliance, Meinecke wholeheartedly embraced the nationalism of nineteenth-century Europe. He accepted the inevitability of struggles between nationalities as representing a natural and on the whole beneficial process of political and moral growth. He did not reject cosmopolitanism absolutely, but he deprived it of all real content in the belief that its concrete expression must always be imperialistic. "The universal idea in the life of states belongs to those spiritual elements that can be the source of blessings only when they remain intangible aspirations."[59]

Meinecke was content then to leave the state's external relations to its own discretion. On the strength of the Bismarckian example, he believed that the autonomous state could recognize its responsibilities and dangers and pursue policies of moderation. And he believed that the marriage of state and nation would provide clearly defined limits beyond which the wise statesman would not go. This series of propositions underwent a profound alteration when Meinecke began to comprehend the full impact of the struggle of 1914-1918. But a parallel series remained unchanged: the individual statesman could never wholly transcend the concrete power needs and values of his own political community. Thus the politics of

[58] *Ibid.*, p. 213.   [59] *Ibid.*, p. 328.

world relations would always be conducted primarily in terms of the individual communities which comprised the world and seldom if ever in terms of the cosmopolitan ideal of the world community. Nation and state, or their counterparts, would always stand between the individual and humanity, and the statesman would always first have to give consideration to the survival of his own constituents. The pattern of world politics would remain a tragic conflict of concrete, tangible interests versus an abstract and glimmering ideal of the human community. The statesman would always have to decide between the two, and his decisions must be left to circumstances and his own sense of responsibility.

CHAPTER V

THE STATE AS A POWER
ORGANIZATION

THE postulate that the state is and should be an autonomous entity, relying on its own resources in an anarchic world, led Meinecke logically to the proposition that the state will tend to subordinate the values of mankind to its own interests. It also led to a parallel proposition in the realm of domestic politics: the state's chief concern is the optimum allocation of its own resources to insure survival. The conclusion then followed that the state will tend to subordinate the values of its individual citizens to its supreme need for power.

Meinecke's reading of history and politics saw international conflict as the chief threat to the power and existence of the state. He therefore accepted the classic doctrine of Ranke that "foreign policy has primacy over domestic policy, that the internal constitution and development of the state are subordinated to the compulsions imposed by the struggle for power and independence in the outside world. The state must build its internal organization in such a way that it will be in the best possible position to pursue its external interests. From [Ranke's] time down to the present moment, historical research and living experience have again and again confirmed that Ranke discovered a natural law in the life of states and that, apart from temporary deviations, this law has always prevailed."[1]

Meinecke's affirmation of the primacy of foreign policy is one of the key ideas in his interpretation of politics and the state. It

---

[1] *Vom geschichtlichen Sinn, op.cit.,* p. 30. The quotation is from "Rankes Politisches Gespraech," first published in 1924. While it represents a relatively late formulation of the doctrine of the primacy of foreign policy, it is only a more abstract and didactic expression of a continuing proposition that is implicit or explicit in all of Meinecke's historical-political writings until after World War II. Cf. *Boyen* II, *op.cit.,*

had profound implications not only for his approach to political phenomena as a historian and philosopher but, naturally enough, for his attitude toward the institutions and policies of his own German state. In view of his hostility toward the concept of "natural law," his use of the phrase in this context is indicative of the emphatic nature of his assumption. Insisting on the relativity and differentiation of human values as against the natural-law tradition which tended to absolutize and standardize them, Meinecke was nonetheless willing to concede absolute and universal validity to the more egotistic components in human life, and specifically to the proposition that the state's first concern is and must be to protect itself from external threat.[2] Even here, however, there was an implicit modification of the absolute position when Meinecke acknowledged "temporary deviations" wherein the law might not apply. Nor did he regard the primacy of foreign policy as an unchallenged absolute.[3] But he constantly approached the conduct of states from this perspective and treated the primacy of foreign policy as a dominant tendency if not a natural law.

This dominant note is struck again and again. Throughout his treatment of the Prussian Reform era, Meinecke consistently portrayed the commands of foreign policy in sharp relief. We have already seen him recording the fact that France's revolutionary power gave enormous acceleration to internal political life in Prussia. The work of Stein and the reformers gained most of its dynamic from the fears engendered by the menace of Na-

---

p. 434; *Erhebung, op.cit.*, p. 76; and Meinecke's article in *Die Hilfe*, no. 47, November 22, 1917, "Vaterlandspartei und deutsche Politik," pp. 700-701.

[2] ". . . state egotism, the ruthless impulse to power and self-assertion, even though it expresses itself in historically conditioned and differentiated forms, is nonetheless in its essence timeless, unconditional and part of the nature of the state." "Grundzuege unserer nationalen Entwicklung bis zur Reichsgruendung Bismarcks" (1915-1916) in *Preussisch-deutsche Gestalten, op.cit.*, p. 40.

[3] Cf. "Vaterlandspartei und deutsche Politik," *op.cit.*, cited and discussed in Chapter VIII, below.

poleon. Municipal, agricultural, and educational reforms, although ends in themselves, were also tailored to the objective of making the state better able to resist foreign encroachment. Meinecke saw Stein's supreme and unrealized reform, the creation of a national representative body, as "a proud and mighty weapon for a war of liberation." "The political rights which the nation would have achieved through the establishment of a Reichstag were designed primarily to create enthusiasm and strength for the struggle."[4]

After Napoleon's defeat, for a short time foreign policy considerations continued to act as spurs to reform, despite the fact that Boyen and Humboldt were almost the only members of the original reform group still in positions of power. Meinecke attributed much of Boyen's success after 1814 in pushing through so many of his liberalizing military reforms to the ambitions of the Prussian king and his prime minister to obtain generous benefits for Prussia at the peace settlement. "If the King and Hardenberg now so willingly accepted Boyen's military reorganization, one of their essential considerations was clearly the forthcoming Congress of Vienna at which they hoped to impress the rest of Europe with the spectacle of the Prussian state in the armor of universal military service. Here again one sees the relationship between internal and external policies, between the impetus to reform and the drive for power."[5]

All these observations served to support the generalization that "the strongest stimuli to vigorous internal reforms usually stem from the state's external situation."[6] But Meinecke did not mean to restrict the impact of international politics to the stimulation of reform. On the contrary, he saw foreign policy once again the paramount factor in bringing the Reform era to a close. After the prospects for a united Germany under Prussian leadership had been destroyed in the Congress of Vienna, he judged as futile the hopes of Gneisenau and many of the

[4] *Erhebung, op.cit.*, pp. 164-165.
[5] *Ibid.*, p. 226.
[6] *Ibid.*, pp. 76-77.

other reformers that they could temporarily set aside the problem of German unity and concentrate on Prussia alone as the object of further internal reform. Gneisenau underestimated the difficulties "if he believed that Prussia, relying only on itself, could achieve this objective . . . in the given international situation. The external and internal life of a state stand in too intimate a relationship to allow an intense concentration on internal matters while leaving external affairs fallow over a long period of time. The external political situation in which Prussia now found itself—the Holy Alliance with its spirit of conservatism—could not be without influence on domestic affairs. This was doubly true in that the external system found a domestic ally in the party of the nobility and in the representatives of a conservative bureaucracy, both of whom had witnessed with resentment and suspicion the burgeoning of a freer national life."[7]

When the revolutionary movements of 1848 temporarily ended the ascendancy of the conservative and anti-national forces, Meinecke again located the center of these movements in the realm of international politics, both at the level of the German nation as a whole and at the level of the Prussian state as a Great Power in its own right. Thus Meinecke devoted the entire second part of *Weltbuergertum und Nationalstaat* to a study of problems which must be understood to a large extent as those of the foreign policy of Prussia vis-à-vis its German milieu. Here the polarity of Prussian patriotism - German nationalism reflects and replaces the familiar polarity of nationalism - cosmopolitanism, and the supreme issue is one of choosing between Prussian and German interests. The struggle between liberals and conservatives assumes a secondary role in the central drama of the fate of Prussia as an autonomous political entity.

In this perspective the ambivalence of the Prussian rulers toward the Frankfurt Convention was less a reflection of the

[7] *Ibid.*, pp. 222-223.

balance between the liberal and conservative forces within Prussia than it was of a concern on the part of those in power for the maintenance and growth of the Prussian state, whatever its political complexion. For this reason the Prussian ministers "with one hand resisted the demand that Prussia sacrifice its existence as a state. At the same time they extended the other hand to the men of Frankfurt and were ready to cooperate in the establishment of a national federal state under Prussian leadership. But [they wanted] a federal state in which Prussia remained Prussia. It was just this hegemonial desire which moved them to give the octroyed [Prussian] constitution so markedly liberal a content, for only a liberal Prussia could assume the leadership of Germany."[8]

Here domestic policy is portrayed as completely subordinate to foreign policy considerations, and the constitutional idea is reduced to the level of diplomatic tactics. Ranke was Meinecke's chief exemplary of this approach. Active himself in the Prussian government's deliberations concerning the constitution, Ranke remarked that "the constitutional instrument must be regarded, without favor or antagonism, as a form by which people today desire to live. The constitution must be so constructed that one can live with it."[9]

Certainly Ranke's acceptance of the constitutional idea was a response deriving from a concern for the internal stability of Prussia, and he believed that a constitution was necessary to restore that stability. But stability was not an end in itself; it was at the same time a prerequisite to the role that Ranke felt Prussia must play in Germany. He believed that Prussia could no longer live alone and that part of its power and significance

[8] *Preussen und Deutschland, im 19. und 20. Jahrhundert*, Munich and Berlin, 1918, p. 12. This book is a collection of essays and lectures which Meinecke had published individually between 1896 and 1917. The quotation is from a lecture entitled "Preussen und Deutschland im 19. Jahrhundert" given on April 19, 1906. The book will hereafter be cited as *Preussen und Deutschland.*

[9] *Rankes Werke*, 49-50, p. 592ff. Quoted in *Weltbuergertum, op.cit.*, pp. 456-457.

in European politics was now bound up with the influence which it was able to exercise in the rest of Germany. Were Prussia to go its own way against the tide of sympathy for the constitutional idea in all of Germany, Ranke believed that it would have to give up the customs union it had forged and suffer a heavy loss of power and prestige both within Germany and in Europe at large. Thus Ranke saw the strongest reason for supporting a constitutional organization for Prussia "not in the demands of his contemporaries nor in Prussia's internal problems, but in Prussia's relations with Germany. There was the single choice of 'exercising influence or submitting to it.' . . . And in order to exercise influence, Prussia now had to make the constitutional idea a reality."[10]

The same ascendancy of external power considerations over internal political goals is found in Meinecke's picture of 1848-1849 at the level of the whole ensemble of German states. He identified the dominant popular passions of the period as being more concerned with unified German national power than with democratic reform. Of these popular passions he wrote that "The truest and most characteristic aspect was the burning desire to take Germany's fate into their own hands. . . . However much the democratic aspirations for freedom often seemed to overshadow all the others, for the most part it was still power —so long and painfully absent—which the Germans longed for. At long last they wanted to act in the world. Of all the demands of 1848 none evoked such a response as the two demands for a German navy and a German emperor."[11]

The First World War brought Meinecke's arguments for the supremacy of foreign policy to a climax. He reviewed the rise of Prussia to the status of a Great Power and concluded that its leadership of Germany and the authoritarian system which dominated the internal politics of Prussia-Germany were ineluctable necessities imposed by Germany's European environ-

[10] *Weltbuergertum, op.cit.,* p. 457.
[11] *Erhebung 1914, op.cit.,* p. 15.

ment. "The predominance of Prussianism in Germany and of the traditional Prussian-conservative tendencies in Prussia itself is based not simply on force, nor is it really the product of economic and social relationships. It is rather the result of the vital needs of every great European state." These needs were summed up as the security of the state from external threat: "In the final analysis the constitutional life of the German Empire will continue to be determined by the exigencies of power politics. Our defense . . . against the outside world requires that we continue to place our reliance on Prussian militarism and the 'Prussian system' in domestic politics which serves that militarism."[12]

During the early part of the war Meinecke's defense of the military influence in Prussian-German life became an impassioned outcry against Germany's detractors. He countered the accusations that German militarism had usurped functions of the civil government and had made the Germans into an aggressive people by challenging critics to deny the proposition that Germany needed a "combat-ready people because of England's envy and because of our geographical position between France and Russia. How can we forget the sufferings which our helplessness forced us to experience ever since the Thirty Years' War? It is . . . iron necessity that requires us to develop a maximum of military power. It is the only sure guarantee of our independence."[13] As the war years progressed, Meinecke continued his defense of the German emphasis on military power. Indeed, he even foresaw the need for an increased emphasis in the future.[14]

[12] *Weltbuergertum, op.cit.*, pp. 524 and 531. The second quotation is from an afterword which Meinecke wrote to accompany the third edition published in 1915.

[13] "Kultur, Machtpolitik und Militarismus" in *Deutschland und der Weltkrieg* (Friedrich Meinecke, Otto Hintze *et al.*, editors) Berlin and Leipzig, 1915, p. 641 (hereafter cited as "Machtpolitik").

[14] *Staat und Persoenlichkeit*, Berlin, 1933, p. 198. This book is a collection of Meinecke's essays written during World War I and the era of the Weimar Republic. The reference is to "Reich und Nation von 1870 bis

The pattern of Meinecke's analysis so far reveals three specific themes. In the era of the Prussian Reform he established a positive relationship between a vigorous external policy and the liberalizing of internal institutions. Thus he criticized Frederick William III for his reluctance to engage in a contest with Revolutionary and Napoleonic imperialism and asserted that a more robust power drive on the king's part would have compelled him to use the instrument of reform before the catastrophe of 1806 forced his hand in that direction.[15] Similarly, the reform period itself was seen as the proper response to the pressure exercised by Napoleon and as a basis for further vigorous external activity in the post-Napoleonic world. Thus for Boyen "Prussian power politics and liberal reform were only different functions of the single idea of Prussia's political and national personality."[16]

Secondly, in his analysis of Germany's position in world politics after 1870, Meinecke established a positive relationship between energetic foreign policy and authoritarian forms. He argued that German geography and history demanded the kind of rigid organization which distinguished the authoritarian state. "An internal predisposition and external fate have made us into a people of discipline and organization. As the late-comers and newest candidates for world significance, we could not rise out of the terrible encircling pressures of the outer world without this armor."[17]

The patent contradiction between the two opposing positive relationships which Meinecke developed can be partially attributed to the fact that he was judging the impact of foreign policy on domestic affairs in two different historical periods. But to say that foreign policy may demand a liberal state in

---

1914," first published in the *Internationale Monatshefte*, vol. XI, No. 8, 1917.

[15] *Erhebung, op.cit.*, p. 76.

[16] *Weltbuergertum, op.cit.*, p. 338.

[17] "Reich und Nation von 1871 bis 1914" (1917) in *Staat und Persoenlichkeit, op.cit.*, p. 198.

one era and an authoritarian state in another does not reveal the full dimensions of the problem.

As we have already seen, Meinecke was often a sharp critic of authoritarian institutions in Germany, and this criticism goes far in balancing his defense of German militarism and elite rule against the reproaches of foreign critics. Indeed it is precisely the attitude of defensiveness which is the distinguishing mark of Meinecke's discussions of the illiberal aspects of German political life. Unhappy necessity is the tone of the argument which justifies the "Prussian system." On the other hand, we shall see Meinecke turning once again to the positive relation between external pressure and internal reform in his interpretation of the meaning of the First World War. And in his treatment of the positive relationship between foreign policy and liberal institutions there is always the note of creativeness, of seizing the opportunity to build a better and freer community in the face of external danger. The Fichtian concept of the "creative tension" between nations and Meinecke's belief that nations as well as personalities develop moral stature only in the process of conflict and adjustment with the external world are clearly evident.

Meinecke would have liked to believe with Ranke that contests between states were contests of "moral energy," that the superior moral force was usually ultimately victorious,[18] and that this moral force was reflected in the ethical development of a community toward greater internal freedom. He was realistic enough to see that the exigencies of foreign policy often worked the other way to make a state restrict the freedom of its citizens and to rigidify the internal political hierarchy. But there was always the normative note that wise policy should respond to foreign dangers by seeking to achieve a greater degree of individual consent to and participation in affairs of state.

Given this attitude of mixed hope and faith, Meinecke's vigorous if defensive vindication of the authoritarian tradition

[18] *Staatsraeson, op.cit.,* pp. 479-480.

of Germany becomes even more contradictory. The intellectual and emotional tensions created by the contradiction might have become insupportable were it not for the third aspect of his analysis of the interaction of foreign and domestic politics. This was the primacy of foreign policy as such, without any qualification as to whether vigorous pursuit and defense of state power would favor liberal or illiberal internal government. Meinecke's basic proposition was that man's civic life is a creature of relations between states rather than within states, that "the polarity between revolution and counter-revolution in the internal life of the state . . . is secondary to the great issues of power politics in foreign relations."[19] This was the decisive theme of which the relationships between foreign policy and specific domestic political institutions were only variations. It was Ranke's guiding thought in his stand on the Prussian constitutional issue in 1848-1849 and Meinecke's basic assumption in his evaluation of that issue. Not only did it permit Meinecke to temper his censure of the arbitrary aspects of German political life but it led him generally to underplay the issues in domestic politics.

In 1848-1849 Ranke had treated internal political life and the constitutional idea which symbolized it primarily on the level of tactics. A Prussian constitution was a means of extending Prussian influence in Germany and of coming to terms with the dominant political mood. For Meinecke the constitution was much more than that. It was necessary and desirable as an end in itself, and that end was to protect modern society and the individual from tyranny.[20]

Meinecke was far more profoundly concerned with the liberty of the individual and of domestic political institutions than was Ranke. But his persistent tendency was to deal with the problem of these liberties in terms of Ranke's primacy of foreign policy, which in practice becomes a formula conceding an absolute

[19] *Vom geschichtlichen Sinn, op.cit.,* pp. 29-30.
[20] "Constitutions, statutes and settled rights are an absolute necessity of political life." ("Liberalism and Nationalism in Germany and Austria" in *The Cambridge Modern History,* vol. XI, New York, 1909, p. 57.)

right of the state to override the wants of its citizens in the name of state security. Meinecke believed in constitutional government, but he preferred a constitution which did not permit the liberties of citizens to interfere with the state's external policies. He argued that the conduct of foreign policy was the most basic and delicate of the state's functions and that it must be free of pressure from mass passions. "Foreign policy is and always will be in large measure a matter of trust—a dictatorship based on trust."[21]

Here, then, was the crux of Meinecke's position in the polarity of foreign and domestic politics. Civil liberty and popular participation in affairs of state must be striven for in harmony with the peculiar nature of the state as a power organization. Foreign policy, the protection of the power organization in a world populated by actual or potential opponents, is the basic function of the state. Realistic goals for civil society must take this first political fact of life into account and must be fashioned in accordance and not in conflict with it.

The constitution must protect the state as well as the people. Its mission must be to effect an optimum relationship between the liberty of the citizen and the state's need for power. Meinecke could not accept the idea that a constitution should hand over all rights and responsibilities of governing to the people. Rather he saw it as an instrument for defining the competencies of the people, on one hand, and of the state on the other. Each set of rights and responsibilities should be inviolable, the government refraining from interfering with the established privileges and immunities of the citizenry and the people refraining from attempts to control certain defined functions of government. The government had no right to abrogate freedom of speech and opinion; hence Meinecke opposed the repressive policies which Bismarck directed against the German socialists. But the citizen had no right to force his often uninformed and

[21] *Probleme des Weltkriegs*, Berlin, 1917, p. 112. This book is a collection of essays written during World War I. The quotation is from "Die Reform des Preussischen Wahlrechts," first published in 1917.

immature judgment on the government in matters of extreme delicacy and danger; thus the requirement that foreign policy, the chief among these delicate and dangerous matters, be conducted in terms of a "dictatorship of trust."

As long as Meinecke believed that the traditional aristocratic, military, and bureaucratic elite of Prussian-Germany would exercise this dictatorship of trust with a feeling of responsibility for the state and the people as a whole, he would not concede that it should be controlled by anything other than its own conscience and reason. Only when the war years convinced him that the governing elite had lost its sense of responsibility did he contest the dictatorship. And then his solution was not to abandon the idea of dictatorship but rather to reform the elite and give it the broader base which he felt would insure the revival of a community of trust and consequently of a responsible dictatorship in the realm of foreign policy.[22]

Whatever the elements which composed the elite, the fear that an uninformed and easily misguided public opinion might ignore the primacy of foreign policy or misinterpret its meaning compelled Meinecke to seek means to insulate foreign policy from public control. And in so doing he left unprotected the Achilles' heel of his own ideals of liberty for the individual in civil society. Given his emphasis on the fundamental role of foreign affairs in the life of the state, he found it a difficult task to draw the line between the necessities of state and the freedom of the individual.

The "dictatorship of trust" inevitably involved more than the actual conduct of foreign relations; it also served as the legitimization of institutions which powerfully affected domestic politics. In Germany's case these institutions were an aristocracy, a military establishment, and a bureaucracy which claimed for themselves the major role in the creation and development of the German Empire and which preempted a corresponding share of political power. From 1871 until 1914 these institutions, but-

---

[22] Cf. Chapter VIII, below.

tressed by the real and imagined requirements of Germany's uneasy position in world politics, coexisted with a reasonably open society in which the individual had very considerable freedom to express his opinion, join the party of his choice, and make known the criticisms he might have of government and politics in Germany. But as the war years deepened into crisis, the "dictatorship of trust" reached out to swallow up the whole of German life.

Meinecke had qualified the idea of the dictatorship of trust by stating that foreign policy must be conducted in terms of such a dictatorship "in large measure." The qualification implied that there are and should be some public controls, including, presumably, the ultimate right of the citizen to contest the direction and directors of foreign policy if that policy was clearly placing the community in intolerable peril. But the contention that all other values were secondary to the protection of the state from external threat buttressed the power of the dictatorship so as largely to offset this rather vague limit to its authority. If all other values in the state were subordinate to foreign policy requirements, there was little basis for protest or for practical recourse against the dictatorial elite which could invoke the potent symbols of military danger to justify the sacrifice of one value after another to the German war effort of 1914-1918.

The basic difficulty of Meinecke's approach, which the hypertrophy of German militarism so dramatically illustrated, was that he did not construct a true polarity between state security and individual liberty. He had asserted that "it is the supreme and also the most difficult task of modern culture to harmonize the inalienable rights of the individual and the moral-spiritual ideals of humanity with the stern and unyielding demands of the state which by nature is egotistic and domineering."[23] But the balance of his arguments in concrete issues favored the side of power and security against the idea of civic liberty, and the primacy of foreign policy was one of the chief expressions of this balance.

[23] *Erhebung, op.cit.*, p. 125.

Woven into the whole development of Meinecke's argument for the nation-state was another expression of the balance. At one level, as we have seen, this argument is a plea that the state become something more than a power organization. In order to do so it must rest on the sentiments of the nation.[24] At another level, however, the argument reveals the underlying assumption of the primacy of power, in temporal as well as analytical terms. It implies a sequence in which the establishment of the power organization precedes the development of those cultural and moral values which make the state more than a power organization. Meinecke did not mean to contend that political freedom had to wait until the relatively late appearance of the national idea in history. The essence of his theme was that in any age human freedom had to wait until the accumulation and consolidation of power had created the elements of social stability. First there must be power; then men can turn their attention to other matters. This postulate necessarily required that if power was threatened, men must turn from and sacrifice other pursuits in order to protect the power which was the foundation of their total existence.

Meinecke's analysis of the idea of the nation-state also contributed to the preponderance of the power factor in a far more direct manner. The transfer of values and loyalties from the cosmopolitan idea of mankind to the national idea, inherent in his identification of the nation-state as the true macrocosm, imbued the nation-state with such high functions as to place the question of the desirability of its survival practically beyond argument. All the value and power needs of the individual, the family, the church, of economic interests and social groupings, and of the distant ideal of humanity could not balance the mighty concentration of values which Meinecke attributed to the nation-state. If he had not assigned such towering importance to the national state, he might have treated the primacy of foreign policy as a tactical rule by which states live but which might be

[24] Chapter II, above.

repudiated by individuals and societies when the game of state survival interfered with other crucial values. But pictured as the concrete bulwark of all man's values, the nation-state could and must demand the total subordination of the individual to its own needs.

There was a deceptiveness in both the polarity between nationalism and cosmopolitanism and in the polarity between the need of the state for power and the right of the individual to freedom. In the one, the cosmopolitan ideal was so abstract that it was practically ineffective against the concrete interests of the individual states. In the other, the analytical and temporal primacy of power and the identification of the nation-state as the natural framework for the organization of power robbed the individual of any source of strength outside the nation-state with which to resist the state's demands. In this light the state, following the rule of the primacy of foreign policy, appears as a Janus-like barrier confronting and separating the individual and humanity, ever tending to control the one and deny the other.

CHAPTER VI

THE STATE AS A CULTURAL
INSTITUTION

"THE DREAM I DREAMED," Meinecke wrote in his memoirs, "together with so many of my generation in the years before the First World War was to realize within ourselves a harmonious unification of the legacies of Goethe and Bismarck and so to arrive at a new synthesis of spirit and power. It is true that Bismarck and what he taught us were uppermost in our conscious thoughts and deeds. But Goethe's world was there too as an indispensable complement."[1]

These words are a faithful reflection of Meinecke's mood and method as he probed into the history and contemporary life of Hohenzollern Germany in the pre-1914 world. The dominance of Bismarck was evident in Meinecke's adherence to the concept of the primacy of foreign policy and in his insistence upon the necessity for state egotism in the state's dealings with the external world and with its own citizens. Yet Goethe, the symbol of cosmopolitanism and individuality, indeed, of distaste for the state, did in fact remain an "indispensable complement" in his thinking. The "inalienable rights of the individual," the assertion that the nation-state "must harbor within itself a vein of universal life"[2] were part of the Goethe heritage.

Hence, power and spirit constituted still another polarity to add to those which Meinecke had constructed between real and ideal, between nationalism and cosmopolitanism, and between the state and the individual. At the same time, Meinecke's words that Bismarck was uppermost in conscious thought once more indicated the deceptiveness of these polarities. In seeking a synthesis between power and spirit, he repeated the process by

---

[1] *Erinnerungen, op.cit.*, p. 284.
[2] See Chapter IV, above.

which, in concrete situations, he conceded the primacy of authority over liberty. For he sought the synthesis by attempting to construct the world of Goethe within the confines of the power state.[3]

This procedure was implicit in Meinecke's enthusiasm for the era of the Prussian Reform. His delight in the cultural and spiritual riches of the age of Goethe, Schiller, and Kant was matched by his ardent desire that these riches should not be confined to "a class privilege . . . enjoyed [only] by the scholars."[4] The ideal of humanity which the German poets and thinkers embraced "demanded its own universalization."[5] It must spread beyond the few free spirits and become the ethos of whole peoples. But we have already seen his criticism of the cosmopolitan ideal as a means to the desired end and his arguments for identifying the individual nation and state as the carrier of culture. Hence the nation-state must be made the instrument to provide the necessary education, economic conditions, and political organization.

Meinecke sensed the tragic nature of this thesis, for he observed that the cultural achievements before and apart from the Reform "when the German spirit sought and wanted only its own realization certainly reached higher into the realm of the eternal."[6] But he felt that the menace of Napoleon and the crumbling of the old state threatened these achievements with

---

[3] Cf. Louis L. Snyder, *German Nationalism: The Tragedy of a People*, Harrisburg, 1952: "He [Meinecke] was aware of the dangers inherent in Prussianism in its contemplated [*sic*] dualism of power and culture, and throughout his long career he constantly warned his countrymen that they must never turn to one to the exclusion of the other. However, in advocating the powerful political ethos of the Prussian state as basic, he was, in reality, a victim of his own historicism, which glorified the state as the carrier of history and placed culture in a subsidiary position to power" (pp. 271-272). Dr. Snyder's criticism has considerable validity, as far as it goes. However, he attempts to characterize the whole of Meinecke's thinking in these terms, basing his analysis mainly upon Meinecke's writings during World War I. Meinecke's thought goes far beyond this, as will be shown later.

[4] *Erhebung, op.cit.*, p. 48.   [5] *Ibid.*   [6] *Ibid.*, p. 11.

extinction or at least encapsulation. How were the ideals of human freedom and the cultural values developed by German poets and thinkers to be realized by the German people and built into their social organization unless there was a vigorous and free political life? The rebuilding of a state capable of defending itself and of halting the process of internal social disintegration was the only answer which Meinecke could find. "By descending to the state the German spirit saved not only itself and the state from threatened extinction but also safeguarded for the subsequent generations an abundance of inner values and a source of creative strength and happiness."[7]

As has been noted in an earlier chapter, the fact that Meinecke described the process wherein the German intellectuals turned to political tasks as a "descent" is witness to a standard of values which did not identify the state as the paramount objective of man's strivings. The central thread of Meinecke's evaluation of the Reform period is that the state must serve as an instrumentality to realize cultural objectives. Indeed, so far as Meinecke's ultimate ends are concerned, the polarity of authority and liberty, of power and culture, resolves itself into a supremacy of freedom and cultural values. But the reverse is true at the level of means. The state is the chosen means to realize and preserve the spiritual and intellectual endowments of men. Power and authority are the basic requisites of the state; hence they must be the prime factor for those who seek to create a durable cultural community.

While aware of the peril of this pragmatic subordination of culture to power, Meinecke took hope in the belief that the dynamic of the state was itself not wholly hostile to the world of the spirit. In his approach to the power-state of Frederick the Great, Meinecke saw the imperatives of political power themselves forcing political organization to go beyond the calculations of pure power. He characterized Frederick's Prussia as being ruled by the motto, "There can be no kingdom without

[7] *Ibid.*

soldiers, no soldiers without money, no money without a populace and no populace without justice."[8] Frederick was forced
to educate and infuse a sense of responsibility into greater numbers of his subjects in order to govern, defend, and expand
Prussia. Here political ambition appears as a spur to cultural
and spiritual achievement.

This theme is reiterated when Meinecke considers the problems of the Hohenzollern regime in his own time: "The life of
states and peoples admonishes [us] to reconcile . . . every more
profound rift between power and culture. Indeed, the very
power interest of the state requires it." Power is created not only
by the drive for power but also by the spiritual and moral factors
which make the social fabric strong.[9]

In the crisis years of the First World War, the theme once
again appears: "There are two kinds of forces which maintain
the strength and vitality of the nation-state, regardless of its
form of government. One is firm and more stable, the other more
flexible and fluid. The state's institutions must be substantial and
durable: the power and authority of its highest organs, the re-
liability of its administration, . . . above all, the discipline and
toughness of its military arm. And it must have continuity and
historically-rooted and tested traditions infusing all of its institutions. But not one of these institutions could permanently
assert itself either alone or in partnership with the others if
they were not pervaded by the life-stream from the national
community and its social groups. And these [latter], in the final
analysis, emerge from the souls of individuals. This stream of
life produces the spiritual and moral energies and goals which
support the power of the state and which exalt the state itself
into an idea, into one of the greatest spiritual powers of cultural life."[10]

---

[8] *Ibid.*, p. 13. The aphorism is attributed to a Sassanian prince.

[9] "Nationalismus und nationale Idee," *Erhebung, 1914, op.cit.*, pp.
94-95.

[10] "Reich und Nation von 1870 bis 1914" (1917), *Staat und Persoenlichkeit, op.cit.*, p. 165. See also "Grundzuege unserer nationalen
Entwicklung bis zur Reichsgruendung Bismarcks" (1915-1916) in *Preus-*

Here the circle was at full turn. The proposition that human freedom and culture must depend on power is joined by the assertion that the state would be incapable of functioning without the free individuals who give it life. There is a mutual dependency of power and culture, of authority and liberty. The essence of Meinecke's "dream" was that the nation-state would provide the framework within which the interdependence of power and culture could strengthen both elements in the polarity and sublimate the antagonism between the two. Each should be a spur to the other; for the needs of one are intimately related to the functions of the other. It was a more abstract formulation of Boyen's conviction that "Prussian power politics and liberal reform were only different functions of the single idea of the Prussian state."[11]

The interaction of power and culture was the life-giving dynamic of the state and of the individual in society. In serving the state, the statesman served both elements in the dynamic. Thus the statesman's concern for the protection of the state was a concern for an institution which fosters cultural and ethical values. The cultural ends and the individuals which the state served legitimized its egotism. History had amply demonstrated that the state was the outer limit of significant social cohesion and legal relationships. Hence the protection of the state which alone makes possible the realization of spiritual, social, and human values is an end in itself. In this way Meinecke injected moral content into the causal relationship that forces the state to be primarily concerned with its own protection in an anarchic world and which is expressed by the idea of the primacy of foreign policy.

In his own thought and writings, Meinecke applied his formula of the power-culture polarity and projected the hope that

---

sisch-deutsche Gestalten, op.cit., p. 42: "The spiritual liberation and refinement of German life had to occur first in order to release those bold and free-ranging energies which the new practical Germany now began to develop. . . ."

[11] See Chapter v, above.

each element would continuously present a powerful and creative challenge to the other. If he made a massive case for the role of power, he was equally vigorous in building his arguments that the nation-state must be more than power. He had used Ranke as the supreme authority in developing the theory of the primacy of foreign policy. He also used Ranke as the main support in his warnings that state power should not transgress its own limits. Ranke affirmed the power-state, but "he denied that states which were merely power-states supported by soldiers and money [could ever] be nation-states. He denied their capacity for survival."[12]

Ranke, like Meinecke, insisted that the state must fulfill a cultural and spiritual purpose. Ranke's doctrine of the autonomy of the state was not a glorification of an agglomeration of sovereign power. This became clear in the Rankian formulation to which we referred earlier: "[The state's] power and its right to personality are not gifts for random use, not even for mere self-preservation. 'The condition of [the state's] existence is that it create a new avenue of expression for the human spirit, that it articulate this spirit in unique form and reveal it ever anew. That is its mission from God.' "[13]

Here Ranke's view of the state and that of the men of the Prussian Reform joined, and Meinecke could embrace both without contradiction. Ranke's words were almost indistinguishable from those which Meinecke used to describe the objectives of the reformers who strove "not only for the immediate needs of the state but also for the benefit of individual, nation and humanity, for the highest values of culture and personality."[14]

If the state was to create new avenues of expression for the human spirit, it could only mean for Meinecke that the state must be the instrument of man's freedom, for "the idea that the inner freedom of the human being is the highest of all values is one that neither they [the intellectuals of the Reform era] nor

---

[12] *Weltbuergertum, op.cit.*, p. 299.
[13] See Chapter IV, above.
[14] *Erhebung, op.cit.*, p. 87.

modern man can do without."[15] Freedom was the foundation
and objective of the state. With Stein's reforms, "the state was
to rest on the moral freedom and dignity of the citizen and the
man and secure their recognition in all its institutions." And,
Meinecke added, "that is the real core of our modern idea of
political freedom."[16]

Ranke and the reformers were still in harmony in these words
which portrayed the state as a creative instrument of freedom.
But the paths which led to this juncture of agreement were profoundly different. Ranke was primarily concerned with the state-
instrument; the reformers were basically interested in the goal of
freedom. Living in a different age, Ranke did not share the early
skepticism toward the state which Fichte, Humboldt, Arndt, and
other men of the Reform first had to overcome before they went
into the state's service.[17] The reformers did not suddenly embrace the state as an absolute good. Rather, they retained their
own individualities and values transcending and sometimes conflicting with the state.[18] Even Stein, far less of an individualist
than the others, was willing to sacrifice the interests of the concrete state to the goal of human freedom.[19]

The reformers were always challenging the state to demonstrate its service to freedom; if the state did not fulfill this function, it must be resisted or abandoned. Ranke never felt the
antinomy between the state and individual freedom. The state
was the only framework within which man could exist. He was
not free to choose between the state and a condition of state-
lessness. If he sought to live according to an idea of political

[15] *Ibid.*, p. 52.　　[16] *Die deutsche Freiheit*, Berlin, 1917, p. 23.

[17] *Erhebung, op.cit.* "To Humboldt the state was merely a subordinate
means to which the true end, the human being, must not be sacrificed"
(p. 51). Ernst Moritz Arndt "proclaimed that 'man shall be eternally
superior to the state, and the state may not shackle his strength'" (p.
59). "Fichte, too, subordinated the end of the state to the end of the
individual" (p. 51).

[18] "Stein und die Erhebung von 1813" (1913), in *Preussen und
Deutschland, op.cit.*, p. 126.

[19] See Chapter IV, above.

and cultural freedom which transcended the state he would find either that such an existence could continue only at the state's pleasure or that he must set about building a new community which would in turn assume all the characteristics of the state.[20] With this proposition Ranke underlined his profound commitment to the state as the great and primary instrument of human culture.

As always, Meinecke carried within him the ideas both of the reformers and of Ranke. When he reproached the reformers for being unrealistic about the nature of the state, he sided with Ranke. But even the extremes of idealism in the Reform period had their own value. Meinecke found inspiration in the spectacle of man "soaring beyond the real state" and "seeking even the impossible." In those who understand them, the men of the Reform "fired a sense for the eternal which enables us to tolerate the temporal. If the state is not a cold and oppressive power and the nation not a crude, tribalistic concept, we in Germany must pay first homage to their work."[21]

Like the reformers, Meinecke saw the conflict between the individual and the state. But like Ranke, he considered the relationship between human freedom and the organization of the state far more complex and binding. He agreed with Ranke's Aristotelian view that man is inevitably a political animal and

[20] This position contributed powerfully to Ranke's persistent skepticism toward the idea of a politically unified Germany. As we have noted already, he saw the separate sovereign states of Germany as the real sources of both political and moral energy, and he was persuaded that their vigor as sovereign entities would bring to grief any scheme of national unification which would doom them to disappear. These were the considerations in Ranke's mind when he asserted that "the state is a far more cohesive entity than the nation." Cf. *Weltbuergertum, op.cit.,* pp. 296-299.

Bismarck's successful formula for German unification was in fact built on the theory that the individual German states would not "disappear," and he was careful to insure that theory would correspond with practice at least as far as Prussia was concerned. Ranke's old skepticism nonetheless persisted in modified form even after Bismarck's success, which he accorded only a grudging admiration.

[21] *Erhebung, op.cit.,* p. 234.

that the individual must work out his salvation within the framework of a concrete political society. Given the difficulties of changing political allegiances in the modern state system, the presumption must be that the individual is enduringly and pervasively bound to the political society into which he is born and in which he matures. Even when an individual does abandon his political allegiance to his native land, he cannot entirely eliminate his original conditioning. In any case, the most that he can do is to exchange one political fealty for another. Certainly he cannot take a meaningful role in human affairs wholly without attachments to any concrete—and discrete—political community. He cannot serve an undifferentiated mankind.

These convictions spoke against any attempt of the human being to cast off his political nature, and they bound him tightly to the state. They were also a measure of Meinecke's sense of the indissolubility of his personal ties to his German homeland. But since they existed side by side with his recognition of the inevitable conflicts between human freedom and the necessities of political organization, they did not prevent him from vigorous criticism of the state in general and his German political milieu in particular. Indeed, this ambivalence of attitude, together with his agreement with Ranke and the Reformers that the state must be a moral and spiritual community, were at the root of all Meinecke's criticisms of pre-1914 Germany.

However much Meinecke was committed to the Bismarckian state, he was far from believing that it had achieved an ideal political and cultural life. This achievement was still only a "dream," and there was within Meinecke a deep feeling of the hollowness of certain aspects of the German scene.[22] In judging Bismarck's work Meinecke observed that in the events leading up to 1870-1871 "not the many but the few represented the genius of the nation and had to blaze the trail for their fellow

[22] In *Erhebung, op.cit.*, pp. 8 and 9, Meinecke remarks the "longing for the age of Goethe" and asks the question "whether from half-men we can one day again become complete human beings."

countrymen."[23] While affirming that "Bismarck was our necessary Moses," Meinecke asserted that the lack of popular participation in the creation of the Second Reich was its great weakness. "The nation's own achievement . . . was too small. It was too much the instrument in the hands of a mighty leader. It still had to become . . . energetic and mature by virtue of its own activity."[24]

This weakness at the beginning continued to mar the progress of the new Germany. Meinecke used Bismarck's policy toward the German socialists as a prime example, flatly declaring Bismarck wrong in his denunciation of the socialists as 'un-German.'[25] Even the fact that Bismarck took over part of the socialist program did not detract from his error, for Bismarck's social reform was too much "for the people" and not enough "of the people."[26]

For all his defense of authoritarian forms as necessities imposed by Germany's position in international politics, Meinecke was acutely aware of the threat which the authoritarian tradition posed for the successful functioning of domestic political life. He regarded direction from above and lack of participation from below as the chief problem of German politics. He saw not a gradual political maturation and activation of the people but a "growing alienation of the masses from the state."[27] The course which had been set in the 1870's and 1880's remained basically unchanged; the gulf between the ruling elite and the growing working class continued deep.

In describing his abandonment of the conservative party and his increasing sympathy for the liberal and social reform ideas of Friedrich Naumann, Meinecke remarked that "it was my guiding idea [to help] in winning the working classes . . . for the national state—first and foremost because of an inner [con-

---

[23] *Erhebung 1914, op.cit.*, p. 16.   [24] *Ibid.*, pp. 18-19.
[25] *Preussen und Deutschland, op.cit.*, p. 517. The reference is to Meinecke's article, "Bismarck und das neue Deutschland," first published in 1915.
[26] *Ibid.*, pp. 518, 519.   [27] *Erinnerungen, op.cit.*, p. 126.

viction of] the need for an authentic national community." This necessity was made the more imperative when Meinecke considered Germany's relations abroad: "Then too, because [this reconciliation] was the *conditio sine qua non* for . . . a more active German role in world politics."[28] Here again external and internal politics are interwoven in the pattern of liberalism at home and power politics abroad.

Ironically enough, Meinecke in part attributed the failure to reach the desired goal of a true national community to Bismarck's use of foreign policy techniques in domestic government. He suspected Bismarck of deliberately setting the stage for a conflict between the Prussian Diet and the German Reichstag so that the government "could pursue its own policies as the third and strongest power. . . . Its [policies] were and had to be carried out more in terms of foreign than domestic policies. Diet and Reichstag became more and more two powers with differing spirit and direction, so that the government had to make deals first with the one and then with the other. As in foreign policy, the government desired that neither one should be too strong or too weak so that the government could itself call the turn. Much can be achieved by the use of such methods. But there is one objective which can be realized only with great difficulty. And it is just this objective which must be the aim of every authentic domestic policy: a sense of unity in all aspects of public life."[29]

Meinecke's observations led him to two fateful questions: whether the mode of government which Bismarck had established "was always as desirable for the ruled as it was for the rulers" and whether the system carried with it "the warrant of historical durability."[30] When writing *Weltbuergertum und Nationalstaat* in 1906 and 1907, he deliberately and meaningfully left these questions open. After the outbreak of the First World War, inspired by the sense of spontaneity and unity which

[28] *Ibid.*, p. 123.
[29] *Weltbuergertum, op.cit.*, pp. 519-520.
[30] *Ibid.*, pp. 518 and 524.

the Germans demonstrated, he believed the questions could be answered in the affirmative. With the coming of the critical years after 1917, he knew the answer must be no.

In any event, these questions were ever in Meinecke's mind and spurred him to criticize stereotyped attitudes, to weigh possibilities of reform, and to ponder the relationship between power and spirit, authority and liberty.[31] And in this process of reflection, he now began to fear that the idea of the nation could itself become an instrument of tyranny rather than a means to the moralization of politics. He feared that the ruling classes were seeking to monopolize the national idea, that Bismarck's branding of the socialists as "un-German" was a symbol of a general perversion of the national community. He was moved to distinguish the "idea of nationality" from "nationalism" and to identify the latter as a distortion of all that he had argued for in *Weltbuergertum und Nationalstaat*.[32]

"One should serve the state as a free man," Meinecke wrote, "as an individual and man of culture, not as a stereotyped patriot . . . the modern nationalist overemphasizes the right of the objective power. He demands that the individual subordinate himself in a rigid and uniform manner to the needs of the state and nation. In such a situation . . . the interests of a ruling class can so easily be smuggled in. Then the vital and free ideal of the nation becomes a conventional dogma. . . . Nationalism cannot endure a free, many-faceted, and differentiated national culture but only one which is schematized and conventionalized."[33]

Yet it was Meinecke's hope and belief that the unifying and

[31] In his memoirs, Meinecke describes his reflections in terms of still another polarity, the one which was to become central to his second great work, *Die Idee der Staatsraeson*: "The relation of ethics and *Realpolitik* . . . spurred me to more intensive contemplation and investigation. Machiavelli became ever more important in my thinking. . . ." *Erinnerungen, op.cit.*, p. 105.

[32] For clarity's sake, I shall not attempt to reflect the distinction in the text but shall follow customary English usage and employ the word "nationalism" as a generic term.

[33] "Nationalismus und nationale Idee," *Erhebung 1914, op.cit.*, p. 91.

constructive forces of the national idea would outweigh and overcome the divisive and corrosive aspects which it was developing. He was not ready to abandon the nation-state simply because mighty conflicts had risen within its bounds. He knew that "there are basic impulses and demands in the life of the individual as well as of peoples which appear to be in irreconcilable contradiction with one another and nonetheless spring from the [common] depths of life." He did not believe that such contradictions could ever be eliminated and thus accepted the prospect of their continued existence. "Ordinary understanding endeavors to deal with the problem either by dulling these opposites to the point of bland indifference or elects to support one or the other with a one-sided radicalism. The great human and historical perspective, however, knows that antinomy is inherent in the moral life of both individuals and peoples. This is the root of all tragedy, but it can also give rise to the highest degree of vitality when the narrow path is found in which the conflicting forces can be joined together."[34] And Meinecke saw the nation as the narrow path on which the conflicting forces of power and spirit, authority and liberty, could best travel together.

He adhered to the proposition that the nation was man's true macrocosm. Its cohesion was the result of both the propinquity and blood-ties of its members and a relatively common cultural heritage. Thus it partook of both the conflicting forces of power and spirit which "spring from the [common] depths of life" in a way which a non-national state or a super-national universal society could not. Moreover, he felt that the shared fund of experience which propinquity and a common cultural framework bring created that measure of trust indispensable for the free community.

Meinecke was strengthened in these beliefs by his interpretation of the liberalizing influence of nationalism as it had manifested itself since the French Revolution. Nationality was a far

[34] "Deutscher Friede und deutscher Krieg" in *Erhebung 1914, op.cit.*, p. 53.

more inclusive concept than economic, religious, or class status, for it implied political participation and responsibility on the part of all members of the community simply by virtue of their being nationals. It conferred on each citizen the right to be considered as "end in himself" and gave to each "a dignity of his own."[85]

In support of his thesis, Meinecke used as his chief example the central instrument of state power—the soldier. "Human dignity for the soldier could not, as the Enlightenment of the eighteenth century occasionally dreamed, simply be decreed. . . . The way to human dignity for the soldier was via the nation. If he were to regard the arduous duties imposed on him by his profession not merely as external constraints but . . . as inner and personal duties toward the fatherland, then he would achieve that moral personality which was the ideal of the humanitarians."[36] In the French *tirailleur* Meinecke saw this postulate verified in practice. He could be "granted more freedom in fighting because he was more dependable. Moreover, this [freer] way of fighting . . . appealed more to the personal capacities of the warrior and at the same time demanded a more honorable and humane way of dealing with him. . . . The simultaneous rise of nation and individual, the best of the ideas of 1789, was revealed here and demonstrated its practical effectiveness."[37]

These were the ideas, the nation and the individual, which guided the Prussian reformers. They incorporated them in their response to the French challenge, and thus we find Scharnhorst insisting that the soldier must no longer be degraded to the status of a machine. "In order to know victory again, the soldier must once more become a warrior, which means he must achieve personality. He could do this only if he felt himself to be a son of the nation and if the whole people became a mighty reservoir of military strength."[38]

All through Meinecke's portrayal of the Prussian Reform as the agent of Prussian and German nationhood, it was the in-

---

[85] *Erhebung, op.cit.*, p. 181.   [36] *Ibid.*   [37] *Ibid.*, p. 74.
[38] *Ibid.*, p. 109. (Meinecke's paraphrase of Scharnhorst.)

dividual as citizen and soldier which provided the central theme. Surveying the whole gamut of economic and social change in the years 1806-1819, Meinecke returned again and again to the meaning of citizenship and military service. Citizenship meant participation in the affairs of state, and full participation could come only with voluntary service to the state in its function as a military power, the kind of power which demanded the most of the individual. Since the Prussian state faced the mortal peril of Napoleon's military might, the willingness of the Prussian citizen to fight for his country was both the supreme necessity and the supreme criterion from which to assess the achievements of the reformers.

It was Meinecke's judgment that the Prussian Reform had succeeded in infusing the people with the will to fight. The acid test came when Prussia took up arms against Napoleon in March 1813. "Until then, one could always have doubted that the 'people' actually existed. One could have questioned whether the patriots' reform ideas and plans for a popular uprising were not reckoning on a concept of the 'people' which was merely a postulate and reflex of the ideals which the individual reformers shared among themselves. The spring of 1813 removed all doubt. . . . In the discipline and energy with which [Prussia fought] . . . one sensed the will of the nation itself."[39] 'Stein's goal . . . was now a reality: every nerve was strained and every source of energy was tapped and activated."[40]

In Prussia's contribution to the Wars of Liberation, Meinecke saw the dignity of the individual and the dignity of the state joined in an exalted communion of freedom and necessity. "On the battlefield at Leipzig, individual, nation and state . . . gave the best that was in them. The single idea of crushing the tyrant of Europe united the obscure emotions of the ordinary soldier and the calculations of the statesman to the life-work of the great men . . . of the [Prussian] renascence. For them the downfall of Napoleon was the immediate objective of all that they had done. At the same time it was a means to still higher ends and

[39] *Ibid.*, pp. 207-208.   [40] *Ibid.*, p. 210.

was thus both finite and infinite, a great reality and a great symbol. In such a concatenation one can experience the most exalted earthly joy known to men, and this experience was now given to Stein and Gneisenau."[41]

The reformers had united the ideal and the real. They accomplished this unity with the appeal to nationality which animated even the military core of state authority with the idea of freedom and which elicited from the people a spontaneous acceptance of state authority as an organization for purposeful activity. If the soldier could fight as a free man giving service to his fatherland, then the "humanitarian ideal achieved its full meaning in concrete form as a giver of light and life not merely to a small enclave of free spirits but to all their countrymen."[42]

On the battlefield at Leipzig, Meinecke saw the nation not only join state and individual in a tremendous positive achievement. He viewed the nation itself acting as a mighty individual in which reason and passion, spirit and power combined to realize historic ends. For Meinecke, this was the crystallization of a personality which transcended individual human beings, uniting them in a common political and moral endeavor. This was the ideal which the state must incorporate if its autonomous ego was to be justified. And only the national idea could create that voluntary and spontaneous participation of the state's citizens which gave the state a claim to moral personality. Meinecke's deep commitment to the nation-state can be summed up in words with which we are already familiar: "Sustaining and justifying all our thinking about and concern for the state is the profound recognition that the state is an ideal, super-individual corporate personality. This recognition could be fully attained only when the community sentiments and energies of the individual citizens permeated the state and transformed it into the nation-state."[48]

The nation-state was the individual writ large and was thus the political community least likely to oppress the individual.

[41] *Ibid.*, p. 218.   [42] *Ibid.*, p. 181.
[48] *Weltbuergertum, op.cit.*, pp. 10-11.

Indeed, nationhood was the practical political-organizational response to the quest for the liberty of the individual, and Meinecke asserted that "it is . . . no accident that the era of modern national thought follows directly upon an era of movements toward individualistic freedom."[44] Wilhelm von Humboldt, "whose first and lasting love was the individual," was the keystone in Meinecke's argument here. Humboldt saw the individual and "then the nation . . . rising above the individual . . . and steadily deepened his understanding of the causal and natural connections between the two." The result of Humboldt's thought was expressed in a memorandum of December 1813, when he considered the future of German politics: " 'In the way in which nature unites individuals and divides humanity into nations there is an immeasurably profound and mysterious factor which finds the true path of proportionate and gradual development of strength of the individual, who is in himself nothing, and of the race, which expresses itself only in the individual.' "[45] With this statement Humboldt at once affirmed the nation-state as the ideal political organization and posited a unique relationship between individual and nation which no other organization could claim.

Humboldt's position was here very close to those assumptions of Ranke which posited an organic union between citizen and state in great "collective personalities."[46] As we have seen, it was this projection of the characteristics of personality into the nation-state which became the hallmark of the dominant tradition in German political thought. It gave the nation-state a philosophical basis for its own freedom and at the same time imposed on it moral obligation. Meinecke was fully within this tradition in his conception of the nation as the great and natural super-individual within which individual human beings worked out their destinies. Here he recalls Burke's indissoluble contract

[44] *Ibid.*, p. 9.
[45] *Ibid.*, pp. 194-195. The quotation from Humboldt is from Humboldt's *Gesammelte Schriften* (Schmidt edition), vol. XI, p. 104.
[46] See Chapter II, above.

spanning the generations in a "partnership in all science, in all art, a partnership in every virtue and in all perfection."[47]

As Meinecke noted, Burke's reformulation of the contract theory had the effect of breaking down the barriers between the individual and the state and fusing them into an indivisible unit. It was precisely this effect which Meinecke was seeking in a state divested of the qualities of a "cold and oppressive power." Not yet faced with the problem of the total state, he was primarily concerned with finding means to realize the greatest possible participation of all citizens in political life.

If the state was to have a spiritual personality it could not rest upon a mechanical organization of the ruler-ruled relationship, treating the great bulk of its citizens as mere means to its own ends. The essence of Meinecke's transfer of personality characteristics from the individual to the nation-state was the requirement that the nation-state incorporate within itself the ends and values of the citizens which comprise it. The nation-state could not pursue the ends of just some of its citizens nor could it be an expression of only the power aspects of human personality. If the state was a super-individual personality, it must represent all of its components and the whole range of human values.

The endowment of the state with personality, in order that its significance may be fully understood, must be seen against the background of Meinecke's concern for state security. In this concern the idea of nationality also played an important role. Meinecke's arguments for the primacy of foreign policy led him to assert that the uninformed masses could not be permitted to interfere with the delicate and highly complex business of maintaining the state's external well-being. Yet at the same time he strove for greater mass participation in political life, and he insisted that the state recognize its citizens as ends in themselves and not simply as instruments of state power. The result was that he did not call for the displacement of the state ego by the egos of the individuals comprising it. Such a dis-

[47] *Reflections on the French Revolution.* Meinecke cites Burke's famous dictum in *Weltbuergertum, op.cit.,* pp. 138-139.

placement, he believed, was the central error of the philosophy which animated the French Revolution.[48] Rather he sought a fusion between "the inalienable rights of the individual . . . and the inevitably egotistic and domineering nature of . . . the state."[49]

Meinecke felt this fusion could be accomplished by means of the national idea because the nation, like the state, was a historical community, conscious of its own continuity and complexity and not simply a contemporary assemblage of individual egos determined to remove the restraints of the state and substitute individual goals for community goals. Nationality was a more congenial idea to the state than either aristocracy or democracy, both of which Meinecke regarded as less than community-wide in their concerns. In his experience, democracy, like aristocracy, was associated with the interests of a particular socio-economic group whose prime interest was not the welfare of the state as a whole but the seizure of power in order to serve its own specific ends. Both aristocracy and democracy were too limited in philosophical concept as well. The one denied the right of political participation to all but a selected few. The other flouted the law of hierarchy in human organization and replaced the judgment of a trained elite with the transient and fickle will of the majority.[50] Nationality, on the other hand,

---

[48] "At the beginning of the Revolution France sought to solve this problem [of the conflict between state and individual egos] by subordinating the state to the postulates of human rights. It soon experienced a calamitous setback, and the reestablishment of a still more despotic state destroyed in great part the ideals of 1789. The Prussian Reform . . . also experienced setbacks, but perhaps the contact between the state and the human spirit was more intense and more lasting because neither was able even temporarily to command the other. Two forces struggled with each other and neither achieved complete victory. But each absorbed so much of the other in its own being, and each was thereby strengthened to such a degree that both could wish to renew the attempt at adjustment and reconciliation." (*Erhebung, op.cit.,* pp. 125-126.)

[49] *Ibid.*

[50] The criticism of majority rule was an outstanding feature of Meinecke's attacks on the wartime policies of Britain and France. Cf. *Prob-*

was a concept which ignored economic, social, and intellectual distinctions and implied a community in which everyone had a right to participate by virtue of his being a national. Hence, in political terms the national idea was not restricted by the aristocratic thesis of government by the few or the democratic thesis of government by the many.[51] It assumed the participation of all but did not rule out the principle of hierarchy. Thus nationalism was eminently suited to the state in an anarchic world where each state had to depend increasingly both on complex hierarchical organization and wide internal support in order to maintain its external security.

If the joining of the nation to the state required that all nationals participate in the political community, it also imbued the state with other values than power. Meinecke regarded nationality as primarily a cultural phenomenon, deriving from common language and experience and the feeling of kinship which these common possessions inspire. Nationality embodied the whole range of human experience—political, intellectual, esthetic, moral, emotional.[52] Since it embodied these aspects of human personality not as abstract properties but in concrete and familiar institutions and symbols, it lent itself to community organization in a way which was closed to the abstract political doctrines of aristocracy or democracy that cut across cultural

---

leme des Weltkriegs, pp. 67, 68, 110, 113, 114. Despite his desire for full political participation by the citizen, he feared the majority system of government would throw open the gates to demagogues. Meinecke felt his fears were justified most dramatically in the person of Lloyd George.

[51] While Meinecke regarded constitutional forms as a necessity in modern politics, he did not equate constitutionalism to democracy. Moreover, he had some sympathy for Ranke's feeling that the issue whether or not there should be a constitution was less important than the more general one that some form should be found which would assure the people's "spiritual and moral participation in government." Cf. *Weltbuergertum, op.cit.*, p. 299.

[52] It is typical of Meinecke to warn that "It is urgently necessary that our spiritual culture be imbued with esthetic apprehension so that will and intellect will not dry it up and deprive it of warmth." (*Weltbuergertum, op.cit.*, p. 532.)

boundaries and thus did not rest on the intimacy of shared historical experience. Nationality, then, was the ideal means to infuse the state with the many values of human personality and still provide the cohesive forces which the state required, particularly at a juncture when the state was going through a metamorphosis from a power organization to a community embracing and honoring the ends of all its citizens.

By conferring personality on the state via the nation, Meinecke posited the state as a multi-purpose institution rather than an organization animated by the single end of power. So doing, he introduced into the state the same central dilemmas faced by the individual personality for whom power is only one among other ends. Above all, he presented the state with the ethical issues with which every personality must deal. Which of the many values of life shall have precedence? To what degree may one individual treat others as means instead of ends in themselves? Is self-preservation to be maintained at the cost of all other considerations?

But when Meinecke confronted the state with the ethical questions which the individual personality encounters, he did not perceive their full poignancy. Indeed, he did not formulate them in this manner. Investing the state with many values, he did not, in the prewar years, give thorough examination to the possibility that the several values might collide in mortal conflict. He required that the state be concerned with cultural and moral ends and felt that this concern would of itself place restraints on the drive for power. But, significantly, when he asserted that the state must "recognize and honor the spiritual and moral forces in the nation," he added that it must "at the same time press them into its service as a new instrument of power."[53] This prescription indicated not only the dynamic and all-embracing nature of the power-drive—a valid insight in itself. It also implied that the state must accept spiritual and moral forces only if they did not seriously endanger its power objectives.

[53] *Erhebung, op.cit.,* p. 10.

What if they did constitute such a danger? Meinecke's observations on German political life left no doubt as to the answer. Reform, he argued, which would give the masses and thus the opposition parties greater responsibility, could not be realized as long as the opposition left in doubt the extent to which it would protect Germany's military and foreign policy imperatives.[54]

On first consideration, this unambiguous reaffirmation of the primacy of power demonstrates one of two things. Either Meinecke did not effect an authentic transfer of the idea of individual personality to the state because he did not confront the state squarely with the dilemmas of human personality and instead always assumed the value of power to be the deciding factor. Then his picture of the nation-state as a community of power and spirit was nothing more than a tenuous *modus vivendi* between power and non-power values which could be abandoned when power considerations required it. Or, Meinecke assumed that power was also the supreme value in the individual human personality. Then the multi-valuing individual, in this view, was never besieged by authentic ethical dilemmas and would always make his decisions with the power factor as his final criterion. In this case, the transfer of this conception of personality to the state would involve no contradiction.

Actually, at this stage in his thinking, in regard to both the nature of the state and the nature of the individual, the most that can be demonstrated is that which we have seen Meinecke express in his own words: "It is true that Bismarck was uppermost in our conscious thoughts and deeds. But Goethe's world was there too as an indispensable complement."[55] Meinecke did recognize authentic conflicts of value in the state between the state's "egotistic nature" and the "inalienable rights of the individual." He chided Boyen for seeing the state "in too ideal a perspective" because in Boyen's concept of the state "there was

[54] *Probleme des Weltkriegs, op.cit.,* p. 95.
[55] See page 118, above.

no contradiction or conflict between power and spirit, between state, humanity and individual."[56] Indeed, he regarded it as one of the great lessons of the Reform era that state, culture, and individual all have a claim to autonomy and that the autonomy of each meant that tragic conflict among them was inevitable.[57]

The weight of evidence, however, indicates that Meinecke assumed the great decisions in such conflicts would always go to power. The state must be more than power, but power is its first requisite. Power and spirit could reside together, but it was always at the peril of spiritual values. Meinecke hoped and believed that nationality, as a great cultural community which served to balance the power orientation of the state and at the same time offered the state a new element of cohesion, would make the coexistence of power and spirit a more harmonious one. Conflict between the two could never be eliminated, but the national idea offered the best prospect of preventing conflict from becoming brutal and irreconcilable hostility.

These hopes and beliefs, so intimately tied to the hopes and fears for his own nation, in fact obscured Meinecke's view of the polarity of power and spirit. *Weltbuergertum und National-staat*, the summation of Meinecke's pre-war thought, was focussed primarily on the conflict between nationalism and cosmopolitanism. The relationship between ethics and politics was only a sub-theme of the central plot.[58] This concentration on the idea of the nation was both cause and effect of Meinecke's treatment of the power-spirit relationship in the state as a manageable side-issue.

Meinecke's concentration on the national issue had the same obscuring effect in regard to his view of the nature of the individual. The question, what does politics reveal about the na-

[56] *Erhebung, op.cit.*, p. 124.

[57] "Stein und die Erhebung von 1813" (first published in 1913) in *Preussen und Deutschland, op.cit.*, pp. 126-127.

[58] It has already been noted that the conflict of ethics and politics began to assume greater importance for Meinecke only after the publication of *Weltbuergertum*. See page 129, above.

ture of men? was overlaid by the question, what can politics in terms of the nation do to exalt the nature of men? It is clear that Meinecke believed the autonomous multi-valuing individual in order to live in harmony with authority required a multi-valuing state and that the national idea could inspire him with a sense of community and participation which would act as a restraint on his own individual ego. But the relative weight the many values carried within the individual and the role of power in individual conduct were left obscure. At this point it can only be said that the supreme value which Meinecke assigned to individuality would indicate that security was and should be the final imperative for the individual as for the state. Hence we are left with the impression that moral obligation and the need to pursue many values did not extend to the point where the power objectives of state and individual would be sacrificed to non-power considerations.

The limitations inherent in this concept of moral obligation would be most apparent in a time of crisis, and the First World War produced the crisis that revealed them. Meinecke had hoped that the assumption of a spiritual mission and a cultural personality by the state would tend to temper its power-strivings both in regard to its own citizens and toward other states. The recognition that all states were cultural institutions as well as power organizations might serve to soften the image of the Janus-like barrier separating peoples into competing power organizations and balance it with a feeling of sympathy and understanding for the cultural and moral qualities of the several state and national personalities. But in leaving the power core of the state essentially unchallenged Meinecke's hope was unrealistic. Indeed, the assumption of moral and cultural characteristics in the state bolstered its case for the right to promote its security with every means at its command. An external threat to a cold and oppressive power organization might leave the man of culture indifferent. But a threat to an institution which harbored within it a mighty complex of cultural and spiritual values must be passionately resisted.

CHAPTER VII

WORLD WAR I: THE POLARITY OF
POWER AND CULTURE

MEINECKE's response to the outbreak of war in 1914 made apparent his realization that the mighty struggle with all its momentous issues was also the supreme challenge to the picture of the state and international life which he had created. Like any challenge to deeply held convictions, it evoked both a sense of exhilaration and a consciousness of danger. Now more than ever before Meinecke felt called upon to apply the ideas he had found in history and test them against the issues of contemporary life. Now he would have to formulate and fight for a policy for his nation in the light of the personality of power and spirit with which he had endowed it. And though he was a devoted member of his own nation, his concern for the culture of Europe and the nature of international life obligated him to consider the war from the vantage point of a European thinker as well as of a German patriot.

The spontaneity with which the Germans rallied to the national cause when the war declarations came was heartening evidence to Meinecke that Imperial Germany had achieved a high degree of success in welding together a moral community —a greater success, indeed, than Meinecke had dared hope for.[1] The supreme moment came on August 3, 1914, when the German Reichstag unanimously approved war credits. The deep fissures between the rulers and the ruled which Meinecke had made the object of his anxious concern seemed to close in a mighty demonstration of national solidarity against the external enemy. Above all, the German Socialists, along with their coun-

[1] The basic forces of "our recent history . . . were healthier, stronger and more harmonious than any of us realized." (*Erhebung 1914, op.cit.,* p. 29.)

terparts in other countries, had turned their backs on the cosmopolitanism of the Second International and had rallied to their nation-state in its hour of peril. This was "one of the greatest moments of my life," Meinecke wrote in his memoirs. "The seal [of triumph] was placed on two decades of hope, fear, and longing."[2]

In this atmosphere Meinecke relived the days of Prussia's revolt against Napoleon a hundred years before. He saw the Prussian renascence repeating itself in a German renascence which promised to be even more momentous. In 1813 an inspired leadership had only the beginnings of a popular will to work with and mold into an instrument of power. Now, in these stirring days of 1914, Meinecke felt there was a mature popular will capable of responding fully to mature political leadership.[3]

With so benevolent a combination, what might not a nation expect to accomplish? As a spur to great achievement Meinecke now portrayed the spirit of the Prussian Reform and its climax in 1813 as one which transfigured German political thought. "Now it was recognized that nowhere did humanity reveal itself more directly than in one's own people and that no more stirring task could beckon the creative spirit than to build anew and finer the destroyed body of this people. To live and die for the nation now meant to live and die for humanity and for the God who works in humanity."[4] He believed that this same transfiguration, only still more resplendent and heroic, was taking place in the Germany of 1914. "In the midst of the most terrible war in human memory and confronted with a hostile world coalition such as no state has ever before had to face, the German people rises to [defend] its ancient faith in the meaning of reason and human history, in the victory of the spirit over

[2] *Erinnerungen, op.cit.,* p. 137. Writing these words in 1944, Meinecke added that in his old age, "after all the bitter experience of our national life, I still avow those . . . feelings. Certainly we may have overestimated the sentiment making for national solidarity at that time, but that it was strong beyond expectation cannot be denied even today."

[3] *Erhebung 1914, op.cit.,* p. 28.

[4] *Ibid.,* p. 11.

brutal force, in the victory of the ideas which guide it. As in the days of Fichte's Germany we shall carry on this struggle as humanity's people."[5] Perhaps there are no more striking examples in Meinecke's writings of the transfer of universal values from the world at large to the nation-state. With this transfer Meinecke added his voice to those of his compatriots and counterparts in the other warring countries who were striving to sanctify the cause which commanded their loyalties and to claim for it the values of universal truth and reason.

This is the ever-recurring story of the crisis situation which brings with it the almost overwhelming temptation to confuse subjective preferences with objective truth. But it was particularly ironic that Meinecke should also be a victim of this temptation in the light of all his thought and criticism concerning the universalist assumptions of the cosmopolitan doctrines. He had specifically rejected the Fichtean concept of humanity's people[6] only to resurrect it in the heat of emotions generated by the eruption of the First World War.

Yet the moral glorification of the German cause did not prevent Meinecke from often assuming the role of detached observer and judging the struggle, including Germany's participation therein, with an almost cynical eye. He readily endorsed George Bernard Shaw's shaft at the British statesmen and scholars who were sounding the note of "humanity's people" in England's name: "Our national trick of assuming an attitude of righteous indignation is repulsive enough in the strife of hostile parties. In war it is ungenerous and indefensible. Let us take the field openly and leave hypocrisy and bad blood behind us. This war is nothing more than a war for power objectives."[7] It was an agreeable enough task, of course, for Meinecke to endorse Shaw's assessment of British conduct. But he went further and applied the Shavian analysis to all the contesting powers: "This is the language which is congenial to the objective historian, who is accustomed to look upon states as living personalities

[5] *Ibid.*, p. 9.   [6] Chapter IV, above.
[7] Quoted in *Erhebung 1914, op.cit.*, p. 69.

which demand breathing space for themselves and whose power struggles can therefore be justified in terms of the pressures of vital necessity. . . . Today all of us—friend and foe—are pursuing vigorous and egotistic power policies."[8]

Thus Meinecke's thinking in the early war period oscillated between passionate partisanship and analytical detachment, but the objectivity he sought often proved elusive. Indeed, he identified his very efforts toward objectivity as a German virtue. The Germans, he argued, were at least honest enough to admit the egotistic nerve of their policies, whereas Shaw's voice was that of a lonely dissenter in the midst of British smugness. This was itself a rather prideful proposition. In Meinecke's assertion that "the compulsion to conceal the hard substance [of power politics] with sentimental illusions and ideologies is stronger among our enemies than among ourselves"[9] was a suggestion of sanctimoniousness as unmistakable as that which attended British cant.

At every point there was a tendency to see superior merit in the German cause. Still, the basic concept of the nation-state as a culture-power symbiosis made Meinecke draw back from ideas which would portray the struggle between Germany and her enemies as a black-and-white issue. On both sides there were moral energies as well as ego. Indeed, from this observation Meinecke drew confidence that neither side would wholly suppress the other. As far as Germany was concerned, he argued that it was ridiculous to imagine that Germany wanted world hegemony. Germany's whole history, he contended, speaks for a multiplicity of forms and the coexistence of free and strong states and nations.[10]

Here Meinecke revealed his fundamental confidence that the war was being fought between nations conscious of their dual nature as communities of power and spirit. There was an implicit assumption that conflict between such entities could not

[8] *Ibid.*, pp. 69-70, 71.
[9] *Ibid.*, p. 71.
[10] "Machtpolitik," *op.cit.*, pp. 637-638.

reach the disastrous proportions of past wars, where universal forces of religion or ideology divided the world into good and evil and thus created a total hostility. He affirmed the Rankian concept of international relations which "taught us to pay homage to truth and see states as living personalities, filled with the will to life and power—all of them proud, egotistic, and conscious of honor. . . . [Ranke] also taught the inevitability of conflict among these forceful personalities; often it takes the form of peaceful competition, often of measuring one another's power in war. That is the judgment of historical realism which accepts the politics of states as they are and not as they might be according to humanitarian ideals."[11]

This approach allowed Meinecke to view the early months of the war with a certain equanimity. As he recalled in his memoirs, in considering the imperfections of this world he "always ended up with the historical-philosophical consolation that although there was no guaranteed progress toward the good, there was an oft-demonstrated regenerative force that would protect the Prussian-German as well as the Western character from ultimate degeneration and blind alleys leading to irrevocable disaster. The demonic nature of the old power politics and the new demonic forces rising out of . . . nineteenth-century nationalism had not yet become fully apparent to me."[12]

If Meinecke's view of nation-states and their struggles led to a philosophical optimism at the beginning of the war, it is clear that it was not a blind optimism. As far as Germany is concerned, we have already seen that Meinecke was certainly not blind to the dangers threatening his hopes for an increasingly successful national community. The profundity of his concern was dramatically illustrated when he deliberately addressed himself to the internal forces he considered to be dangerous to the nation-state in the very collection of popular-style essays he

[11] *Ibid.*, pp. 636-637.
[12] *Erinnerungen, op.cit.*, p. 200. Here Meinecke comes close to the unfounded optimism concerning the role of nationality in world politics for which he criticized Herder. See Chapter III, above.

published in 1914 as an exhortation to victory.[13] Writing for
a German public in the first glow of patriotic war enthusiasm,
Meinecke confessed that he had written his essay on "Nationalism and the National Idea" before the outbreak of the war;[14]
that he had hesitated to publish it once war was declared in view
of the desire to forget differences in a common effort; but that
he finally felt justified in making it public because the essay
sought to understand the differences and not intensify them
and because "we must also purify ourselves in the war."[15]

Distinguishing between nationalism and the national idea,
Meinecke insisted that "it is necessary to overcome it [national-
ism] with a finer and richer national concept."[16] Then followed
a slashing attack on "radical and arrogant nationalism" and particularly the Pan-German variety of nationalism. He warned
that the class interests of entrepreneurs, officers, and bureaucrats
had too closely associated the national idea with special interests.
The master-race (*Herrenvolk*) idea of these groups "brews up
a strong draught . . . of all the ingredients which might be useful, from the corrupted legacies of the old Prussian bureaucratic
and Junker state to the vulgar exploitation of the ideas of Dar-
win, Gobineau, and Nietzsche. The philosophy of 'race'—of the
'elite race' and 'elite people'—are examples of the general and
considerable responsibility of uncritical racial doctrines for the
degeneration of the national idea. This kind of nationalism among
our educated classes is only too prone to show its teeth, not only
in foreign affairs but also in domestic policy. Above all they see
themselves as an 'elite group' by the grace of God and claim all
positions of social and political power. And this with arrogant
ruthlessness—and astounded indignation when any doubt is expressed as to their rights. . . . This repulsive caste arrogance is
one of the worst hindrances to the objective of making our
people a real world people, creative in both world politics and
world culture. When caste arrogance and ideas of a social elite

---

[13] *Erhebung 1914*, op.cit.
[14] But after the assassinations at Sarajevo.
[15] *Erhebung 1914*, op.cit., p. 84.   [16] *Ibid.*, p. 85.

join with chauvinism the situation becomes really unfortunate. This hard-hearted and loud-mouthed impetuousness discredits us not less than the parvenu attitude of the half-educated."[17]

Meinecke did not direct his shafts exclusively at the ultra-nationalists. He admonished those as well who disdained the state and the national idea in order to devote themselves to their "own precious subjectivity."[18] Whichever side was the object of his attack, the common theme was the necessity of assuring the union of politics and culture which Meinecke had defined as the essence of the nation-state and the justification of its power politics in international life. Hopefully he wrote that the alienation of culture and politics was at an end. But he warned that it must be "exclusively the concern of culture to insure that the alliance which German culture must now effect with German politics be one of freedom and not of slavery. May it grasp the hand of the state and become a weapon of the state in that great conviction, with that sense of an autonomous ethos which Kant preached."[19]

As Meinecke looked beyond Germany to the other warring nations and the struggle as a whole he also saw dangers which threatened his hopes and expectations regarding the conduct of the struggle. Again he identified the divorce between politics and culture as the chief peril—a peril which became inevitable when the national idea degenerated into ultra-nationalism. Such a divorce was indeed "The specific character of modern nationalism with its voluntaristic aspect, its tendency to marshal all the national qualities to achieve political self-assertion. . . . In this process the nations are becoming uniform and militarized. . . . We have recognized the inherent right and reason of this process in full measure—for this very reason we must emphasize the danger of pitfalls and corruptions which threaten it. To sum it up once in an exaggerated manner, the struggles of the nations . . .

[17] *Ibid.*, pp. 87-88.
[18] *Ibid.*, p. 90. Among these he included Gerhardt Hauptmann and the satirical magazine *Simplizissmus.*
[19] *Ibid.* "Politik und Kultur," p. 45.

threaten in the end to be like the rivalries of the student cor-
porations which are distinguished from one another only by
the colors of their caps and armbands but which otherwise are
exactly alike in emulating the ideal of the dashing student. . . .
The ideas which fill the brain of the French, Italian, German,
English and Russian chauvinist are so similar as to be identical."[20]

If, as Meinecke wrote in his memoirs, the demonic forces of
nationalism were "not fully apparent" to him in the early stages
of the First World War, they were vividly enough described.
What was not clear to him was that they were far stronger than
he had hoped and believed. He was sanguine enough, in regard
to German foreign policy, to assert that Bismarck's distinction
"between a healthy politics of interest and an arrogant and ad-
venturous politics of prestige . . . has become part of our flesh
and blood."[21] But his strictures against German chauvinism
were evidence of his recognition that the ascendancy of restraint
was never guaranteed. They spurred him actively to align himself with those who fought the growth of ultra-nationalism.
Hence he moved more definitely into German political life to
espouse and defend publicly a war policy of moderation and a
domestic policy of social reconciliation.

Externally, Meinecke's basic policy concept was that Germany was fighting to preserve the integrity of its "indispensable"
Austro-Hungarian ally against Russian despotism, and, now that
war had come, also for other power goals, but not for world domination.[22] This concept harmonized with his explicit assumption
that Germany was fighting a strictly defensive war. In this defensive operation Germany was attacked by France and England;
the former attacked because of motives of revenge, the latter
because it desired to deny Germany's place in the sun as a world
and colonial power.[23] This interpretation, which was extrava-

[20] *Ibid.* "Nationalismus und nationale Idee," p. 93.
[21] "Machtpolitik," *op.cit.*, pp. 632-633.
[22] *Erhebung 1914, op.cit.*, p. 72.
[23] *The Warfare of a Nation*, Worcester, Massachusetts, 1915, p. 39.

gantly one-sided, even if one allows for propagandistic motives, testified to the limitations of Meinecke's ability to undertake a real political analysis of the European struggle in the first heat of war.

But the notion of Germany's being besieged by attackers did not lead him to the idea of punishing the aggressors for morally reprehensible conduct. Here Meinecke's affirmation that all the contestants were pursuing vigorously egotistic power policies furnished a perspective and something of a counterweight to his narrowly subjective appraisal of Germany's role in the outbreak of hostilities. His too-good case for Germany's conduct was balanced by the fundamental presupposition that Germany was not simply the victim of an immoral struggle for power but was instead an active participant in the struggle which was itself not wholly evil but rather the way of international life.

Without this fundamental view of world politics, the proposition that Germany was the object of aggression could well have led to demands for punitive peace terms which would have ranged Meinecke alongside the ultranationalists he so bitterly opposed. With this view, he could argue for moderation despite Germany's real or fancied grievances. Thus he warned that Germany must not return hate with hate. The national idea justified the struggle for national independence but became corrupt "when the nation is unable to restrain its more ignoble spirits, when the cultural life of the nation is contaminated by hate against neighboring nations and by a brutal will to power which employs every means [to gain its end]."[24]

The caveat against an uninhibited drive for power was itself buttressed by power calculations. "It is politically unwise," Meinecke wrote, "to treat an enemy exclusively in terms of revenge so that he could never again be our friend or ally. High politics is a volatile phenomenon which today divides the atoms and

This book is a translation by John A. Spalding of some of the essays which appeared in *Erhebung 1914, op.cit.*

[24] *Erhebung 1914*, pp. 85-86.

tomorrow can reunite them. . . . Today there may be a feeling across the Channel that England's interest is to destroy Germany. Tomorrow, when it is recognized that this objective is unattainable, [the British] may be convinced of the advantage of a British-German coalition against Russia." On the other hand, while he believed that Russia constituted the greatest danger to Europe, Meinecke did not rule out an agreement with Russia as an alternative possibility.[25] This joining of power considerations and ethical values was one of the pieces of experience which later went into the development of Meinecke's study of *raison d'état* in the postwar years.

In regard to internal policy, the experience of solidarity among all political groupings in Germany upon the outbreak of hostilities encouraged Meinecke to believe that political reform could be pressed more rapidly. He regarded the socialist support of the German war effort as evidence that the working class, so long in opposition to the established state and so long proclaiming allegiance to the international rather than the national idea, now accepted the power requirements and functions of the state. Hence it could be trusted with a greater measure of political responsibility. Now that Germany had experienced a mighty demonstration of national unity, the way was open to ending inequalities and allowing equal opportunity for all.[26] Meinecke urged that the regime end its discrimination against the socialists and that the way to their acceptance of the monarchy be made as easy as possible. The new phase of the national idea must be the mutual recognition and collaboration of the state and the working class.[27]

These words of moderation in regard to foreign and domestic policy constituted the criterion by which Meinecke was to judge the conduct of wartime Germany. But Meinecke himself was

[25] "Sozialdemokratie und Machtpolitik," an essay by Meinecke published in a collection entitled *Die Arbeiterschaft im neuen Deutschland*, Leipzig, 1915, pp. 27-28.

[26] *Warfare of a Nation, op.cit.*, p. 40.

[27] *Erhebung 1914, op.cit.*, pp. 76-77.

not always able to live up to the standards which he had established. Certainly his analysis of the issue of responsibility for the outbreak of hostilities did not bespeak moderation. Again and again he referred to Austria's harsh demands on Serbia as stemming from "a bitter necessity of state," whereas Serbian and Russian interests were "overextended." Russia and Serbia "wanted" to destroy Austria, and Germany and Austria "had to" defend themselves.[28]

Again in the issue of the German invasion of Belgium, Meinecke's partisan appraisal did not do justice to the ideal of moderation. Meinecke justified the violation of Belgian neutrality by asserting that Belgium was in fact unneutral, that it was clear that Britain and France intended to use Belgium as a military base, and that it was better to break a treaty than to have the Allies so dangerously close to the Ruhr. He found the treaty with Belgium and the safety of Germany a clear case of a conflict of duties in which the decisive consideration had to be *salus populi suprema lex esto*.[29] The patness of Meinecke's argument both from the practical and ethical viewpoints is hardly in keeping with the magnitude of the strategic, political, and moral issues involved.

If Meinecke's assessment of the Belgian question at least recognized a conflict of duties on the moral level, his bias is fully revealed on the level of political analysis when he undertook to judge the British response to the crossing of the Belgian frontier. Noting the numerous prominent voices in England who could find no fault with German conduct between Sarajevo and

[28] Cf. "Politik und Kultur" in *Probleme des Weltkriegs*, Berlin, 1917, pp. 20-22 (the article was first published in April 1915); "Der Ursprung des Weltkriegs" in *Zum Geschichtlichen Verstaendnis des grossen Krieges*, Berlin, 1916, p. 332; and "Machtpolitik," *op.cit.*, p. 633. In the article first cited, Meinecke conceded that the Austrian note was a "veiled declaration of war" but argued that only force could bring about a solution to Austro-Serbian differences and that Austria could not have let Serbia go unpunished without increasing the latter's appetite.

[29] "Machtpolitik," *op.cit.*, p. 636 and "Rhythmus des Weltkriegs" in *Probleme des Weltkriegs*, *op.cit.*, p. 133.

the invasion of Belgium, Meinecke asked whether Germany's guilt in violating Belgian neutrality was enough to change the views of this segment of British opinion. He offered only an indirect negative answer to his question by citing the British wartime Blue Book[30] in which the British Foreign Secretary refused to pledge neutrality even if Germany promised to respect Belgian frontiers.[31] Meinecke did not attempt to weigh the pros and cons of Germany's action, nor did he attempt to judge the actual impact of the German invasion on British opinion. Instead he regarded Grey's reply as evidence that Grey was determined to make war on Germany and that the British, who could find no real fault with Germany's actions, merely used the Belgian question as the pretext for declaring war. He failed to subject the Belgian invasion issue to a realistic analysis. His assumption that Britain ought to have tied its hands by pledging itself to a neutral policy in a great European war simply in return for a German promise to stay out of Belgium displays a startling lapse of critical judgment. The best that can be said is that Meinecke did not dwell on the Belgian invasion issue at any length.[32]

A different problem in regard to Belgium provides a further illustration of a weak spot in Meinecke's political judgment. While he regarded Germany's war as a defensive one, it will be recalled that Meinecke also believed that Germany should

[30] Number 123.

[31] *Probleme des Weltkriegs, op.cit.*, p. 32.

[32] Meinecke did later criticize the German invasion of Belgium, but only briefly and in utilitarian terms in *Staatsraeson, op.cit.*, p. 539 and in *Katastrophe, op.cit.*, pp. 68 and 117. Also, Meinecke revised his judgment of Grey in the postwar years to the extent that Grey was pictured as not actively wanting war but as harboring "an attitude [which] . . . made war inevitable." Whatever the justice of Meinecke's revised judgment of Grey's personal position, he certainly showed more realism regarding the greater issues at stake when he conceded that after events had been allowed to take their course up to August 4, 1914, Grey had no choice "but to throw England's sword onto the scales in order to protect British world power from the effects of a German Continental victory." (Review of Grey's *Twenty-Five Years* in its German translation which was published in 1926. *HZ*, 135, 1926, pp. 118-119.)

take the opportunity, once the war was on, to improve her power position in the world. One aspect of this desirable improvement, he felt, was that Belgian hostility to Germany must be counteracted. This would involve making Belgium a German satellite, though not via outright annexation.[33] Though such a solution was morally repugnant to him, he reverted once again to the doctrine of *salus populi* to justify it.[34]

Even more striking than the doubtful moral and political wisdom of this policy was the manner in which Meinecke arrived at a decision to favor it. Presumably hitherto undecided, he believed such a policy to be a *"dira necessitas"* upon hearing a report from an acquaintance that a Belgian political leader had told him that when the Belgians were once free of German occupation they would sign a binding alliance with France and raise an army of 700,000 men.[35] To draw such sweeping con-

[33] "Sozialdemokratie und Machtpolitik," *op.cit.*, p. 29.

[34] *Erinnerungen, op.cit.*, p. 202.

[35] *Ibid.*, pp. 201-202. Meinecke's description of this episode in his memoirs admitted that it represented a "backsliding" from his policy of moderation and that he now recognized that "the natural weight of German power combined with a wise hegemonial policy is more effective than protectorates based on force."

At approximately the same time as he was advocating a protectorate for Belgium, Meinecke inadvertently lent his name to a statement of annexationist war aims promulgated by a group of professors and intellectuals with whom he came into bitter conflict later in the war. He and his close friend and fellow historian, Hermann Oncken, publicly dissociated themselves from the statement and policies of this group in a letter to the *Frankfurter Zeitung* in August 1915. As Meinecke noted, this disavowal did not save him from occasional denunciations as an annexationist as late as the 1930's. (*Ibid.*, pp. 203-204.)

Despite his dissociation from annexationist groups, Meinecke admitted in 1919 that he had harbored annexationist ideas, though he asserted that he had been against any annexations which would have caused "permanent enmities in East or West" and that he had never made "desirable border alterations a *sine qua non* of peace." Nonetheless, he reproached himself for having had such ideas at all, for he regarded the annexationist philosophy as the chief reason for the breakdown of German morale, which, he believed, rested on the conviction that Germany was fighting a defensive war. (*Nach der Revolution*, Munich and Berlin, 1919, pp. 131-133.)

clusions from a second-hand and apparently isolated report seems almost incredible for a man of Meinecke's sophistication. It is certainly evidence of the charged atmosphere of the times and perhaps also of the stresses and strains of a political philosophy which had not yet plumbed deeply enough into the nature of inter-state relations and was suffering shock from the war's revelation of a more profound antinomy between power and culture than it had assumed.

That Meinecke was suffering from a sense of shock cannot be doubted. Nor can it be doubted that the main cause of shock was the violence of the propaganda war that accompanied the military struggle. Meinecke had hoped that the national idea would serve to admonish the warring nations that each—whether friend or foe—had a cultural personality and spiritual worth and that this admonition would require a mutual recognition of the opponent's status as an honorable enemy. Instead, the cultural values of the contestants provided an additional dimension for savage warfare. It was an ironic fulfillment of Meinecke's hopes for the integration of nation and state that the concept of the unity of a state's culture and power characteristics should operate to place the whole of an opposing state's personality under the ban of enmity. If all the facets of national and state life were intimately related, as Meinecke maintained, then there was indeed no aspect immune to attack in wartime.

Meinecke felt deeply and personally the power of the British assault on German values. He responded to it more vigorously than to attacks from other quarters both because the British were the leaders of the Allied propaganda effort and because he had more respect for British opinion than for that of the rest of Germany's enemies.[36] That the *London Times* should label Germany *hostes generis humani,* that British academicians should say that Germans "understand only death," and that the war should be regarded as a religious war were intolerable trans-

[36] "Before the war England seemed to many of us to be the land in which political culture had reached its highest level." (*Probleme des Weltkriegs, op.cit.,* p. 13.)

gressions to Meinecke. "No Pope," he wrote, "has ever hurled more terrible curses at heretics than those with which England—cultivated England—has damned us."[37] He demanded to know why the British were not content with their efforts to defeat Germany militarily, why they sought to make Germany "despised by the whole civilized world." If England had its way, he wrote in exasperation and in words which later came to have a poignancy he did not foresee, "every German who now helps to defend his Fatherland would be branded a pariah . . . because his nation had committed a crime against humanity."[38]

This desperate war of words moved Meinecke to assert that the Allied objective was to bring about Germany's utter destruction as a political entity. His response was to promise that the Germans would resist this threat with every means at their command.[39] This, then, was the total hostility which Meinecke hoped the national idea would avoid. He felt compelled to take up the challenge, heaping obloquy on England and matching at least the respectable British invective.[40]

[37] "Machtpolitik," *op.cit.*, pp. 617-618.
[38] *Ibid.*, p. 617.   [39] *Ibid.*, pp. 617-618.
[40] At this point it may be well to note that Meinecke's denunciations of the Allies were mild in comparison to those of some of his colleagues. (Cf. *Deutschland und der Weltkrieg, op.cit.*) The extremes some British propagandists went to, on the other hand, are illustrated by Cecil Chesterton's charge that Prussian professors encouraged the practice of pederasty. (Cf. "Machtpolitik," *op.cit.*, p. 618.) It should also be recalled that Meinecke was not himself loath to criticize aspects of German life, and he did not simply reject foreign critics out of hand. On the contrary, as the war progressed he paid more and more attention to enemy charges.

In the light of these facts it is appropriate to point out that Louis Snyder's criticism of Meinecke's war attitudes is grossly one-sided. Snyder did not bother to cite Meinecke's violent attacks on the Pan-German mentality in "Nationalismus und nationale Idee" and made no attempt to strike a balance between Meinecke's more extreme moments and his consistent reversion to the underlying theme of moderation.

Snyder is also guilty of a glaring error in translation which he used to make the case against Meinecke's nationalism far stronger than can be justified. In *German Nationalism,* (*op.cit.*, p. 268) Snyder quotes the following passage as a translation from *Erhebung 1914, op.cit.*, pp. 23-

Countering the British charges that Germany's tradition was one of ruthless power politics, Meinecke demanded to know in what way Germany had conducted itself differently from England in the game of national aggrandizement and empire-building.[41] Not only did England have a longer record of power politics and imperialism; it also had committed the cardinal sin of hypocrisy. "The English claim that deceit and force are the essence of the new German power politics. [But] the greatest and most effective deception to which power politics can resort is to conceal its talons and, as Machiavelli said, to 'appear to be all sympathy, loyalty, humaneness, honor and piety.' The worst and most revolting kind of force available to an unscrupulous power politics is that which violates the spirit of truth." Here, Meinecke asserted, England was unsurpassed. Indeed, England's conduct was even more radical than Machiavelli's doctrine, for Machiavelli believed that the liar would be more or less immune to his own lies. But Britain apparently "really believes in its own humanity while conducting itself like a beast of prey."[42]

24: "Foreigners believe that the Germans are the people of organization and method, the respecters of authority and drill. But these foreigners are not more cultivated or gifted than we, the representatives of the old, distinguished Western European civilization. They are the unfree people; they are the people of the barracks and the school." This faulty translation conveys a meaning precisely opposite to that of Meinecke's words. The entire passage, in which Snyder mistakenly saw a German rebuttal, was an attempt to simulate a Western Europe critique of German culture. A correct translation of the passage is as follows: "Now it was said that the Germans are the people of organization and of method, the respecters of authority and drill. These are the means by which they gain their achievements. They are not more gifted or cultivated than we, the representatives of the older and more distinguished Western European civilization; it is only that they understand how to raise the average by means of drill, to make mediocrity capable of achievement. But this makes them an unfree people; they are the people of the barracks and the school. . . . That was the answer of foreigners to our economic growth and to the first stirrings of our overseas ambitions."

41 "Machtpolitik," *op.cit.*, p. 628.
42 *Ibid.*, p. 630.

If some Englishmen conceded British hypocrisy, Meinecke contended, they quickly salved their consciences. He cited Ramsay Muir as a case in point. Muir had admitted " 'England has sometimes played the hypocrite. But hypocrisy is the tribute paid to virtue and except where it is the lie in the soul, it is preferable to the kind of truth which the Great King (Frederick II) cultivated. For it at least recognizes the claims of a standard of conduct higher than that of the jungle.' These words prove," Meinecke wrote, "that the lie has indeed reached into the depths of the English soul."[43]

Here different ideas of morality and truth were pitted against one another. While denying that Frederick and Bismarck or the traditions bearing their mark had embraced the "law of the jungle," Meinecke had staunchly insisted on the need to give power politics its due, to interpret state conduct by criteria which conceded rather than condemned or denied egotistic motivations. Hypocritical concealment of power considerations seduced the practitioner into ever more reckless violations of moral values. What should restrain him if he denied he was violating morality? Honesty with oneself, on the other hand, led to recognition of one's own selfish motives and was a better surety that the power seeker will act with moderation and justice. To recognize hypocrisy and then label it preferable to honesty was indeed the "lie in the soul."

Meinecke nonetheless clearly perceived how Germany's enemies could capitalize on the frank affirmation of power considerations which characterized many German pronouncements on the nature of the state and foreign policy. His attempt to combat the effect of enemy propagandists' citations from Frederick, Bismarck, and Treitschke, to say nothing of Nietzsche and Bernhardi, was the main theme of "Kultur, Machtpolitik und Militarismus." It is necessary, he wrote, to give "clear answer and a justification of the interpretations which the more

[43] *Ibid.* The quotation from Muir is taken from his book, *Britain's Case Against Germany*, Manchester, 1914.

recent German thinkers and statesmen were wont to give in regard to the relationship of politics and morality."[44]

"Kultur, Machtpolitik und Militarismus" was more than a propaganda effort, however. It was one of Meinecke's first systematic attempts to state the problem of morality in political action and, as such, foreshadowed the profounder reflections that were to come in *Die Idee der Staatsraeson*. "The laws of morality," Meinecke wrote, "of brotherly love, of the sanctity of agreements are inviolable. But the duty of the statesman to care for the welfare and safety of the state and people entrusted to him . . . is also sacred and inviolable. What happens when these two duties conflict with one another? Or can one suggest that conflicts of moral duty are in principle impossible? Only superficial men, unrealistic fanatics or abject hypocrites could put forward such a proposition. Every authentic tragedy is a shattering demonstration that moral life cannot be regulated like clockwork and that even the purest strivings for good can be forced into terrible choices and pitfalls."[45]

With these words Meinecke reverted to the concept of polarity between state ego and universal morality which he adumbrated in *Weltbuergertum und Nationalstaat*. But there the conflict between ethics and politics had been softened by placing the ethical commandments at the "glimmering boundaries of experience" and by assuming that the state's service to the cultural nation could both justify and modify its arbitrariness in international relations. Now the crisis of war forced Meinecke to reevaluate these assumptions. Whereas before he took the position that the idea of the nation-state promised a satisfactory means to deal with the antinomy between the commandment of self-assertion and the commandment of moral law, he now began to treat concrete issues in which the conflict appeared as "tragedy." The fact that Meinecke regarded the nation-state as embodying moral good within itself was overshadowed by the proposition that "even the purest strivings for good can be forced into terrible choices and pitfalls."

[44] "Machtpolitik," *op.cit.*, pp. 631.   [45] *Ibid.*

This proposition pulled the nation-state back into the realm of relative values—a realm in which Meinecke had always located it in theory. But once again he demonstrated how tenuous and vague were the theoretical admonitions against the absolutization of the state when measured against the concrete demands of practical policy. The formal thesis was that the conflict between the absolute of state necessity and the absolute of moral law reduced both the absolutes to the status of relative values. From the argument, one could logically draw the conclusion that the safety of the state was as ambiguous a value as the law of personal morality and that, as the occasion demanded, the individual might choose to serve the latter rather than the former. But Meinecke was not yet ready to go this far. "In relations between states," he wrote ". . . conflicts between private morality and state interest are plainly inevitable and as old as world history itself. And historical experience as well as the individual conscience teaches with irresistible force that in such cases the statesman can act only in accordance with the principle: *salus populi suprema lex esto*. This is exactly what Bismarck meant when he said that 'state egotism is the only healthy basis of the great state.' "[46]

Thus the conflict is resolved once again in favor of the state ego. With this solution Meinecke contradicts himself, for there is no authentic tragic choice when there is a clear hierarchy of values making the choice automatic. Meinecke attempted to soften the contradiction by asserting that there were nonetheless "limits to state egotism and power politics which may not be transgressed in the name of an inevitable conflict of duty. The limit is constituted [by the principle] that a state should not seek more power than is necessary to its safety and to the free development of all the energies of its people."[47] But the limitation merely meant in practice that a state so proscribing itself —and the proscription was not without considerable flexibility —could and should automatically decide to violate moral law

[46] *Ibid.*   [47] *Ibid.*, p. 632.

in the name of its own welfare. State objectives which were not in accordance with these limitations could and should be rejected automatically in obedience to the moral law. Hence Meinecke's limitations did no more to incorporate the idea of tragic choice than his original proposition.

The absence of a true sense of tragedy in these formulations is underlined by the examples Meinecke selected to illustrate situations in which the state transgressed the proper limits of power politics. He cited the Boer War and the Italian desertion of the Triple Alliance as examples which could not be justified by the existence of a conflict of duty. But he discovered no similar examples in the history of German conduct.[48] Indeed, he had explicitly maintained that the most morally controversial of German acts—the invasion of Belgium—could find justification in terms of conflict of duty. Meinecke accused Britain of "deifying the interest of the moment" and of making the pragmatic proposition of "That is true which is useful to me" the maxim of its policy.[49] In the heat of his passionate attacks on hypocrisy, he did not see how closely his own subjective reasoning was joined to this principle.

How estimate the quantum of power necessary to the safety of the state? Meinecke conceded that it could not be determined with mathematical precision and that there could certainly be diverse interpretations.[50] His explanation of why he judged the Boer War and Italy's abandonment of the Central Powers as examples of excesses in power politics was hardly comprehensive. In the case of the Boers, he argued that a war in South Africa was not vital to metropolitan Britain's security. Seen in the perspective of Englishmen already settled in South Africa, however, the problem takes on a different coloration. As for Italy, he found no "compelling reasons" for her decision in 1915. But in the light of Italy's exposed position in the Mediterranean and the ultimate defeat of her one-time allies, there are powerful

[48] *Ibid.*
[49] *Probleme des Weltkriegs, op.cit.,* pp. 13-14.
[50] "Machtpolitik," *op.cit.,* p. 632.

arguments to show that her decision to join the Entente was intimately related to the safety of the Italian state. In any case, the distinction between the conduct of England and Italy in these specific instances and the German invasion of Belgium suggests that Meinecke's criteria for judging between "healthy" and "unhealthy" power politics were shaky indeed.

One basis for more reliable objective criteria was already present in Meinecke's caveat on power politics. The thesis that the state must serve "its safety *and* . . . the development of all the energies of its people"[51] implied that the state has two supreme objectives. It implied that the state may find itself in a position where the pursuit of its safety is inhibiting "the free development of all the energies of its people." In the realm of such a contingency the idea of tragic choice gains real meaning. The true dilemma looms up when the state as a power organization and the state as a cultural institution are no longer in harmony, when there is no longer a unity between power and culture but conflict, when the power strivings of the state begin to rob culture of the autonomy which Meinecke conferred upon it.

We have already seen Meinecke's fears for the health of German culture in his castigation of the power-mania of the radical nationalists and Pan-Germans. Yet these concerns were greatly mitigated by the demonstration of spontaneous devotion to the German state symbolized by the initial support of all the parties for the German war effort. Certainly it might be hoped that the reconciliation between the German state and the German socialists who had so long been in conflict promised a shift in the internal political situation. Such a shift would be away from the political and cultural chauvinists and toward those whose record of opposition to the power of the state seemed a warranty that the state's power requirements would be subject to close scrutiny. The internationalist tradition of the socialists might be expected to strengthen that feeling for the "universal vein of life" which Meinecke admonished the nation-state to nourish. Above all, the

[51] Italics mine.

healing of the breach between the German monarchy and the German socialists seemed at last to provide the German state with an authentic opportunity to serve the free development of all its people and not just some. With such happy auguries it was unthinkable to Meinecke that Germany should be denied the chance to realize the exalted objective.

Much was at stake; hence much leeway could be permitted the state regarding the means which it selected to preserve its safety. As the full dimensions of the war became plainer and the Allied propaganda onslaught against German values became more intense, Meinecke's readiness to justify German war acts in the name of safety grew correspondingly. When unrestricted submarine warfare was first adopted in February 1915 to overcome the effects of the British blockade he greeted the move with the phrase "*à corsaire corsaire et demi.*"[52]

Everything in Meinecke's arsenal of arguments supporting German war policies depended, however, on a continuing conviction that the preservation and expansion of German power were compatible with and even necessary to the realization of cultural objectives. Indeed, they were dependent on a general view of history in which liberalism, optimism, and the idea of progress were dominants. At the outbreak of the war Meinecke expressed the belief that in the historic interplay of cultural and power values there was visible "a gradual ascent. The cruder methods and objectives of power politics give way to the nobler and more humane. A higher degree of humanitarian [values] in power politics does not, it is true, mean that power politics is practiced with less energy and sacrifice. But [it does mean] that higher and more spiritual values of culture are embraced, represented, defended and disseminated by it."[53]

Once the war began to appear to Meinecke not as a defender and disseminator of culture but as an antagonist and oppressor, he would have to abandon his initial affirmation of the war and Germany's role therein and take up the position of critic.

[52] "Machtpolitik," *op.cit.*, p. 642.
[53] "Politik und Kultur" in *Erhebung 1914, op.cit.*, p. 45.

CHAPTER VIII

DEFEAT AND REVOLUTION: THE POLARITY
OF POWER AND CULTURE

IN HIS MEMOIRS Meinecke identified his warning against nationalistic extremism, written on the eve of the outbreak of World War I, as the turning point in his thinking about the relation of national and trans-national values.[1] "Hitherto I had taken the path which led from cosmopolitanism to the nation-state, seeking at the same time to prevent the former from being wholly swallowed by the latter. Henceforth I began to go the opposite way—from the nation-state, which continued to be my home, to the cosmopolitanism which was under such heavy attack and which was so necessary to regain. My steps were at first unconscious and halting, but events saw to it that they continued in this direction."[2]

Actually, the direction was not set until two years of war had provided an abundance of evidence that many of Meinecke's propositions about the nation-state in general and Germany in particular could no longer be supported. In 1914 and 1915 his hopes and expectations were that cultural values could maintain their autonomy while serving the state. In 1916 Meinecke saw German culture not as the creative bringer of balance and purpose to the state but as dominated by hysteria and lack of restraint. "Particularly among the educated and nationally-minded classes" Meinecke found an all too eager espousal of the most extreme power objectives of warring Germany. Decrying the fashion of grandiose speculations concerning German expansion, he warned that Germany's greatest need was "criticism and self-

[1] He refers to "Nationalismus und Nationale Idee" in *Erhebung 1914*, *op.cit.* Cf. Chapter VII, above.
[2] *Erinnerungen, op.cit.*, pp. 200-201.

control."[3] Using the terms "exaltados" and "moderados" to describe the expansionists and their opponents, Meinecke asserted that the conflict between the two was taking place at every level of German society and that unless the moderados gained the upper hand Germany would be in mortal danger. "Let us for once say it openly," he wrote, "the true heirs of Bismarck's *Realpolitik* are today the moderados and not the exaltados. The power frenzy of the latter is simply sentimentality. Bismarck with his cool sense of the possible and the achievable would have mercilessly criticized and suppressed their fantastic demands."[4]

Not only did Meinecke recoil from the spectacle of German war aims extremism. The war itself had become an extremity: "The war has become hypertrophied."[5] The terrible sacrifices of life in the struggle at Verdun and on the Somme moved Meinecke to question the very sense of the war and to reach the conclusion that such sacrifices no longer had purposeful meaning. In such a war one could not look for victory or defeat. Sensible policies required a compromise peace.[6] The warring states, in their struggle to gain power advantages, were killing the nerve of their greatness as cultural personalities.

It was one thing for Meinecke to take nationalist extremism to task as he did in July of 1914 and quite another to concede in the spring of 1916 that this extremism had become the dominant force among articulate non-socialist Germans. In the fall of 1915 Meinecke was still able to speak of the war as a natural, manageable, and not unbeneficent phenomenon;[7] a year later it had become "hypertrophied." Hence 1916 rather than 1914 appears as the more important turning point, for it was in 1916 that Meinecke was questioning the fundamental propositions of

[3] *Probleme des Weltkriegs, op.cit.,* p. 38. The quotation is taken from the lead article of this collection of wartime essays whose title is the same as that of the book. "Probleme des Weltkriegs" was first published as an article in June 1916.

[4] *Ibid.,* pp. 45-50.

[5] *Ibid.,* p. 59. The quotation is from "Staatskunst und Leidenschaft," first published in September 1916.

[6] *Ibid.,* pp. 59-60.   [7] Cf. Chapter VII, above.

his political thought. He was conceding that the national idea had failed to provide effective limitations to the power drive of the state. With this concession he reopened the whole issue of the proper basis for the state.

The reassessment of this issue had a number of profound consequences. In regard to Germany as Bismarck had created it, Meinecke moved from affirmation to criticism. In the realm of political activity, he exchanged the position of interpreter of existing institutions for one of active reformer. In international relations he abandoned the view that the nation-state system was a successful and desirable system and instead perceived it as perhaps a historical necessity but one fraught with danger. In philosophical method he stressed more strongly the idea of polarity and emphasized more the potentialities of conflict than of unity in the polar relationship.

It had been a central thesis throughout Meinecke's prewar political writings that Bismarck's Germany was a viable political entity, that it represented a balance between authority and liberty which offered the optimum prospects for growing internal freedom and continuing safety from external threat.[8] Gradually this belief was chipped away. In order to realize these prospects Meinecke's goal before and during the war was the reconciliation of the state and the working classes, and such reconciliation meant giving the working classes a more powerful political voice. By the beginning of 1917 he was disillusioned as to the willingness of the ruling groups to effect the reconciliation. Angrily he protested that "We must bring into the open what is in countless hearts: We do not want to be ruled in Prussia any longer by Junkers and corps students . . . every last hangover of the old spirit of caste and special privilege is evil. The German people has matured to the point where it can call sons from its

[8] Meinecke's contention in 1915 that Bismarck had created a "people's state with authoritarian forms" which has demonstrated its vitality in time of trial was typical and is evidence that his prewar views extended into wartime. Cf. "Bismarck und das neue Deutschland" (1915) in *Preussen und Deutschland, op.cit.*, p. 513.

midst to serve in any leading position which Junker heritage or Junker sympathy has [hitherto] monopolized."[9]

In his plea for electoral reform in Prussia Meinecke named the spirit of the Prussian bureaucracy along with the three-class suffrage system as spoilers of the "finest and most sacred gift the war has given to our national life: the winning of the working class to the nation-state, the nationalization of the whole nation."[10] In late 1917 Meinecke launched an even more vigorous attack on the representatives of heavy industry and conservatives in general as enemies of electoral reform.[11] Finally, in November of 1918, on the eve of the revolution, Meinecke expressed his belief that the far-reaching constitutional changes introduced in October of 1918 were an absolute necessity, that Bismarck's system was not adaptable enough to create a popular state which could withstand the crisis of defeat.[12]

In his first appraisal of the causes of the German revolution Meinecke observed that Bismarck's state had encompassed all the social forces in Germany except the social democratic workers, and that "the social democratic problem could no longer be solved with the instruments of the authoritarian state." And he agreed with Engels' devastating criticism that Bismarck " 'did not comprehend the historical situation which he himself had created.' "[13] Turning to the ruling groups who inherited the German state from Bismarck and took it into war, Meinecke placed first blame for the revolution on them: "Perhaps, then, it was the rigid obstinacy and the political adventures of those who have hitherto been the privileged [classes] which finally

[9] *Die deutsche Freiheit, op.cit.,* p. 32.

[10] *Probleme des Weltkriegs, op.cit.,* p. 105.

[11] "Vaterlandspartei und deutsche Politik," in *Die Hilfe, op.cit.,* p. 70.

[12] *Nach der Revolution,* Munich, 1919, p. 4. This is a collection of essays written during the period between the fall of 1918 and the fall of 1919. The present reference is to "Am Vorabend der Revolution," first published November 20, 1918, but written in early November before the outbreak of the revolution.

[13] *Ibid.,* pp. 28-29. The quotation is from "Ursachen der Revolution," first published in March 1919.

made the revolution inevitable. Annexationism, submarine warfare and resistance to reform—at the end of the road . . . stood military collapse. In all these things they overtaxed their strength and ought not to be surprised that they suddenly find themselves prostrate."[14]

It was Germany's tragedy, Meinecke had argued, that militarism and authoritarian forms were historically necessary to its very existence. Without these forms "Brandenburg-Prussia—small, fragmentized and hemmed in by stronger neighbors—and Germany, similarly fragmentized and surrounded, could not have won the struggle to achieve national unity. One must keep in mind all the miseries of German history since the Middle Ages—the tragedy of the confessional conflict, the terrible catastrophe of the Thirty Years' War, the helplessness in the face of a Louis XIV or a Napoleon. Then one can understand how the military strength and spirit of Prussia could be regarded as the indispensable shield of the German people."[15]

But though these forms and the social groups they favored had to be powerful, Meinecke asserted that they should not have been allowed to become all-powerful.[16] If there were no other contenders for power in the national arena, then the stimulus to serve the nation wisely was weakened and the policies of the ruling elite would be designed to serve the interests of that elite rather than those of the nation as a whole. In Meinecke's view, this was in fact what had occurred: the special interests of those in power rather than the national interest blocked the way of Stein and all his reforming successors in their endeavors "to rebuild the authoritarian state into a popular and communal state."[17] Authority was praised over liberty not to save the state but to preserve the perquisites of the rulers.

Consequently, Meinecke saw the latter-day development of Bismarck's Germany running directly counter to his conviction that "the inner freedom of the human being is the highest of all values."[18] Throughout the war, despite his concessions to the

[14] *Ibid.*, p. 38.   [15] *Ibid.*, p. 15.   [16] *Ibid.*, p. 16.
[17] *Ibid.*, p. 22.   [18] Cf. Chapter VI, above.

power state, Meinecke continued to affirm this conviction. In 1916 he was attacking contemporary German utilitarianism as a philosophy which "thinks only about the whole . . . forcibly fitting the individual into the whole . . . [and] expressing itself most typically as ruthless nationalism."[19] At about the same time he warned the Prussian state that it was "faced with the question whether it should seek strength more in external authority or in an inner trust between government and people [and that] it should not hesitate for a moment [to choose the latter]."[20] And in an article written expressly to provide deeper insight into the past as an inspiration for wartime Germany he reminded his readers that the basic conviction of the great men of the Prussian Reform was "that the human being has a dignity of his own and may never be treated merely as a means to an end."[21]

The political institution in Imperial Germany which represented one of the most flagrant violations of this Kantian principle of the Prussian reformers was the three-class suffrage system in Prussia. When Meinecke moved into the role of active reformer it was this institution which received the brunt of his attack. Before the war he was still doubtful as to the need for its reform.[22] Its historical justification he had anchored firmly in the concept of the primacy of foreign policy: the Prussian Diet under the three-class suffrage system could be counted on to protect Germany's military and foreign policy imperatives; the opposition, particularly the Social Democrats who vigorously denounced power politics and war, gave reason to doubt both its

[19] *Preussen und Deutschland, op.cit.,* p. 470. The quotation is taken from "Der deutsche Geschichtsunterricht und die modernen Beduerfnisse," first published in 1916.

[20] *Weltbuergertum, op.cit.,* p. 533. The quotation is from an afterword which Meinecke added to the third edition (March 1915) and which was probably revised for the fourth edition (January 1917).

[21] *Preussisch-deutsche Gestalten, op.cit.* ("Grundzuege unserer nationalen Entwicklung bis zur Reichsgruendung Bismarcks," 1915/1916), p. 13.

[22] *Weltbuergertum, op.cit.,* p. 527.

patriotism and its wisdom in matters of foreign policy.[23] Therefore its voice should be kept weak, and this is precisely what the
three-class system did.

Once the war had demonstrated the loyalty of the Social
Democratic workers and other critics of the regime, however,
the old dependence on discriminatory suffrage was no longer
justified—it had become a "barrier . . . between monarchy . . .
and people."[24] Reform of the Prussian electoral law had become
a "national necessity" and those who opposed it were placing
their narrow class interests ahead of the national interest.[25] Now
the shoe was on the other foot: formerly the national interest
and the opponents of unequal suffrage in Prussia were in conflict; now the conflict was between the national interest and the
defenders of unequal suffrage.

It should be noted that here again in championing reform
Meinecke found it congenial to argue fundamentally in terms of
foreign policy needs: "We are arguing not from the standpoint
of democratic ideals but from the premises of purely state interests."[26] He recalled that in advocating greater popular representation it was Stein's purpose to fire popular resistance to
Napoleon.[27] So, a hundred years later, a heightened sense of
participation and responsibility was the urgent need to bring out
that extra effort on the part of the masses which might make the
difference between victory and defeat. The reform of the Prussian electoral laws would add another weapon to Germany's war
arsenal, for "The power instruments of the state include not
only soldiers, cannon, and discipline but also those moral quali-

[23] *Probleme des Weltkriegs*, *op.cit.*, pp. 95-97, 106. Cf. also "Sozialdemokratie und Machtpolitik" in *Die Arbeiterschaft im neuen Deutschland, op.cit.*, p. 21.

[24] *Probleme des Weltkriegs*, *op.cit.*, pp. 95, 106, 108.

[25] *Weltbuergertum*, *op.cit.*, p. 533. Meinecke gave public support to
Prussian electoral reform less than a year after the outbreak of the war.
Cf. "Preussen und Deutschland," *Frankfurter Zeitung*, April 2, 1915.

[26] *Probleme des Weltkriegs*, *op.cit.*, p. 93.

[27] *Ibid.*, p. 85.

ties of a nation which can flourish only in the atmosphere of moral and political freedom."[28]

Embrace freedom, the argument ran, in order to increase power. And here, demoting freedom to the role of an instrumentality rather than treating it as an end in itself, Meinecke once more brings into question his previous contention that the freedom of the individual is the highest of all values. How could this contention stand alongside the implications inhering in the concept of the primacy of foreign policy? Logically, the two could not stand together. Meinecke was in this sense no further along in his thinking than before and during the early part of the war when the balance of the polarities of power and spirit, state and individual was always on the side of power and state.

In mood, however, there was a distinct change in position. For the first time there appeared the explicit emphasis that foreign policy was not the only determinant of the life of states. "It would be a step backward," Meinecke wrote, ". . . if credence were given to the idea that a national political will has its foundation solely in reactions to foreign dangers, and if the cultural and intellectual activities of individuals were accorded only a modest share in the process."[29] Still more positive was the statement that "The internal demand for the freedom of the maturing nation is in its way just as justified and organic an impulse [as that of seeking security from external threat]. This demand must struggle with the first and more powerful impulse."[30]

It is true that Meinecke had long regarded the nation-state as an ensemble of autonomous values. But the ensemble was perceived as an essentially harmonious one under the aegis of the primacy of foreign policy. Now, however, the autonomy which Meinecke stressed in regard to individual will and de-

[28] *Ibid.*, p. 94.

[29] *Preussen und Deutschland, op.cit.*, p. 55. The quotation is from "Zur Geschichte des aelteren deutschen Parteiwesens," first published in 1917. Meinecke added that such an idea would certainly be congenial to a "muscular Pan-Germanism."

[30] "Vaterlandspartei und deutsche Politik," *Die Hilfe, op.cit.*, p. 701.

mands for freedom in civil society was pictured as clashing with the demands of foreign policy. Meinecke was no longer content with an analytical system that made the civil society an unambiguous creature of its international relations.[31] The claims of foreign policy might come "first" and the impulse behind these claims might be "stronger," but the impulse to civic freedom is as important as the first and stronger impulse.

Above all, the will to civic freedom must contest the primacy of foreign policy, must "struggle" with it, in order to keep the latter within bounds. With this proposal Meinecke recognized that the doctrine of the primacy of foreign policy could be carried too far, that it could infringe on values which he felt must be upheld. Thus he was unwilling to accept Seeley's dictum that "the degree of freedom in a state varies inversely with the political pressures on its borders." He feared that such a formulation could be used as "justification for absolutistic militarism" and proposed instead his own thesis: "More truly and simply one may say that the quantity of power instruments and the degree of power organization varies directly with the pressures exercised on the borders."[32] The nation which faced danger from abroad was not doomed to be unfree but faced the truly inspiring challenge of cultivating and strengthening its freedoms in order to withstand the impact of the necessarily increased emphasis on power. Here was the test of a great nation. And it was the enduring fame of the men of the Prussian Reform that they had met the test by coupling "the issues of the constitution with the struggle for survival"[33] and so had sought national safety in greater liberty for the nation's citizens.

This is essentially the idea upon which Meinecke wanted to build a hundred years later. He wanted to seize the opportunity which the war offered to inject more freedom into the German state, not simply to make the state more powerful but because

[31] Cf. Chapter v, above.

[32] "Die Reform des preussischen Wahlrechts" in *Probleme des Weltkriegs, op.cit.*, pp. 93-94.

[33] *Ibid.*, p. 87.

freedom was an end in itself. Even while he clung to the primacy of foreign policy doctrine, Meinecke showed his concern for freedom as such when he asserted that this very doctrine, which had so often been labeled as "reactionary," was "our best weapon against today's reactionaries." The reactionaries' policy of conquest and annexation, he argued, would rob Germany of freedom of action in foreign policy since it would perpetuate a hostile coalition against her. But, more than that, "A policy of force externally compels a policy of force internally; robbery abroad leads to . . . rapaciousness at home."[34]

If, by this argument, Meinecke sought once again to show the causal impact of foreign policy on domestic politics, he also demonstrated that, in value terms, the nature of the civil society was uppermost in his thoughts. Extremist policies abroad were deplored because they threatened freedom at home. Here at last was a position which conceived of foreign policy as the servant and not the master of domestic political life. At this time, however, it was a position on which Meinecke had only a tenuous hold, for the doctrine of the primacy of foreign policy was closely interwoven with a number of other propositions to which Meinecke was perhaps even more deeply committed.

One of these propositions, with whose implications Meinecke continued to be concerned throughout his remaining years, was that democracy's contribution to the free society was at best an ambiguous one. We have already seen the intimate connection between his attitudes on democracy and on foreign policy—that the delicate functions of foreign policy could not be trusted to the rough and tumble of democratic politics.[35] Consequently Meinecke made the realm of foreign policy the citadel of mo-

[34] "Vaterlandspartei und deutsche Politik," *Die Hilfe, op.cit.,* p. 702. Cf. also a speech which Meinecke gave at the founding meeting of the *Volksbund fuer Freiheit und Vaterland* on November 14, 1917. The speech is reprinted in *Um Freiheit und Vaterland,* Gotha, 1918.

[35] Chapter v, above. The similarity to ideas expressed in the *Federalist* and by such contemporary Americans as George Kennan and Walter Lippmann is worthy of note.

narchical and aristocratic practices and called upon the proponents of democratic reform to respect that citadel.

But Meinecke urged limitations on democracy quite apart from his concern for foreign policy. For all his endeavors on the side of democratic reform, he was not a democrat. His ideal state was that which promoted the freedom of the individual personality, and he was very unsure as to democracy's capacity to realize this ideal. In *Weltbuergertum und Nationalstaat* he observed there were two kinds of modern individualism: the first "stemming from natural law was democratically inclined and sought equal rights for all; the other, aristocratic in its intellectual predilections, strove for the liberation and cultivation of the best."[36] Throughout his life, it is clear that Meinecke's sympathy was with the latter type of individualism, that he tolerated the former only as an historically necessary political form, not without certain virtues but wholly lacking in virtue if it did not make possible the realization of aristocratic individualism as well. In his reflections on the German revolution of 1918 Meinecke made his position clear enough. Describing himself as embracing an "aristocratic and humanistic cultural ideal" Meinecke wrote "I am no lover of democracy, but democracy cannot be avoided."[37]

Thus Meinecke's distaste for democracy stemmed first of all from a set of general cultural preferences.[38] His basic fear was that the values and institutions of society would come to be dominated by those who had no training to prepare for a responsible and appreciative treatment of them. His attacks on

[36] *Weltbuergertum, op.cit.,* p. 10.

[37] *Nach der Revolution, op.cit.,* pp. 110-111. The quotations are taken from "Ein Gespraech aus dem Herbste 1919," an imaginary dialogue between two friends, one of whom is designed to represent the views of Erich Marcks, an eminent historian who was one of Meinecke's closest friends but whose conservative views led later to a cooling of this friendship.

[38] Cf. *ibid.,* pp. 462-467 (from "Die deutsche Geschichtswissenschaft und die modernen Beduerfnisse," first published in April 1916) and *Erinnerungen, op.cit.,* pp. 261-263, 275-276.

extremist nationalism were only one aspect of his larger concern with what he thought to be falling cultural standards in Germany. The mass state, he felt, was a danger to individual freedom. And this "loss of personal freedom . . . was not restricted to the realm of political objectives. As bearer of the political movement, the rising middle class has the desire to lead the masses to the fruits of culture; this threatens culture itself by [encouraging] superficiality. It could become impatient with those who dared to rise above the conventional level."[39]

The peril to intellectual freedom emanating from the mass society was in Meinecke's view intimately linked to the peril to the freedom and security of the state. This attitude is vividly registered in his contention that "the most dangerous sources of passions which muddy the waters of statecraft in our age . . . are the unregulated and uneducated power instincts of whole nations which can shove and push the pilot as he stands at the helm. The mightier the military, economic and technological sources of strength of the modern nation, the greater the danger. And still more dangerous is it when the governmental forms of the nation-state make it easier for ambitious and unscrupulous upstarts to reach for the controls. . . . One must say it openly . . . modern parliamentary and democratic states lack certain necessary brakes."[40]

These words were written before Ludendorff's usurpation of civilian control in 1917 had demonstrated that the semi-absolute state of the Hohenzollerns also lacked necessary brakes. Meinecke recognized that Ludendorff's rule was in fact such a demonstration,[41] but even after this recognition he continued to identify an excess of democracy as the more dangerous threat.

In particular, Meinecke denied that democracy and popular control of the government militated against war. On the con-

---

[39] *Preussen und Deutschland, op.cit.*, p. 391. The quotation is taken from "Heinrich von Treitschke," first published in the spring of 1914.

[40] "Staatskunst und Leidenschaft" in *Probleme des Weltkriegs, op.cit.*, pp. 66-67.

[41] "Ein Gespraech aus dem Herbste 1919," in *Nach der Revolution, op.cit.*, p. 122.

trary, he asserted that the prelude to the war declarations of 1914 "demonstrated what we had already surmised; the greatest danger to peace today is not in the first instance the secret politics of cabinets and diplomats but the influence which mighty popular movements exercise over them."[42] He was convinced that the participation of the masses in politics brought a new element of irrationality into the conduct of states. Prophetically he feared that the masses would demand and respond to massive power demonstrations rather than to the intricacies of rational diplomacy.

But, paradoxically, he was also the champion of introducing the masses to political responsibility. His espousal of nationalism, his devotion to the era of the Prussian Reform, his dedication to the idea of the free personality—all required such championship of him. Responsibility and the free personality were synonymous, and Meinecke's objective was the free personality not merely for the few but as a characteristic of the entire nation. Thus he preached the necessity of equality of suffrage in Prussia, with minor modifications, in order to put an end to a system which placed severe limits to mass influence on policy and repressed a sense of responsibility on the part of those discriminated against.

Hence Meinecke was faced with the delicate problem of increasing the sense of responsibility of the masses without "handing the entire state over to them."[48] His solution was to approve the concept of universal suffrage and therefore to support reform of the Prussian electoral law but at the same time to resist parliamentarism. Universal suffrage would serve to increase both the sense of responsibility and the actual influence of the masses on public policy. But it would not be the locus of the ultimate power of decision in the state, for the parliaments elected by universal suffrage would not be supreme—that is, they would not

---

[42] "Sozialdemokratie und Machtpolitik" in *Die Arbeiterschaft im neuen Deutschland, op.cit.,* p. 25. Cf. also *Probleme des Weltkriegs, op.cit.,* p. 110.

[48] *Probleme des Weltkriegs, op.cit.,* p. 92.

have the authority to elect or depose the prime minister and his government. This authority was to remain in the hands of the monarch.[44]

In this way Meinecke hoped to "secure independence of leadership by monarch and statesman from the popular moods of the day."[45] He anticipated that the government would have to rule in basic harmony with the parliament but felt that its formal independence of votes of confidence would enable it more often to support policies on their merits rather than on the basis of what the majority would accept. It was Meinecke's understanding that wise policies are not always popular policies, a belief which made him pause again and again before the problem of democratic government and seek some compromise between the rule of the many and the rule of what he hoped was an educated and rational elite.

Defeat and revolution made many of Meinecke's proposals for reform of the Hohenzollern state obsolete. Moreover, he now felt compelled to embrace the majority principle of government in the face of the revolutionary tide, convinced that it stood as the only available bulwark against the threat of Bolshevization imposed by a revolutionary minority.[46] Here Meinecke took an opposite tack from his deprecation of majoritarianism. But he never lifted the majoritarian idea to the level of a principle, adhering to it only as a tactic. He remained a believer in the proposition that the "most valuable stimuli in historical life would continue to emanate from great individuals and not from the masses."[47]

Indeed, Meinecke's fundamental approach to politics was one which refused to give absolute status to any specific institutions

[44] *"Die deutsche Freiheit,"* *op.cit.,* p. 36.
[45] *Probleme des Weltkriegs, op.cit.,* p. 67.
[46] *Nach der Revolution, op.cit.,* p. 118.
[47] "Heinrich von Treitschke" in *Preussen und Deutschland, op.cit.,* p. 191. Meinecke used these words to describe Treitschke's position but he could as easily have applied them to himself. See, for example, "Des Kronprinzen Friedrichs Considerations sur l'etat present du corps politiques de l'Europe," *HZ,* 117, 1917, p. 42.

or techniques of rule. Strongly as he defended the institution of monarchy, he was ready to accept its demise in Germany as the result of the monarch's own ineptitude along with deeper causes and the heavy pressure of the Allies. But he retained his belief in the necessity of an executive with some measure of independence from the will of parliament. Hence he was one of the first to propose that the new German constitution should provide for a strong plebiscitary president on the American model. He envisioned the German presidency as a substitute for imperial rule (*"Ersatzkaisertum"*) which would serve as a community bond and source of authority transcending the individual parties.[48]

What Meinecke was really concerned with was the continuation—or revival—of conditions which would favor the development of the free and creative individual. He expressed this concern in vivid and prophetic phrases as he attempted to portray his feelings on the outbreak of the revolution: "We felt that irreplacable values were being threatened with extinction—not only old and familiar institutions which could after all be replaced by others, but also the innermost prerequisites of authentic culture. Spiritual freedom for the individual would face a much graver threat in a long-enduring dictatorship of the proletariat than from the pressure of the old authoritarian state. Yes, one could live one's spiritual life in the old state. One could differentiate himself and be an individual to his heart's content."[49]

It was Meinecke's hope that the individual could survive in a

[48] Cf. *Erinnerungen, op.cit.,* pp. 258-259, 276-277, "Verfassung und Verwaltung der deutschen Republik" in *Die Neue Rundschau,* vol. 30, January 1919, pp. 10 and 16, and Hajo Holborn, "Verfassung und Verwaltung der deutschen Republik," *HZ,* vol. 147, 1932, pp. 121-122. Holborn notes that Meinecke had enough foresight to concern himself with the danger that no party in Germany could gain a majority and that the resultant necessity of resorting to coalition groupings would doom Germany to a succession of unstable governments in the absence of a strong presidency.

[49] *Nach der Revolution, op.cit.,* p. 51. The quotation is from "Der Nationale Gedanke im alten und im neuen Deutschland," first published in December 1918.

democratic republic, and his conviction that such survival was impossible in a rigorous Marxist system, which caused him to rally to the republic's defense as the most effective bar to the triumph of Bolshevism. He believed that "the idea of personal autonomy was present in democracy and democratic socialism as well as in liberalism"[50] and that together with the continuing bond of nationality it could provide the basis for a new state acceptable both to those previously committed to the monarchy and to the socialist masses who had hitherto been excluded from political responsibility.[51]

Meinecke found many shortcomings and weaknesses in the concept of a democratic republic, but he asserted that "The republic is today the state form which least divides us." "Looking to the past, I remain a monarchist at heart; looking to the future, I shall be a republican in reason."[52] Here Meinecke's reactions to democratic forms recall those of Ranke in 1848 toward constitutional forms which we have already noted: "The constitutional instrument must be regarded, without prejudice or antagonism, as a form by which people today desire to live. The constitution must be so constructed that one can live with it."[53]

Less resigned and more hopeful are Meinecke's thoughts on the republic as the new bearer of the national community: "that is the immortal meaning of the national idea, that it always seeks and must seek to reveal itself in new forms and that it nonetheless preserves its spiritual continuity in all these metamorpho-

---

[50] *Preussen und Deutschland, op.cit.,* p. 63. The quotation is from "Zur Geschichte des aelteren deutschen Parteiwesens," first published in 1917.

[51] In *Nach der Revolution* (p. 113) Meinecke makes one of his markedly rare evaluations of Bolshevism: "I see in Bolshevism not an organic growth of our historical world . . . as [I do] in the case of democracy but one of those pathological growths which are common enough in periods of decay. It is a modern chiliasticism, a fantastic and crude belief that one can conjure up a heaven on earth by totally destroying the old sinful world."

[52] "Verfassung und Verwaltung der deutschen Republik," *op.cit.,* p. 2. Cf. also *Nach der Revolution, op.cit.,* p. 63.

[53] Chapter v, above.

ses."[54] These reflections too recalled an earlier judgment of Meinecke's. In his last book published before the war, he quoted the words of Josef von Radowitz that " 'Political truth is by nature not absolute truth but is relative according to time and place' " and that " 'A government can operate positively and energetically, whatever its constitution, as soon as it achieves true authority. By itself, a constitution can neither create nor hinder authority.' " "Radowitz sacrificed every state form to the changing times," Meinecke wrote, and so he "moved from the transcendental and absolute sphere of his earlier ideal into the [broad] current of historical life."[55] This was the current in which Meinecke's own thinking was immersed, and these were the attitudes he assumed when he faced the German revolutionary crisis of 1918-1920.

Meinecke's reversals of position were more striking and, on the surface at least, less forthright in the sphere of foreign policy. We have already noted Meinecke's brief dalliance with annexationist ideas.[56] His admission of "backsliding" and his frank concession that "it would have been better had I not had [such ideas]"[57] appear to contradict another postwar reflection in which he pictured himself and his political associates as anti-annexationists: "The basic idea of our circle was always to protect Germany from defeat and revolution. Hence we strove for a conciliatory peace with our opponents and fought against annexationism and intensified submarine warfare, [both of] which prevented such a peace."[58]

The key phrase here is "which prevented such a peace." Meinecke was not averse to territorial annexations at an earlier stage in the contest when German prospects were brighter. Indeed, he was not against annexations in principle. But neither was he

[54] *Nach der Revolution, op.cit.*, p. 63.

[55] *Radowitz und die deutsche Revolution*, Berlin, 1913, pp. 532 and 533.

[56] Chapter VII, above.

[57] *Nach der Revolution, op.cit.*, p. 132.

[58] *Ibid.*, p. 44.

for annexations in principle, and this can be said of him both during the earlier and later phases of the war. He did not join the "exaltados" in making territorial aggrandizement a fixture of German war aims. On the contrary, as early as 1914 he believed that a *status quo ante* peace would represent a considerable achievement for Germany.[59]

Thus he may be justified in claiming to have fought annexationism if we interpret the word in its strictest sense—that of making the idea of annexation into an article of faith—an ism. But it would perhaps have been better had Meinecke eliminated all ambiguity. If this were done on the basis of his own contemporary testimony, a picture would emerge showing Meinecke during the early part of the war in occasional support of annexations and "border rectifications" in East and West. It would also show him treating annexation as a serious and delicate problem, not as the first fruit and natural result of victory but as problematic and almost as an *ultima ratio*.[60] Finally, it would show him in the latter part of the war taking up an active opposition to annexationist war aims and denouncing those who still preached a peace of victory and territorial gain as wholly out of touch with reality and subversive of the hopes for internal stability and a reasonable peace settlement.[61]

Somewhat the same kind of criticism could apply to Meinecke's positions on unrestricted submarine warfare. We have noted earlier that during the first phase of unrestricted use of the submarine in 1915 Meinecke endorsed it as a proper coun-

[59] *Erinnerungen, op.cit.,* p. 198, and *Nach der Revolution, op.cit.,* pp. 12, 132 and 137.

[60] Cf. Meinecke's discussion of this problem in "Probleme des Weltkriegs" *op.cit.,* p. 57. Also see his earlier remarks on annexations as a tactical problem in "Praeliminarien der Kriegsziele," *Das Groessere Deutschland,* July 31, 1915, pp. 1001-1014, and in "Friedensaufgaben," *Leipziger Tageblatt,* January 1, 1915.

[61] Cf. "Demobilmachung der Geister," *Frankfurter Zeitung,* September 23, 1917, "Um Elsass-Lothringen," *Frankfurter Zeitung,* October 21, 1917, and "Verstaendigungsfriede und Heeresleitung," in *Adele Gerhard als Festgabe,* Berlin, June 8, 1918.

ter to the provocations of British techniques of maritime warfare.[62] But he also gave his endorsement to the fateful reintroduction of unrestricted submarine warfare in January 1917, portraying it this time as a justifiable response to the refusal of the Allies to discuss Germany's peace offer of December 1916.[63]

After the war, however, Meinecke denounced the submarine policy as disastrous folly and directly contributory to the totality of Germany's defeat: "Our defeat first became inevitable . . . with the entry of America into the war. We ourselves invited American entry by our decision to pursue radical submarine warfare. . . . This was our Sicilian expedition . . . the leap into reckless adventurism."[64]

Reflecting on the causes which led Germany to repeat the errors of Alcibiades, Meinecke properly refused to fix the blame on individuals: "It would obviously be false and superficial to place the responsibility only on those individual personalities who pushed through the fateful policy. Behind the policy there must have been more general historical tendencies. A particular political mentality must have been at work, and this mentality must have been the fruit of an entire political and spiritual milieu. Thus it was in Athens at the time of Alcibiades and so it was with us. . . . Certain historical forces which had hitherto supported and protected Germany's existence overreached themselves and set the stage for tragedy."[65]

The nub of Meinecke's argument was that the military had wrenched the decision from the reluctant Bethmann-Hollweg in violation of Clausewitz's principle that war is subordinate to politics: "With us, however, war and the soldier overwhelmed

---

[62] Chapter VII, above.

[63] "Since our misguided opponents have rejected a compromise peace, we had to draw on new and sharper weapons [of unrestricted submarine warfare] so that we can at last force an early peace. We refrained from using these before they became necessary. . . ." (*Probleme des Weltkriegs, op.cit.*, pp. 135-136.)

[64] *Nach der Revolution, op.cit.*, pp. 11-12. The "Sicilian expedition" phrase was Bethmann-Hollweg's.

[65] *Ibid.*, p. 13.

politics and the statesman."[66] But it is difficult to judge how much responsibility for this ominous situation Meinecke assigned at this period to the German chancellor to whom he felt close both personally and politically.[67] In his memoirs, Meinecke made it clear that he considered Bethmann's failure successfully to oppose the demands of the military as prime evidence of his shortcomings as a statesman.[68] But in his immediate postwar evaluation Meinecke was ambiguous. At one point he observed that the civilian leadership with its doubts and reservations "had to be silent" in the face of the "warlike energy of our military commanders."[69] At another point he acknowledged that "A Bismarck-nature would not have permitted Ludendorff's rise to the status of a co-executive." But this was a criticism less of Bethmann than of the Kaiser who "would not tolerate a Bismarck-nature beside him."[70]

In any event, it seems apparent that both Meinecke and Bethmann were to a very considerable extent victims of that larger milieu of which Meinecke spoke. Meinecke implied that the military leaders should have known that a renewal of unrestricted submarine warfare must bring with it American belligerency, and that this knowledge ought to have prevented them from taking the fatal step.[71] Yet according to Meinecke's own political precepts it was clearly a function of civilian leadership to provide such insights and then to base decisions on them. The fact that Meinecke, as well as Bethmann, endorsed the submarine decision, even if reluctantly, is compelling evidence of the intellectual and moral as well as political authority of the German military.

In later denouncing the policy of unrestricted submarine war-

---

[66] *Ibid.*, p. 14.

[67] For Meinecke's description of his relations with Bethmann-Hollweg see *Erinnerungen, op.cit.*, pp. 214-217, 223-224, 225-227, 232-234, and 246-250. See also *Probleme des Weltkriegs, op.cit.*, pp. 55-56 for a contemporary characterization of Bethmann by Meinecke.

[68] *Erinnerungen, op.cit.*, pp. 233 and 249-250.

[69] *Nach der Revolution, op.cit.*, p. 14.

[70] *Ibid.*, p. 17.   [71] *Ibid.*, pp. 13-14.

fare, then, Meinecke was condemning mistakes in which he himself participated. Indeed, he implied as much in this comparison of Germany and Athens when he saw the whole ethos of a society at work in a particular decision which subsequently proved disastrous. As far as his own personal views are concerned, it may be said that Meinecke was no more opposed to unrestricted submarine warfare in principle than he was to annexation. His belated opposition to the policy stemmed mainly from his belief that the advantages had been outweighed by the disadvantages of bringing the United States into the war. He was certainly not among the submarine enthusiasts. As in the case of annexation proposals, he looked on the unrestricted use of submarines as a two-edged and risky weapon to be employed only after other and less problematic means proved insufficient.[72]

In the realm of the general war and peace aims of German foreign policy as in the more specific issues regarding means Meinecke preached the virtues of limited objectives and moderate ambitions without always being wholly consistent. In his memoirs Meinecke described the principles of the group to which he belonged as ruling out a goal of first rank world power for Germany.[73] But just before the outbreak of the war, he had endorsed the Kaiser's big navy policy as a necessary concomitant of the equally necessary expansion of German political and commercial interests overseas and had affirmed that Germany's role was to be one of the Great Powers of the world.[74] In "Kultur,

[72] Cf. "Unsere Lage," *Leipziger Tageblatt*, March 30, 1916. Also see *Erinnerungen, op.cit.*, p. 222, for Meinecke's support for the idea of joining the announcement of resumption of unrestricted submarine warfare with a statement declaring Germany's intention to restore Belgian sovereignty after the war. He hoped this would strike a note of peace and so lessen the harsh reaction which was sure to follow.

[73] *Erinnerungen, op.cit.*, p. 279.

[74] "Deutsche Jahrhundertfeier und Kaiserfeier" in *Preussen und Deutschland, op.cit.*, pp. 37-38. This is a speech given by Meinecke on June 14, 1913. (Hereafter cited as "Jahrhundertfeier.") In another early postwar publication, Meinecke recalled his support of the big fleet program and conceded that he therefore shared responsibility for Germany's debacle and that in general he had set Germany's power goals too high.

Machtpolitik und Militarismus" and elsewhere, moreover, Meinecke asserted that it must be an aim of Germany to destroy British control of the seas and to extend to the oceans that balance of power which England sought to promote on land.[75] While Meinecke never deviated from his position that it was not Germany's purpose to seek world dominion, the aim of breaking English maritime supremacy represented so revolutionary a change in the distribution of world power that it was illusory to suppose it could be achieved as the result of a "compromise peace."[76] Also Meinecke had little to say about the Treaty of Brest-Litovsk. Even the criticism to which he subjected it in the spring of 1918 was balanced by his argument that the Bolshevik threat justified the harsh terms and the far-reaching German military and political demands.[77]

Actually, Meinecke's stand on war aims, as he himself conceded, tended to fluctuate according to Germany's military prospects during the course of the war. Thus the several articles calling for a balance of power on the seas were all written in 1915 when Meinecke's "expectations rose" concerning a decisive German victory.[78] He accepted the draconic treaty which took Bolshevik Russia out of the war on the grounds that Germany needed absolute security in the East at a time when all her energies were required to defend her position in Western Europe—a position now mortally threatened by the growing contribution of American power to Allied strength. For Meinecke

(Cf. Meinecke's review of Philipp Hiltebrandt's *Das Europaeische Verhaengnis* in *HZ* 121, 1920, pp. 118-123.)

[75] "Machtpolitik," *op.cit.*, p. 643. Cf. also "Sozialdemokratie und Machtpolitik" in *Die Arbeiterschaft im neuen Deutschland, op.cit.*, p. 29, and "Bismarck und das neue Deutschland" in *Preussen und Deutschland, op.cit., passim.*

[76] Meinecke referred to the kind of peace he envisioned as a "Hubertusburger peace," the reference being to the Peace of Hubertusburg between Austria and Prussia in 1763.

[77] "Grundfragen deutscher Nationalpolitik" in *Die Neue Rundschau,* vol. 29, June 1918, pp. 731-737.

[78] *Nach der Revolution, op.cit.,* p. 132.

and those who thought as he did, German renunciation of radical alterations in the international political system was thus more of a conclusion derived from the war experience than a presupposition which controlled their attitudes from the start.

Another example of the difficulty Meinecke occasionally experienced in reconciling principle and practice is furnished by his admonitions that emotions should not be allowed to overwhelm reason in political activity. At the very moment that he warned against hate and revenge as the poorest of counsellors, Meinecke accused England of having embraced these counsellors. Meinecke's thesis here, as elsewhere, was that a current enmity should not be regarded as an eternal enmity, and that if England rejects the counsels of hate and revenge Germany should be willing to consider a restoration of good relations. But he immediately rejected much of the practical value of his prescription by opining that such a change of heart in England appeared to him as highly unlikely.[79]

But whatever deviations are evident, it is clear that they are indeed deviations from the principle of moderate aims and methods. Meinecke's condemnations of those who entertained grandiose ideas of Germany as premier world power were as frequent during as after the war. His growing insistence during the war that Germany must extricate itself from the dangerous situation in which both Russia and Britain were enemies was an earnest of his rejection of the idea of world hegemony: such extrication was "not possible without a curtailment of our commitments, without retrenchment and abstentions in one direction or the other."[80] Moreover, he convincingly demonstrated the courage of his convictions by publicly supporting the Reichstag resolution of July 1917, which called for a peace without annexations or indemnities, and by joining and becoming a mem-

[79] *Probleme des Weltkriegs, op.cit.,* pp. 18 and 19.

[80] *Ibid.,* pp. 53-54. Cf. also *Erinnerungen, op.cit.,* p. 208. Early in 1915 he still accepted the two-front enmity as an unfortunate but unavoidable necessity. Cf. "Bismarck und das neue Deutschland" in *Preussen und Deutschland, op.cit.,* p. 529.

ber of the executive committee of the *Volksbund fuer Freiheit und Vaterland*, an organization of trade unionists and intellectuals which formed the chief extra-parliamentary opposition to the chauvinist *Vaterlandspartei*.[81]

His great fear was that extravagant objectives would lead Germany down the fateful path taken by Louis XIV and Napoleon who "collapsed under an excess of continental and colonial power aims."[82] Indeed, this was the chief danger which Meinecke foresaw for both sides in the war. He warned the Allies that war aims which envisaged stripping Germany of her colonies, detaching German territory in Europe and reducing Germany to military impotence were Napoleonic and Roman in concept and belonged to "the arsenal of the universal monarchy."[83] As such they would fatally overtax Allied strength. Neither side, he insisted, could strive for total victory without bringing disaster upon itself.

Meinecke's pleas for moderation and mutual tolerance stemmed in large part from a rational calculus of adjusting ends to available means. None of the contesting powers had the strength to rule the world. But alongside the practical considerations of reconciling aims and capabilities was the value-judgment that was at the heart of *Weltbuergertum und Nationalstaat* and which Meinecke reaffirmed in "Kultur, Machtpolitik und Militarismus": "the significance and direction of modern European history leads not to universal monarchy but to a vigorous multiplicity of strong nations which will rebel against any attempt to establish universal rule."[84]

Here spoke once again that nationalism which embodied the ideal of moderation because it saw each nation as a spiritual, cultural, and moral personality whose right to an autonomous existence was inviolable. That one nation should dominate all the others was unthinkable in this context. This was the cos-

---

[81] *Erinnerungen, op.cit.*, p. 235.
[82] *Probleme des Weltkriegs, op.cit.*, p. 53.
[83] "Machtpolitik," *op.cit.*, p. 643.
[84] *Ibid.*

mopolitan root of Meinecke's nationalism: the recognition of the relativity of national values—the assumption that each nation was only an individual historical expression of humanity and its associations. It was a fundamental recognition that there were other and higher values than nation and state—namely, those at the core of a system which permitted and fostered a multiplicity and diversity of political and cultural forms. These were the values for which Meinecke's heroes of the Prussian Reform era stood, and these were the values that he invoked against the chauvinists and imperialists among his contemporaries. This was the conception of the world which functioned as the stabilizer in Meinecke's thinking about German objectives and which permitted him to go only so far with power and national self-interest considerations before trying to reconcile them with a sense of obligation to the transcendent community of nation-states.

In its finest expression this admixture of cosmopolitanism and nationalism is candid enough to admit that no nation can look upon itself as the chosen instrument of universal right. We have already seen how Meinecke emphasized this insight in *Weltbuergertum und Nationalstaat* only to falter in its application during the first heat of war.[85] In the ensuing years he returned to his earlier position. In 1917 he republished an earlier essay on Fichte in which he granted the contemporary political effectiveness of Fichte's ideas on the superiority of the Germans. But he observed that Fichte's glorification of things German could be regarded by the historian only with distaste: "Fichte's attempt to exalt the idea of the German nation into the sphere of the eternal and divine resulted in a defiling of the true nature of the nation."[86] And then came the admonition to modesty: "Nor can we any longer accept . . . [Fichte's] thesis [that the Germans are] *the* original people and the standard of the world because history has taught us the unique value and right to

[85] Chapters IV and VII, above.
[86] "Fichte als Nationaler Prophet" (first published in 1908) in *Preussen und Deutschland, op.cit.*, pp. 146-147.

existence of the other cultural nations and because we know only too well that all cultural values did not originate with us and that we have always had to learn from other nations too."[87]

This theme was taken up again in Meinecke's 1913 tribute to the Kaiser which was also republished in 1917: "Every people finds its own way to these sacred [national] values . . . we do not entertain the arrogant notion that the paths which other people take are false."[88]

But it was during the war itself that Meinecke formulated perhaps the profoundest of his conceptualizations of the relation between the individual nation or culture and the world society. We have seen how Meinecke's insistence on the rights of cultural and political entities to be treated as autonomous individuals exposed him to the danger of absolutizing these individualities despite his concern for the larger society in which they found their existence. Now, in a 1916 analysis of the European community, he fulfilled his self-imposed goal of transcending narrow national concerns by portraying this community as a mighty symbiosis of Latin and Germanic cultures in which each had an equally important and valuable role to play. He saw this symbiosis as a continuing one with the two great cultures needing one another as modification, counter-poise, and challenge. And he followed this with the crucial generalization that envisioned an organic unity between the individual culture and its larger cosmos: "Let us once and for all free ourselves from the narrow conception that individuality is something with immutable outlines and complete unto itself. It is intertwined with all other individualities and is itself always in the process of becoming."[89]

Meinecke developed this theme in another essay published in 1916. "The modern nations have become what they are not

[87] *Ibid.*, p. 143.

[88] "Jahrhundertfeier" in *Preussen und Deutschland, op.cit.*, p. 22.

[89] "Germanischer und Romanischer Geist im Wandel der deutschen Geschichtsauffassung" (first published in 1916) in *Preussen und Deutschland, op.cit.*, p. 121. Hereafter cited as "Germanischer und Romanischer Geist."

only by virtue of their own resources; the characters of the individual nations are not something given and unchanging through the centuries. Rather, nations have grown within the framework of more comprehensive cultural communities, and an immeasurably large part of their spiritual treasure derives from these larger communities. . . . As with individuals, the full personality of a nation emerges not at the beginning but at the height of its development. Even then it does not for a moment remain unchanging but presses forward with further innovations. A rigid, dull-minded and dogmatic national feeling naturally cannot free itself from the idea that the spirits of nations are unchanging gods or idols which demand narrow cultism and absolute subordination. Our heart, however, beats faster and with a feeling of freedom when we understand that nations like individuals belong to the process of eternal becoming. . . . Every generation must create the nation anew and add new values to inherited values. Germany is more a challenge than a given quantity."[90]

With these words Meinecke provided the theoretical foundation for a nationalism and a state loyalty which was the direct opposite of xenophobia, chauvinism, and reaction. These formulations defined the greatness of a nation in terms of its tolerance, its openness toward other nations, and its capacity to absorb new experience.

This was the kind of national consciousness which Meinecke commended to his fellow Germans. It was also the kind, he had to concede after the war, which went into eclipse before the onslaught of an uncritical and immoderate nationalism. It was ironic that all the charges he had leveled at Germany's foes Meinecke now had to address, as a final judgment, to Germany itself. During the war it had been his hope and belief first that the ultranationalists were in the minority and then, with their growing power undeniable, that they would eventually retreat

---

[90] "Grundzuege underer nationalen Entwicklung bis zur Reichsgruen-dung Bismarcks" (1916) in *Preussisch-deutsche Gestalten und Probleme, op.cit.,* pp. 7-8.

before the better sense of the German people. Thus it was a bitter task which Meinecke had to perform when he felt compelled to acknowledge that German nationalism was more dangerous than other nationalisms, that the Germans were in a situation which "induced us to rush into world politics with burning eagerness but without the statesman's far-sightedness and moderation. . . . After the outbreak of the war . . . [Pan-German] influence over the educated classes increased dangerously from year to year. Wide circles of the upper bourgeoisie lost all sense of political proportion" and so made possible the triumph of the annexationists and submarine warfare enthusiasts.[91]

The conception animating Meinecke's 1916 essays on the Germanic and Latin cultures and the background of German unification represented a refinement and in a sense a culmination of his earlier ideas on nationalism and cosmopolitanism. But elsewhere he was forced to occupy some positions in glaring contradiction to previous concepts of nationality and nationhood. The burden of Meinecke's argument in *Weltbuergertum und Nationalstaat* had been that the nation-state forms the ideal political community. Thus Germany's achievement of national unification was adjudged to be both necessary and desirable. By implication, certainly, this achievement was recommended to other nationalities as well. In his subsequent essay on Fichte, Meinecke expressed his conviction of the nation-state's necessity perhaps even more strongly than in *Weltbuergertum*: "National life without a nation-state is for us like a sword without a sheath. Only by means of the power politics of the state and all that this *implies can the great and real interests of the nation . . .* be protected in competition with other nations. And as far as the intellectual and cultural interests of the nation are concerned, they certainly need more freedom from the state, but they cannot do without its protection and encouragement."[92]

It comes, then, as something of a surprise to find Meinecke

[91] *Nach der Revolution, op.cit.,* p. 25.
[92] "Fichte als Nationaler Prophet" in *Preussen und Deutschland, op.cit.,* p. 140.

revising the relationship of state and nation at the outset of the First World War and advancing the proposition that *"the community of the state has and must have primacy over the community of the nation. . . . The sense of nationality . . . must not demand an absolute and tangible congruence of the state and nation but must be content with the essential values of national culture."*[93]

It is true, of course, that Meinecke had long before emphasized the arguments of Hegel and Ranke that the nation could not ride roughshod over existing political arrangements and that the state's interests and the nation's interests must be reconciled if a successful nation-state was to be realized.[94] It is also true that Meinecke's argument could be directed against the ultra-nationalism and expansionist aims of the Pan-Germans and German chauvinists in general. But the outstanding fact is that his discussion was devoted mainly to the problem of the minority groups in Germany and Austria-Hungary. Meinecke was obviously concerned that the doctrine of the nation-state as the ideal political community would be turned against the Central Powers (as, of course, it was) and could inflict grievous damage upon their war effort.

Consequently Meinecke urged Poles, Czechs, Rumanians, and other minority groups to accept the idea that "The national culture of a great people can very well tolerate and even rejoice in the existence of a diaspora as long as foreign states do not forcibly suppress the nationality of the diaspora."[95] To justify his position he pointed to German-Swiss, German-Austrians, and Baltic Germans as examples of the diaspora which Germany tolerated and, in his view, benefited from. Also, his argument posited that minority rights should be protected and that the states with minorities had a solemn obligation to permit and indeed encourage cultural autonomy. But he made it clear that

[93] "Staatsgedanke und Nationalismus" in *Erhebung 1914, op.cit.,* p. 80. (Meinecke's italics.)
[94] Chapter II, above.
[95] *Erhebung 1914, op.cit.,* p. 79.

the state's political and territorial integrity could not be sacrificed to this obligation.[96]

This last qualification revealed better than anything else the contradictory position in which Meinecke now found himself. It was precisely because the political concerns of existing states had come into conflict with the national interest that Meinecke had stressed the political unification of Germany as an historical necessity. He could, of course, claim some consistency in warning against Slav and Italian irredentisms as long as he gave his blessing to a state of affairs in which large blocs of Germans lived outside the German homeland. But here his arguments could only apply to already established states with the great bulk of their nationals already incorporated. He would never have tolerated for Germany his own argument directed to Eastern Europeans that irredentism even in respect to "core elements of a national community has the right to demand a hearing . . . only if all other state and national interests are considered simultaneously."[97] This could mean for some nationalities (the Czechs and Poles, for example) that they had no "right" to a national political existence at all if this existence conflicted with the vital interests of existing multi-national states.

It is understandable if in 1914 Meinecke was reluctant to be too explicit in drawing conclusions from the principle that the state has primacy over the nation. His hope was that the Central Powers could count on the cooperation of their minority groups. But by 1916 the general stresses and strains which the war had engendered were only too apparent in the specific realm of German-Slav relationships. Hence in "Probleme des Weltkriegs" Meinecke returned once more to the problem of nation and state, and this time in more unmistakable language.

Much of the essay is an appraisal and criticism of Rudolf Kjéllén's writings on the war and the foreign policies of the powers. Meinecke readily agreed with Kjéllén's dictum that "Geopolitical necessities . . . always outweigh ethnological necessi-

[96] *Ibid.*, pp. 79-80, 83.
[97] *Ibid.*, p. 79.

ties."[98] In harmony with this approach, Meinecke declared flatly that nations have no *a priori* right to political unity or sovereignty but must earn the right to claim recognition from the existing society of nations by fulfilling a number of specific conditions. The only *a priori* right which Meinecke conceded to the nations was the right analogous to "the right of the individual as against the state: . . . the right to free . . . development of its spiritual force and individuality." And then followed the proposition that explicitly contradicted at least the spirit of much of Meinecke's earlier writings. "The nation which can freely develop its language and literature can achieve a spiritual unity of itself; political unity is not an unconditional requirement."[99] Here Meinecke echoed the words of the anti-national conservatives whose efforts to drain the nationality concept of its political potency by stressing simply its cultural aspects he so vigorously attacked in his study of Germany's path toward unity.[100] Meinecke conceded that modern national groups were not likely to be content simply with a "cultural nation" and that a drive toward an independent nation-state was an immanent part of the national idea. But he came perilously close to cant when he attempted to blunt this point by observing that there are many desires in this world which cannot be fulfilled and that "mature character . . . can be healthy and creative even in an [attitude of] resignation."[101]

From the point of view of realistic political theory, however, "Probleme des Weltkriegs" represents a significant clarification of Meinecke's thinking about the state and the nation. He noted that merely the listing of all the many irredentas, which Kjéllén undertook, sufficed to parody the irredentist idea. "It is obvious,"

[98] "Probleme des Weltkriegs," *op.cit.*, p. 43. (Meinecke's paraphrase.)
[99] *Ibid.*, pp. 46-47.
[100] Chapter II, above.
[101] *Ibid.*, p. 48. There is a particularly ironic contrast between these words and Meinecke's passionate insistence on the right of national self-determination when arguing for German retention of the Saar. Cf. "Frankreichs Ansprueche auf das Saargebiet," *Deutsche Allgemeine Zeitung*, January 19, 1919.

he wrote, "that one cannot operate here with universally valid axioms, that it would mean unloosing a war of all against all were one to grant the right . . . to every nationality still politically dependent to create its own nation-state."[102]

With these words Meinecke took a clear stand against doctrinaire ideas of national self-determination. At the same time he refused to entertain the idea of freezing the status quo. There were no pat solutions to the question of which nations shall form nation-states and which shall not. The answer would vary from case to case as a compromise between "biological and historical and cultural considerations."[103]

This position gave to Meinecke's subsequent theorizing about the state a flexibility not previously apparent. The explicit refusal to identify the nation with the state permitted him to range beyond the time-bound idea of nationality. At the same time it stood as a rebuke to the Pan-German imperialism of the Hohenzollern Reich and to the brutal glorification of race and nation in the Nazi era. It is true that these insights were the result of very practical considerations and were gained in the process of some rather ungraceful reversals or modifications of previous propositions. But it is also true that they contributed to a widening of Meinecke's horizons and represented an authentic forward step along the path which Meinecke described himself as following from "the nation-state back to cosmopolitanism."

If practical considerations forced Meinecke to revise certain of his approaches to the nation-state, equally practical and far more compelling considerations demanded that he reevaluate his analyses of the foreign policies of the nation-states and of the international system in which they operated. We have already seen that he regarded the war as hypertrophied and a compromise peace as the only alternative to disaster for the contestants. And we have also seen him denounce the extremists who ignored the havoc being wreaked by the gigantic struggle and label them responsible for the disasters which did in fact over-

[102] "Probleme des Weltkriegs," op.cit., pp. 44-45.
[103] Ibid., p. 45.

take Germany. But beyond the issues of practical policy alternatives concerning the war rose the much more portentous question of the viability of the international system which permitted such a catastrophic conflict to take place. Meinecke felt the need to address himself to this problem as well.

Meinecke's earlier conceptualization of international relations had posited a kind of *laissez faire* liberalism in which a basic harmony could be expected if states were left to their own devices. He accepted as his own Hegel's observation that there is no magistrate above sovereign states. Moreover, he built onto this observation the proposition that any attempt to erect such a magistracy could lead only to tyranny. The number and diversity of nations and states were so great that universally binding rules of conduct for them all could be realized only by fiat of a conqueror.

Even were such uniformity possible of achievement under conditions of freedom, Meinecke would have been antagonistic toward it. He did not look upon diversity as an unfortunate hindrance to the attainment of the good. Rather he saw diversity itself as a positive contribution to the realization of the good and the beautiful. And he was clearly committed to the belief that the conflict which diversity occasionally—and inevitably—engendered was also not without benefit. In short, he was not far removed from those who have argued that war can be a stimulus to civilization, morally as well as technologically. As he expressed it in postwar retrospect, he had "regarded war as a result of the natural power egotism of states, but not simply as a process of natural necessity. It was also an indispensable though irrational means to slough off the outdated and outworn and to generate great new historical forces and individualities."[104] Meinecke was certainly removed from all who made

[104] *Nach der Revolution, op.cit.*, p. 73. An example of some rather purple patriotic oratory along this line—and such examples are relatively rare—is the following: "Even where concern for our own existence forces us to take up arms, we honor in our opponents the spirit of humanity which can achieve its full radiance only in the development

the empirical observation into a theoretical norm and who saw in war the key to political and cultural greatness. But he accepted the egotism of the state as a necessary component of its dynamic and war as a necessary product of conflicting state egos.

All these assumptions were brought into question when Meinecke surveyed the full extent of the wreckage that the war had left behind in Germany and all of Europe. Since he had declared the war to be hypertrophied as early as 1916, it is possible to agree with him that it was not simply the pangs of defeat that caused him to realign his political thinking.[105] But the distance and suddenness of Germany's fall from power to powerlessness had a stunning impact which is apparent in all of Meinecke's immediate postwar writings.

"Before our eyes," Meinecke wrote, "war itself has become something other [than it was]. Formerly it was a blood-letting, now it has become a blood-bath of the nations."[106] The belligerents could not afford the terrible sacrifices of life and treasure which they nonetheless delivered up. Their very power seduced them to struggle on to the point of exhaustion, for they no longer had to fight on stored energy but were now capable of transmuting the sum of their functions into combat strength. In a penetrating characterization of "total war" Meinecke saw modern culture being threatened by its own successes as the parent of modern warfare. "Now the participants in the struggle . . . are not merely the fleets and armies of the nations but whole peoples with their entire animate and inanimate inventory, with their agriculture, their commerce, their technology, their science and their cultural achievements. . . ."[107] The fate of the defeated

---

of the whole spectrum of its diverse colorations. And these colors, in turn, these irreplaceable individual values of national cultures—how can they be realized other than by the development of all the powers of will and spirit in the nation and by a determined defense of all their achievements—if necessary in hot and bloody struggle?" ("Jahrhundertfeier" in *Preussen und Deutschland, op.cit.,* pp. 22-23.)

[105] *Nach der Revolution, op.cit.,* pp. 73-74.

[106] *Ibid.,* p. 74.   [107] *Ibid.,* p. 75.

was collapse, revolution, and, so Meinecke then thought, permanent impotence in international relations.

Such a development was clearly at odds with Meinecke's previous picture of the international system as encompassing a number of vigorous and autonomous nation-states. From the perspective of 1919 he recalled his earlier thesis that the tendency of modern world history was not toward universal monarchy but favored a continuing multiplicity of nation-states. This thesis had seemed to him to represent "the summation of modern historical research since Ranke."[108] With the superimposition of the World War and the peace settlement of Versailles, the tendency began to look different. The course history was taking seemed to be undermining and killing off nation-states. Instead of a world shaped by the decisions of a multiplicity of vigorous political entities Meinecke foresaw a system in which the victorious Allies monopolized effective power while the other nations were condemned to become mere objects of world politics.

This division of the world into the all-powerful victors and the powerless vanquished was the result not simply of the physical destructiveness of war in a highly complex civilization. Meinecke also charged it to a deliberate policy of the victors. For the first time, he contended, the vanquished nation was not brought back into the European "family" after a war but was labeled a pariah. With this development the idea of the European family of nations was itself destroyed, and there remained only the power of the Entente. Lacking counterpoises, this power was absolute and so presented the prospect of a world hegemony analogous to that of Rome.[109]

[108] *Ibid.*, p. 72.

[109] *Ibid.*, pp. 75-78. Meinecke here intermingled political insights and blind spots in a telling manner. He identified England and America as the core of Entente strength and dismissed France, as well as Italy, as a second-class power. But while he was correct in asserting that England and America had it in their power to rule the world, he was wrong in his assumption that their collaboration in such an enterprise was all but a foregone conclusion. Particularly in regard to America, Meinecke

But not only was the hitherto prevailing structure of world power shattered. Even more important for Meinecke was the fact that he had construed a causal link between freedom and cultural creativity and the system of sovereign nation-states: "We viewed each nation's liberty to live its own life as the precondition and guarantee of the individual personality's right to freedom and uniqueness and hence of continuing vigor in the development of all . . . cultural values."[110] Here again was the fundamental equation of national and individual liberty, the conception of the nation as the ideal political and cultural unit, which formed the basis of Meinecke's prewar political thinking.

If Meinecke posited the end of the nation-state system, then its most precious products were also doomed unless there was some other set of conditions in which they could continue to flourish. In the period immediately following the war's end, Meinecke could do little but speculate, and his speculations carried little conviction. He suggested the League of Nations could serve as a counterweight against the feared Anglo-American hegemony—"the idea of the League of Nations is a moral protest against world dominion; it will therefore become one of the most important instruments to keep alive the distaste of the [world's] peoples for world rule, to save them from a weary submission to the misdirections of world history and thus to save what can be saved of the values vital to [the individual] nations."[111]

From this thought Meinecke proceeded to the proposition which constituted his most drastic reversal of position: "In the perspective of world history the era of unadulterated and naked

---

failed to see that a nation might exhibit an indifference to international power, at least for a long enough period so that its indifference would have very profound effects on world history. He also obviously underestimated the regenerative powers of modern industrial society. As a result of all this, his forecast of a *"pax anglo-saxonica"* with Russia and Germany remaining beyond the pale of power and Japan held in check by England and America was badly out of touch with reality.

[110] *Ibid.*, p. 73.
[111] *Ibid.*, p. 101.

autonomy of states and nations is clearly at an end. . . . It is true that before the war I regarded the idea of a League of Nations simply as a cosmopolitan idea. And it is also true that even an authentic League of Nations places restrictions on the traditional autonomy of nations. But after the experiences of this war it is a most sacred duty at least to make an earnest effort to find another basis for the relations of peoples with one another. . . . The synthesis of cosmopolitanism and nationality, once possible only in the minds and lives of the greatest and freest spirits, now requires external forms and guarantees as well."[112]

This was a far cry from Meinecke's earlier thesis that only when the cosmopolitan idea remained an "intangible aspiration" could freedom be served and tyranny avoided.[113] In fact, however, Meinecke did not move so far from his original position. He was skeptical enough concerning the prospects of the League to see it "in the foreseeable future only as an ideal, . . . an admonition to the consciences of ruling nations whose practical effect can only be certain ameliorations and modifications of the pressures to which we are subjected."[114] Moreover, the only realistic prospect for the salvation of Germany's spiritual freedom and vitality was if "future political liberation" remained the "passionately-desired goal."[115] Finally, the League was certainly not the end of power politics, since it was envisioned as an instrument of resistance against Anglo-Saxon domination. An effective League demanded restrictions on national sovereignties, Meinecke argued, and warned against the error of the Greek city-states whose insistence on their own independence engendered the disunity that facilitated the rule of Rome. What Meinecke was doing here was in effect to lay the groundwork for a new power struggle in the largest dimensions between two worldwide coalitions.[116]

[112] *Ibid.*, pp. 101-102.   [113] Chapter IV, above.
[114] "Weltgeschichtliche Parallelen" in *Nach der Revolution, op.cit.*, p. 102.
[115] *Ibid.*, p. 99.   [116] *Ibid.*, pp. 97-98, 101-102.

It is evident that Meinecke's thinking was still very much in flux and that he was still searching for a new equilibrium between freedom and order among both nations and individuals. The nagging realization that modern war was too destructive to be tolerated drove him to embrace a number of contradictory positions. It forced him to depend for a time more on exhortation than analysis.[117] But it also spurred him to constantly renewed efforts to probe the nature of politics and political conflict.

Above all, the catastrophe wrought by the struggle of 1914-1918 profoundly altered the course of Meinecke's subsequent research. He had resolved to undertake a far-ranging study of political conduct at least as early as 1914.[118] However, as he noted in his memoirs and also in his introduction to *Die Idee der Staatsraeson*, he had originally planned to focus on the relationship of political and historical understanding in the belief that an intimate connection existed between the rise of modern empirical statecraft and modern historical research. "I saw the unifying element," he wrote, "in the growing sensitivity to the highly individual and concrete interests of states which had its source in Machiavelli. And while still working on *Weltbuergertum und Nationalstaat*, the sense for individuality in life and history in general seemed to me to be the real central root of modern historical consciousness."[119]

Only after the war did Meinecke come to the conclusion that the relationship between political and historical understanding was less significant than he had supposed. This conclusion provided an additional impetus to Meinecke's desire to turn his attention directly to politics. Moreover, in his treatment of politics he was no longer content to deal simply with the "interests

[117] Thus his plea that "World history must not end with the suicide of humanity or the enslavement of one nation by another. . . . Faith in the meaning and reason of history must defy this darkest of fears." (*Nach der Revolution, op.cit.*, p. 67.)

[118] Cf. *Erinnerungen, op.cit.*, pp. 190-191. Meinecke here describes how he set forth his research plans in his initiation speech in the Prussian Academy to which he was elected in 1914.

[119] *Ibid.*, pp. 191-192.

of states" in the sense of portraying a series of more or less skillful exercises in the realm of power politics. This was far too utilitarian an approach to the problems of foreign policy which had assumed such awesome proportions in the perspective of the First World War.

Meinecke recorded his change in outlook in characteristic fashion at the close of his introduction to *Staatsraeson*: ". . . let us also acknowledge the personal motives which led to the selection of the problems here to be studied. It will not escape the reader of both books that they have grown out of the problems treated in *Weltbuergertum und Nationalstaat*. During the first years of the World War with their stirring and solemn but still hopeful atmosphere I conceived the plan of tracing the relationship between statecraft and historical understanding and of demonstrating that the doctrine of the interests of states was a forerunner of modern historicism. But with the shattering experience of [Germany's] collapse the real core problem of *raison d'état* in all its terrible significance came more and more to the fore. The historical mood had changed."[120] Meinecke supplemented this acknowledgment in his memoirs: "[Before the war] we had greater confidence and faith than we have today in the beneficent meaning and content of power politics and in the warlike clashes of nations. . . . It was in this [earlier] frame of mind that I wrote *Weltbuergertum und Nationalstaat* and portrayed the elimination of universal and cosmopolitan motives from the theory and practice of statecraft as a great achievement of the middle nineteenth century. I still hold this opinion, for it made possible the realization of Bismarck's Reich. But the negative aspects of this development received too little attention. Power politics and *Realpolitik*, once freed of universal principles—and universal principles are basically ethical principles—could only too easily degenerate into a . . . politics of violence. . . . In my disappointments I have not gone to the other extreme to join Burckhardt in condemning power in itself

[120] *Staatsraeson, op.cit.,* p. 27.

· 202 ·

as evil. It is only a temptation to evil. But I began to perceive the demonic nature of power in a far different and more penetrating manner than in the prewar period. Thus my plans for a history of statecraft changed into the history of the idea of *raison d'état*."[121]

The doctrine of the interests of states was thus too utilitarian to absorb Meinecke's attention in the postwar years. But it was also too pragmatic since it sought to analyze political conduct from the point of view of a particular state; its adherents left off their investigations at that point where there was nothing further to be gained for the state in question. The concept of *raison d'état*, however, sought to transcend this kind of pragmatism and to comprehend the whole state in terms of its internal composition and its external environment. To understand *raison d'état* meant to understand not simply the short-range alternatives but also the long-range ambiguities of political action. Meinecke now began to penetrate beyond the techniques of state survival to questions which touched on the state's capacity and right to survive.

It may also be noted that with this concentration of interests, Meinecke was moving from the more concrete to the more abstract. Hitherto concerned primarily with the nation and more specifically with the German nation,[122] Meinecke now tapped the whole of European history since the Renaissance in a quest to discover the nature of politics. Also, the central issue of politics and ethics was no longer so intimately connected with the problem of nationalism though it still shared the stage to a certain extent with problems of historiography.[123]

Finally, it should be remarked that despite all these developments and changes of attitude, it would be incorrect to assume that Meinecke's thinking had now become precisely the opposite of what it was before the war. There is no question but that it

[121] *Erinnerungen, op.cit.*, pp. 193-194.

[122] Prior to *Staatsraeson*, all Meinecke's major published works dealt with German history and particularly nineteenth-century German history.

[123] Cf. *Staatsraeson, op.cit.*, p. 24.

was more somber, that it had abandoned optimism, and that it was far more realistic as a result of the experiences of 1914-1918. Walther Hofer tellings characterized these changes when he noted that "In the place of syntheses and harmonies [in *Welt-buergertum und Nationalstad*] . . . now appear dissonances and antinomies. Discrepancy, dilemma, dialectic, polarity, demonic —now only such terms can capture the true essence of historical life."[124]

Yet as has been made evident, Meinecke was dealing with history in terms of polarities and dilemmas in his very earliest historical works. We need recall only his early remarks on the conflict between the ego of the state and the rights of the individual and the polarity of nationalism and cosmopolitanism to support the contention that there is a basic continuity in his thought structure and that this continuity resided in his essentially dualistic philosophy of history and picture of the world. It is of course true, and it has been our argument and Meinecke's explicit admission, that while he recognized the dilemmas and conflicts to which such a world gives rise, he often failed to understand their profundity until the shock of the World War and Germany's defeat. But Carlo Antoni's criticism of Meinecke goes much too far when he asserts that as a result of the war "Instead of the 'joyful belief in the unity of nature and spirit' Meinecke offers an inconsolable picture of eternal and incurable conflict between the two principles. History can in no way be wholly justified but is an enduring mixture of moral life and the instinctive [use of] force. The evil, betrayal and butchery in history remain evil, and no higher synthesis can change their nature. The world does not perfect itself. History is hopeless."[125]

[124] Walther Hofer, "Friedrich Meinecke: Eine Skizze," in *Europa Archiv*, vol. v, March 20, 1950, p. 2900.

[125] Carlo Antoni, *Vom Historismus zur Soziologie*, Stuttgart, 1951, p. 145. It is worth noting that in the writing of *Das Zeitalter der deutschen Erhebung* in 1905 Meinecke was using terminology and ideas which Antoni apparently regarded as belonging only to the postwar period. Cf. for example Meinecke's evaluation of Fichte and some of his contemporaries: "They saw and appraised the individual more in terms of

If Antoni can properly point to an overdose of optimism in Meinecke's prewar attitudes, he paints far too simplistic a portrait by neglecting to see that Meinecke was clearly aware of the conflict between "nature and spirit" long before the war. And the question of achieving "perfection" in this world Meinecke had certainly left moot despite the "gradual ascent" which he once professed to see in the process of world politics.[126]

Above all, Meinecke did not henceforth regard history as "hopeless" simply because he now explicitly rejected the idea that mankind would achieve perfection therein. On the contrary, the vigor of his writings and political decisions after the war suggested a hopefulness which did not depend upon a perfectionist philosophy.[127] Moreover, the creativeness of his scholarship and the profundity of his insights after a staggering succession of bitter disappointments manifested an intellectual preparation for the altered conditions of the postwar world which few of his peers could match.

---

his spiritual essence than in the light of his physical and earth-formed nature in which and from which he also lived. They saw the world in the marvelous unity of nature and spirit, but their thoughts gravitated more to the spiritual pole of this unity than to the natural. . . . [When] Fichte said 'The spirit lives, not the flesh,' he offered us a central truth but not reality." (*Erhebung, op.cit.*, p. 52.) See also *Erhebung 1914*, p. 94: "It is again necessary . . . to find a new synthesis between state and culture, between spirit and power. There will always be an antinomy remaining, one that can never be wholly overcome. . . . All historical life is always only an oscillation between thesis and antithesis."

[126] Chapter VII, above.

[127] Antoni, as a student of Croce and Hegel, is evidently analyzing Meinecke in terms of the monism and perfectionism for which Meinecke sharply criticized Hegel. Antoni also reflects some of the criticism which Croce directed at Meinecke in *History as the Story of Liberty*, London, 1941.

CHAPTER IX

THE UBIQUITY OF POWER

WHATEVER the inconsistencies and contradictions into which Meinecke was driven by the shock of war and defeat, it is clear that he had come to one fundamental and very simple conclusion. Power politics desperately needed some kind of restraint. When crisis came, Meinecke's ideal of the nation failed to operate as a moderating element in the clash of state egos. On the contrary, it had degenerated into an ultra-nationalism which undermined what rationality there was in the conduct of the struggle.

The autonomous nation-state which Meinecke had pictured as the most reliable defender of individual liberty and cultural creativity revealed all too clearly that it could be a dangerous enemy of these values, particularly when engaged in a contest for survival. Meinecke now faced the timeless conundrum of who is to guard the guardian. Hence his quest was no longer one of building a case for the greatest possible freedom for the nation-state in the most incorporeal of international societies. Rather it went in the opposite direction, seeking some means of control over state sovereignty to prevent it from wholly destroying the values which Meinecke wanted to protect. This is the most tangible of all the evidence that he was indeed "following the path back to cosmopolitanism."

But Meinecke was making his way slowly and carefully. He was far removed from those of his contemporaries who jumped on the League of Nations bandwagon once Germany's defeat became apparent.[1] His skeptical attitude toward the League has

---

[1] Cf. *Ernst Troeltsch, Spektator-Briefe*, Tuebingen, 1924, p. 1: "After our difficult situation could no longer be concealed, all too many of those who had enthused over a victorious peace imposed by [German] power now exhibited the same kind of childishness in pinning their hopes

already been indicated in the previous chapter, and we shall note it again presently. More important, he also avoided the temptation to engage in the great and not very edifying debate concerning the war-guilt issue—a temptation to which so many German historians succumbed. Instead he was moved to undertake a study of politics in which the crushing problems of his own time were viewed, in a phrase he often favored, *sub specie aeterni.*

The disaster of 1914-1918 had demonstrated that state power needed controls. An imbalance had arisen between political assertion and ethical restraint. If controls were to be established and a balance restored, it was necessary to achieve a better understanding of the nature of the phenomenon which was to be controlled and balanced. This was the central purpose of *Die Idee der Staatsraeson* after its metamorphosis from Meinecke's original project of relating the economy of modern statecraft to the growth of historical understanding.

Addressing himself, then, directly to the problem of power, Meinecke first made explicit a basic and governing assumption: any scheme of social organization was doomed to failure which thought to avoid the evil effects of power by seeking its elimination. The whole of his historical work had testified to the ubiquity and persistence of power considerations in every field of human activity. They were present in the most exalted creations and transactions of the human spirit. Perhaps Meinecke never expressed this insight more tellingly than in his memoirs when he recalled how his first visit to Florence had spurred his interest in Machiavelli; he gazed on Machiavelli's monument in Santa Croce and was "moved to wonder by the difficult problematic of power politics in the midst of a world of beauty."[2]

Thus Meinecke was immune from the first to utopian projects

to Wilson and the League of Nations for whom they had previously been at such pains to show their contempt."

[2] *Erinnerungen, op.cit.*, p. 43. The visit took place in 1905. Meinecke noted that the experience in Santa Croce was one of the first in a series that was to culminate in the writing of *Staatsraeson.*

whose aims to purge the state of power-striving and egotism he could regard only as self-deception. Too many examples were at hand to demonstrate the unreality of such objectives. The French Revolution began by proclaiming the subordination of the egotistic state to the individual who had hitherto been its victim and ended by transforming the state into almost pure violence. Moreover, the state was animated, after all, by the egos of individual human beings, and since it was their egotisms in whatever form which made for conflict, one could not overlook the fact that even the derogation of the state in favor of the individual could have egotistic connotations. Thus Meinecke had long before cited Clausewitz's observation that "It always seemed to me . . . like egotism when a man is so proud of his worth as a man that he can regard his worth as a citizen with indifference."[3]

More recently, the World War and the Treaty of Versailles had provided a superabundance of evidence that high-minded goals of world betterment could go hand-in-hand with shrewd calculations of self-interest. And as Meinecke reflected on his own hopes for German victory, he certainly experienced within himself the poignant revelation that objectives which he had identified as in the interest of the well-being and happiness of all mankind, on closer examination turned out to be intimately joined to subjective and egotistic preferences. Here another recollection which Meinecke recorded without comment is indicative: "But when I once . . . tried to explain the deranged mentality of the German people in terms of their mistreatment under the Versailles Treaty, my Danish friend Aage Friis countered with the question 'Had Germany won, would it have dictated a more moderate peace?' "[4] On the other hand, if noble purposes are un-

---

[3] *Erhebung, op.cit.,* p. 120.

[4] *Erinnerungen, op.cit.,* p. 194. Meinecke's passionate postwar *mea culpa* in regard to his near-orthodoxy in evaluations of Bismarck is also illustrative: "We historians were among the foremost participants in this canonization of the development of the nation. We never tired of demonstrating that all earlier attempts to solve the national problem were faulty, untenable and utopian nor of measuring them against Bis-

accompanied by power calculations, they are likely never to be fulfilled. This was the basis of the charges which Meinecke more than once laid at the door of the Prussian Reformers. They too often underestimated the role of power and egotism in men's actions and thus formulated programs whose implementation was too dependent on human selflessness. "The obstacles [to the goals of the Reformers] . . . resided in the nature of the ideals with which they now sought to conquer reality as well as in the nature of reality itself. . . . The man of moral self-determination which they called for was and is the rarest flower of cultural life. And the concrete state must often obey commandments of a cruder kind; its laws must reckon with the average man. The Reformers did not always recognize that, and one must not entertain illusions about the immediate effectiveness of all their policies."[5] As we have seen earlier, Meinecke sought to show that this misreading of reality by the Reformers led them astray in both domestic and international politics.[6]

Thus it was Meinecke's argument that policies formulated in ignorance or defiance of power considerations were bound to be either ineffectual or hypocritical. From what has gone before, it is evident that he believed that hypocrisy was more often the likely result. If Meinecke was aroused by what he labeled as British cant during the war, he was even more incensed by Wilson's ideological crusade after America had become a belligerent. Even while he himself bitterly criticized the war policies of the German government, he heaped scorn on Wilson's deemphasis on American and Allied power objectives and his endeavor to make the war one of "constitutional forms." Meinecke charged that the Western Allies were aping the Holy Alliance and that Wilson was "playing the role of Metternich if

---

marck's achievement as a fool-proof criterion. Oh, we felt ourselves all too secure in the world which he created and all too easily became haughty and overbearing toward those who had once conceived of a different kind of German unity." (*Nach der Revolution, op.cit.,* p. 54.)

[5] "Jahrhundertfeier" in *Preussen und Deutschland, op.cit.,* p. 29.

[6] Chapters II and III, above.

he insisted on functioning as president of the world and forcing
. . . a constitution on us. The sin of both against freedom . . .
is the same. . . . It is perfectly clear: they desire to democratize
us in order to disorganize us."[7]

So also did Meinecke evaluate the League of Nations. In the
previous chapter it was noted that he urged his fellow Germans
to support an "authentic" League. But it was obvious that his
"authentic" League would be one in which the distribution of
power would be very different from that which the Treaty of
Versailles established. His forebodings during the Armistice
negotiations that the League would be only an expression of
American world hegemony[8] were of course nullified by the
American refusal even to become a member of the League. But
during the early postwar period these forebodings became convictions that the League, whether American-, British- or French-
dominated, was destined to be an instrument to serve the interests of the victor powers rather than the welfare of the world
society. A different and "authentic" League would "presuppose
the destruction or dissolution of Anglo-Saxon world rule. Peoples in possession of such an enormous power as the Anglo-Sax-
ons now enjoy will under no circumstances jettison it in the
name of sentiment and good will. The League of Nations which
they now offer us with a haughty gesture is only an ill-made
disguise for their own world control."[9]

From all these considerations Meinecke drew the conclusion
that the remedy for the abuse of power is not to ignore or
attempt to suppress the power calculus but rather to expose

---

[7] *Die deutsche Freiheit, op.cit.,* pp. 25-31. Meinecke's sentiments were
representative of the intellectuals critical of the imperial regime. Adolf
von Harnack's introduction to this book which was primarily a response
by a group of these intellectuals to Wilson's war message of April 2,
1917, was even more blunt: "I do not like to use strong words, but there
is nothing else for me to do but say the truth: this is the most shame-
less, arrogant and hypocritical pronouncement that a head of a great
state has made to another people since the days of Napoleon" (p. 3).

[8] *Erinnerungen, op.cit.,* p. 269.

[9] *Nach der Revolution, op.cit.,* p. 100.

it as fully as possible to the light of day. This was, of course, not simply a conclusion based on newly accumulated evidence. It was also a reaffirmation of his earlier thesis that the Germans had needed to understand the nature of power before they could achieve statehood and that subsequently and consequently it had become a particular virtue of the Germans to dare to call power politics by its real name and not by a morally more gratifying but misleading appellation. Through all the process of abandonment or modification of earlier propositions, Meinecke could not and did not relinquish the fundamental thesis that power plays a mighty role in human affairs. The war experience only served to make this thesis an even more integral part of his thinking.

Hence his impatience with those who constructed abstract political systems without the power calculus, and hence his insistence that one must not turn one's back on power, as the Wilsonians often argued, but must pay it greater heed than ever before. Only by the closest scrutiny of every political organization could the power aspirations which were inevitably present be fully revealed and provisions made to prevent the abuse of power. No human institution was immune to such abuse; when we consider Meinecke's previous attitudes, it is hardly surprising that he was not prepared to suggest that democracy and the then current proposals for a world order were exempt from this rule.

Thus Meinecke's study of *raison d'état* became, in one sense, an exercise in the detection of power motives. And in this sense it was but a continuation and systematization of previous efforts. The distinction was in the difference of attitude between the prewar and postwar exposés of the power calculus. Formerly they were undertaken largely to explain and to justify the role of power in history and particularly in German history. Now their purpose was to spur men to realize the dangers to which they were subject in a world of unregulated power and to urge them to seek effective controls.

Despite the difference of attitude, however, there was common to both periods an undeniable fascination for the spectacle of power politics as such. It was the fascination of ever more striking discoveries of the role of egotistic reckoning in the establishment and preservation of human institutions, of the intricate efforts of men to clothe their cruder motives in garments of righteousness. There was an intellectual joy in uncovering the ironies of selfish calculation in exalted places and in measuring the extent to which glowing ideals were alloyed with baser metals. But there was also awe and wonder that egotism and moral consciousness were often intimately bound together so that the one could not be touched, by the outside observer, at least, without moving the other. Indeed, egotism only too often seemed necessary to the realization of moral goods transcending the ego.[10]

All these propositions were present in Meinecke's thought in more or less developed form before and during the war; some were either explicit or implied in his earliest writings. Now, however, he was using a broader framework in which to present his ideas and was seeking more precise and unambiguous evidence. The vast changes that the war had wrought in Europe and the world impelled him to find a more secure platform from which

[10] A typical formulation was Meinecke's observation on the eve of the German revolution that while it was time for self-criticism, such criticism did not mean a rejection of one's past *in toto* and that "if we find defects in our past, we shall never forget that defects and merits are often rooted together." ("Am Vorabend der Revolution" in *Nach der Revolution, op.cit.,* p. 2.)

A prewar formulation which is notable both for its clarity and its curiously parochial point of view may be found in his study of Radowitz published in 1913. "Nineteenth-century German history abounds with bewildering junctures of apparent opposites and divergencies of things that were originally joined together. The same human breast often gives rise to both creative and destructive forces. What appears to be toxin or antitoxin for a particular period is often transformed by its effects into its opposite. The opponent of a particular course of action can find himself unexpectedly fighting side by side with those who have defended this action. Thus the opposing camps of our political and intellectual parties are not so simple and easily distinguishable as is generally the case in other countries." (*Radowitz und die deutsche Revolution, op.cit.,* p. 1.)

to appraise political life than that which the nation-state had offered. Before the war it was Meinecke's hope and belief that nationalism had provided a viable solution to the problem of power. His subsequent disappointment led to a more consistent position: there are no "solutions" to the power problem. At best there are only more or less successful adjustments to it, and it is the fate of every age to face and grapple with the ancient challenge which power considerations presented to ethical and cultural values.[11] Hence his desire to examine a succession of historical eras in order to arrive at a theoretical formulation of the problem of power politics transcending time and space. Hence also his determination to ferret out the power element in events and institutions in a multitude of diverse examples in order to guard against parochial viewpoints and overhasty conclusions.

Die Idee der Staatsraeson, as the product of these desires and resolves, was thus more diverse and abstract than the bulk of Meinecke's previous writings and it breathes a markedly different atmosphere. Machiavelli was presented as the embodiment of the challenge of power politics, and the varying success with which subsequent European thinkers and statesmen dealt with Machiavelli's ideas constituted the core of the book. The questions which Meinecke implicitly put to each were: are the imperatives of power given their due or not? If so, what kinds of controls are suggested to prevent the abuse of power? If not, in what guise or disguise does the power calculus express itself?

Above all, it was necessary to learn how to detect the power drive, to cultivate a feeling for its ubiquity. Here the simplest method was to expose the moral idealist employing the weapons of Machiavellianism. Thomas Campanella, the Italian monk who became an eminent apologist for the power methods of Richelieu, furnished a typical example. Campanella's writings were directed toward the creation of an ideal state of justice and morality and were replete with denunciations of Machiavelli and the un-

---

[11] Cf. *Staatsraeson, op.cit.*, p. 340.

scrupulous power politics he preached. But in the building of his ideal state, Campanella was a willing borrower from Machiavelli's arsenal. Thus Meinecke remarked that along with the usual condemnations of *raison d'état* (here he used the Italian phrase *ragione di stato*), one could discover the "crassest Machiavellianisms." As an example he quoted Campanella's prescription for conduct in a newly-conquered land that was drawn directly from Machiavelli's *Prince*: "He who acquires a new land . . . must humble the leading personages, change the laws, raze the fortresses, and root out and banish the royal family. All this must be done at once on the day of victory and must be identified as the work of the soldiers and of the leader of the army. Conciliatory policies, on the other hand, must not be inaugurated all at the same time after the victory has been achieved, but must be introduced one by one and in the name of [the ruler] himself." Meinecke found no dearth of similar recipes: "In order to protect a kingdom" Campanella contended, "one must encourage divisions and enmity among the powers whom one fears, as the Spaniards do between the Turks and the Persians and among the barons of . . . France." The Dominican monk further argued that "any religion which contradicts 'natural politics' need not be observed."[12]

If one looked carefully, such earthy maxims could be found in many a utopian scheme. Sometimes they would appear as simple exceptions to the rules of morality for ordinary states. Thus Johann Kessler, an obscure seventeenth-century German court philosopher, served his Lutheran prince by demanding that he subject himself to the rule and judgment of God and, on the other hand, by urging that in extraordinary circumstances he was " 'allowed to violate even innocence in the name of the public weal'. . . . Even were he an angel, occasions would arise when he would have to turn his back on the good in the name of the common welfare. . . . [Kessler] warned against wars of conquest . . . but he did not shy away from granting the right,

[12] *Ibid.*, p. 129. The quotations and paraphrases from Campanella are taken from his *Aforismi politici* (1601).

in the name of one's own security, to 'pluck the feathers' of any neighbor growing too strong and dangerous. Indeed, though it violated all divine ordinances and the law of nations, in case of extreme necessity it was permissible to instigate rebellions in such a [neighboring] state."[13] As Meinecke remarked, "Along with morality, law and life and property could be gobbled up by the Leviathan of this *raison d'état*."[14]

The same could be said of the young Frederick the Great's *Anti-Machiavel*, which sought to discredit forever the political teachings of the Florentine. When confronted with "the doctrine that treaties need be observed only so long as they serve the interests of the state, . . . Frederick pronounced it a wicked and villainous policy, 'for one needs to deceive only once to lose the trust of every prince.' And still, possessed by a dark and strong premonition of things to come, he felt obliged to add that there were unfortunate situations (*nécessités fâcheuses*) in which a prince had to break treaties and alliances. Of course this must be done correctly: he must notify his allies in good time and must take this step only 'when the welfare of his people and a very great necessity oblige him to do so.' "[15]

Among many theoreticians and particularly among experienced politicians, however, one was less likely to discover such frank prescriptions for power. Therefore it was necessary to probe behind the façade of stated aims and objectives in order to detect ulterior motives and purposes. As we have noted, such detection was among the prime functions of Meinecke's study of *raison d'état*. Consequently, he provided a host of illustrations from Machiavelli's day to his own.

In his discussion of the role of prestige in international politics, he stressed Richelieu's contention that prestige involved "not only external deference but also the winning of sympathy

---

[13] *Ibid.*, pp. 172-173. The quotation and paraphrases are taken from Kessler's *Detectus ac a fuco politico repurgatus candor et imperium indefinitum, vastum et immensum Rationis Status boni principis* (1678).
[14] *Ibid.*, p. 173.
[15] *Ibid.*, pp. 371-372.

and trust" and that prestige or " 'reputation' was the expression for the practice already in vogue of manipulating and winning over world public opinion by claiming supposedly moral and idealistic motivations for one's own power politics." For concrete evidence he went on to cite the observation of Richelieu's contemporary, Duke de Rohan, that "Spain's reputation . . . was based essentially [on her practice of] concealing her plans in the mantle of piety and great zeal for the welfare of the Catholic religion. Rohan observed that 'this is a wonderful means of holding the people in awe. . . . It is a deception, of course, but it brings solid results.' "[16]

This kind of deception, Meinecke had contended, was also the trademark of British diplomacy. In *Staatsraeson* he repeated his wartime charges that British hypocrisy was so complete that Englishmen had managed to persuade even themselves that they served only higher purposes.[17] Now he also went further to assert that British hypocrisy really was naïve, that "the English mentality is incapable of fathoming the problematic of power politics." But here Meinecke immediately changed tack by observing that this British incapacity is due to "a practical instinct that does not want to probe [too deeply]."[18] Hence naïveté and incapacity suddenly take on the aura of wisdom: by choice the Britisher does not attack the problems of power politics with the weapons of philosophy because he does not wish to publicize the secrets of political strength. Elsewhere Meinecke equated this "unconscious expediency" to "political instinct which the German is usually lacking." His observation that "Bismarck was a great but rare exception"[19] strongly implies that Meinecke regretted this lack.

[16] *Ibid.*, p. 216. The quotations and paraphrases of Rohan are from Rohan's *De l'Interest des Princes et Estats de la Chrestienté* (1638).

[17] *Ibid.*, pp. 491-492.

[18] *Ibid.*, p. 495.

[19] *Ibid.*, p. 492. From the character of the minor changes which Meinecke made in the text of the third edition of *Staatsraeson*, it is apparent that he had done far too little research in English thought to justify

One is therefore uncertain whether Meinecke did not rather envy the British the gift for cant which he imputed to them. In any case, his recognition of an "unconscious expediency" introduces further complexities in the nature of power politics. Not only must the student be alert to deliberate artifice but also to unintentional deception regarding political motivation. Meinecke had already suggested this problem in his treatment of the French Huguenot Gentillet. The pious Gentillet attacked the teachings of Machiavelli and insisted that moral principle and not expediency must be the basis of politics. Indeed, he blamed the Saint Bartholomew massacre and the civil war in France not on Catholic fanaticism but on the Machiavellian Medici clique whose practices demonstrated an unscrupulous atheism rather than Catholic conviction. But Meinecke was moved to question whether Gentillet's endeavor to ease the religious controversy between Catholics and Protestants did not represent "an unconscious obedience to the laws of political expediency. For since his [Protestant] party was only a weak minority in the nation, it could hope to assert itself only if it enjoyed trust and favor among the moderate Catholics. . . ."[20] And this observation was followed by the generalization which brought into full view the difficulties attending any analysis of motive: "That is the peculiar quality . . . of actions guided by *raison d'état*: one can involuntarily let himself be led by its principles and at the same time indignantly disavow them. For one's consciousness

---

the rather sweeping judgments he undertook to make. Cf. his dropping of More as the first practitioner of "British cant" (p. 491 in the first and third editions) and his alteration of the judgment that the "English mentality is incapable of fathoming the problematic of power politics" to read "the *average* English mentality . . ." etc. (p. 495 of the first and third editions). (My italics.) This far-reaching modification was unaccompanied by any other changes and hence appears to indicate that Meinecke felt himself on unsure ground here.

Meinecke's relative *neglect of English thought* was one of the main criticisms in Hermann Oncken's review of *Staatsraeson* in the *Deutsche Literaturzeitung*, vol. 47, 1926, pp. 1304-1315.

[20] *Ibid.*, p. 66.

penetrates the ramifications of one's own life only incompletely."[21]

Here was a realm of irrationality with which the outside observer would surely have his own peculiar difficulties in attempting to penetrate. Meinecke was highly sensitive to this problem, and he usually used external evidence with extraordinary care and skill in order to gain entrance into the region of hidden motives. Thus he was able to suggest that Gentillet's hostility to Machiavelli's doctrine was not simply that of a "devout Huguenot. Above all, it was the French seigneur [in him] who resisted . . . and who realized that his whole world and way of life, the traditions, honor and interest of his class were threatened . . . should only the devilishly cold calculations of princely advantage rule the state."[22] So also was Meinecke able to see —more clearly in the perspective of defeat—the concealed motives of the German ruling groups who were too concerned with the maintenance of their privileged position to attend properly to the safety of the state as a whole and of whom some at the same time exhibited considerable sincerity in their claims that the welfare of the state was indeed their first concern.[23]

Thus class or any other grouping and perhaps the individual too could have a hidden *raison d'état* of its own which might clash or coincide with *raison d'état* proper. Meinecke certainly saw that supreme allegiance and all that it implies could be brought to other altars than the nation-state and therefore that one always had to look for power considerations among those who denounced the power of the state. With his observations that the interests of Europe could be served on occasion by the same power calculations which were being made on behalf of an individual state,[24] he also revealed his understanding that power could function as a double agent, supporting the state and a community beyond the state. Yet he insisted on a qualita-

[21] *Ibid.*
[22] *Ibid.*, p. 68.
[23] *Nach der Revolution, op.cit.*, pp. 21-23.
[24] *Staatsraeson, op.cit.*, pp. 324-325.

tive differentiation of the state from other human institutions on the basis that self-interest as the over-riding consideration was the rule for the state and was (or ought to be) the exception for all other organizations.[25] This differentiation had profound consequences for Meinecke's whole approach to the problem of politics. Insofar as it betrayed a subjective preference for the sovereign state as the supreme form of human organization, it was a telling illustration of Meinecke's contention that "consciousness penetrates the ramifications of one's own life only incompletely."

In any case, whatever degree of blindness may have afflicted Meinecke in regard to his own conceptions of the state, he was perceptive enough to warn against imputing moral purity to any human organization, including the state. This admonition was central to the thesis of *Staatsraeson* and appears again and again throughout the book. It is clear that his warning did not mean that he begrudged these institutions their concern for power and self-interest. On the contrary, he contended that such considerations were necessary to the vitality of any organization. Self-interest, after all, was a potent goad to rational and efficient and even creative activity. His warning simply sought to remind that conferring absolute value on any human institution meant one was absolutizing the selfish interests which inevitably inhered in it along with its more exalted objectives.

Meinecke's concern with the role of self-interest, however, was not simply the negative one of pointing to its universal existence in order to preach against the worship of things human. The full complexity of the subject was revealed only when one probed its relation not only to rational and creative activity but also to moral achievements. Could self-interest also be the sire of virtue? This was, of course, Machiavelli's contention. His *necessitá*—understood as the imperative of survival—was the spur to that virtue which built the state. "The greater the *necessitá*, he insisted, the greater the *virtù*, and many things which

25 *Ibid.*, pp. 16-17.

reason is not strong enough to attain are achieved by force of necessity."[26]

Machiavelli's *virtù*, however, was in essence a capacity for living successfully, for outwitting an indifferent or sometimes spiteful fate. Thus it bore only faint resemblance to that virtue which is conceived in terms of self-denial and altruism. After all, the practice of Machiavelli's *virtù* demanded that one learn how not to be good.

Therefore, while Machiavelli was the agent who had done most to provoke all the subsequent soul-searchings in Western history concerning the nature and justification of power politics, and while he provided profound insights into their problematics, Meinecke contended that Machiavelli did no more than define the issues. The full dimensions of the relationship between self-interest and morality began to reveal themselves only in the process of time as thinkers and statesmen took up the challenge of Machiavelli and attempted to reconcile it with the traditional morality of Western and Christian civilization.

It was Meinecke's examination of the responses Machiavelli elicited from his intellectual heirs and enemies which made *Staatsraeson* more than simply an exercise in the detection of power motives. The central design of his inquiry into four centuries of thought on the problem of *raison d'état* was to draw on the tremendous resources of modern history for guidance in seeking a satisfying answer concerning the relation between the demands of power and the commands of ethics. The thesis that the relation was a positive and usually fortunate one, to which so many German intellectuals subscribed in the prewar world—and Meinecke had often enough been among them—was now far too simple for him. Thus he was moved to probe all the aspects of the association and to come up not with a simple positive correlation but with an ambiguous reciprocity.

Machiavelli's *virtù* had little to do with moral sensibility. But Meinecke found examples enough to establish a relation between

[26] *Ibid.*, p. 47. Meinecke's paraphrase of Machiavelli is based on the *Discourses* (I, 1 and I, 6).

power strivings and authentic moral achievement. We have already noted Meinecke's reference to the regime of Frederick the Great in which it was contended that Frederick was forced by the requirements of power to establish justice in the state.[27] Frederick's state "had to seek support in the moral forces emanating from the life of the people. It required a conscious code of honor among its officers; it had to educate its civil servants to duty and responsibility and its subjects to work and diligence. It also had to attempt to develop their intelligence through schooling and instruction."[28]

It was undeniable that political ambition was here at least contributing to the shaping and strengthening of moral values. In *Staatsraeson* Meinecke was able to cite additional examples as evidence of such a process. He noted Hobbes's assertion that one need not fear "that the Leviathan would misuse its power to enslave and maltreat its subjects . . . [because] the power-wielder would be compelled by his own interests to rule with reason and advance the public welfare."[29]

If there is cause for doubt regarding the validity of this proposition by the author of *Leviathan*, there can be little room for skepticism when confronted with the historic fact of the growth of such a phenomenon as religious tolerance. Here Meinecke turned to the example of sixteenth-century France: its problem was that a "relentless struggle for the preservation of the old Church would propel the state into the arms of Spain and would require the renunciation of all these power objectives that could be attained only in contest with Spain. Recognizing this, the party of the 'Politicians' . . . first bent every effort toward the reestablishment of internal peace via concessions of toleration to the Huguenots who then found it easy to cooperate in forging a united political front against Spain. Here the political root of the modern idea of tolerance is clearly exposed. The true interests of France required tolerance in order to safeguard the

---

[27] Chapter VI, above.
[28] *Erhebung, op.cit.*, p. 13.
[29] *Staatsraeson, op.cit.*, p. 265.

freedom of the state from foreign influence and to develop its external strength."[80]

The significance of these processes clearly goes beyond their function as illustrations of the concept of enlightened self-interest. Here it is unnecessary to attempt to solve the ancient problem of whether there is an authentic element of morality in this concept. For present purposes it is enough to stress that concrete moral, spiritual, and cultural values are being generated by the operations of state interest, and that once generated they have a dynamic of their own which can achieve a very high degree of independence from the power calculus of the state. They can in fact become so potent that the state would hesitate to violate them even though other circumstances might make it expedient to do so. In such a situation, of course, these values are themselves likely to have become vested interests, and the irony of the inevitable corruption of the ideal in its concrete form becomes clearly evident.

Not only in the development of the civil society but also in the relations between states could considerations of interest give rise to moral conduct. It has already been pointed out that Meinecke's case for moderation and restraint in Germany's war policies and aims rested to a very great extent on power deliberations. Thus he scored the "exaltados" for their lack of realism— that realism with which Bismarck would have demolished their grandiose power fantasies.[81] He returned again to the theme in his postwar writings. "Only a Bismarck-like self-denial and realism could have protected us . . . from the dangers to which we were exposed by our rapid rise to power."[82]

Meinecke used the power argument to admonish both Germany and her wartime enemies. Thus in the middle period of the war he was farsighted enough to see that power excesses by the European nations would only succeed in destroying Eu-

[80] *Ibid.*, p. 190.
[81] Chapter VIII, above.
[82] Review of Philipp Hiltebrandt's *Das Europaeische Verhaengnis*, Berlin, 1919, in *HZ*, vol. 121, 1920, p. 121.

rope's position as the power center of the world. After calling for a compromise peace, Meinecke turned to France and England to warn them that even if they succeeded in completely destroying Germany "it would be a Pyrrhic victory in the worst sense. They would then themselves be exhausted and powerless to prevent the United States and Japan, as the only intact world powers, from automatically rising to the top and determining the course of world politics. Japan's hand in particular would be strengthened by a number of trumps which she would exploit to the hilt. . . . If England wants to remain militarily and financially strong enough to protect its power position after the war, it should not now undermine that position by a war policy whose final goal can be achieved, if at all, only by disarming itself."[33] The passage of forty years has produced an abundance of evidence that this was good advice indeed.

Advice of enduring significance was also contained in Meinecke's plea to his own countrymen not to let the passions of war becloud their political judgment. Here he looked at the problem of Japan from a different angle: "The complex of issues over which the war is now being fought can disintegrate; the advantage which this or that [course of action] seems to offer us today can become a serious disadvantage tomorrow. And today's enemy can become our friend day-after-tomorrow —or at least can become an instrument for advancing our interests. Our position vis-à-vis Japan, for example, is distinctly different today [1915] from what it was in August 1914, when the Japanese presented us with their brazen ultimatum. For today Japan threatens the interests of Russia, England and America in China and so has become an embarrassment to our opponents. Is it really so out of the question that we shall once again experience a certain community of interest with Japan? Should this happen, we must avoid shouting anathema one day and Hosanna the next. Instead we must keep our eyes open and our tempers

---

[33] "Staatskunst und Leidenschaften" (1916) in *Probleme des Weltkriegs, op.cit.*, pp. 62-63.

cool and attempt to master every aspect of the Japanese problem."[34]

Meinecke defined the cultivation of such an approach as "political culture." Certainly it was a model of cold calculation of interest without a hint of ethical deliberation. Yet it is not without irony to observe that a public discussion of this kind could be tolerated in the authoritarian atmosphere of Imperial Germany. Such a discussion—urging moderation toward an enemy belligerent and looking forward to the reestablishment of friendly relations without necessarily first demanding his total capitulation—would be difficult to conduct in a contemporary democracy. And few would deny that moderation and curbing the passions of hatred and revenge may be virtuous as well as expedient.

Of course, as we have seen previously, it was not merely power calculations which animated Meinecke's political reasoning.[35] He did not want to see the great fabric of creative individuals, social achievements, art and ethics which Western civilization had woven ripped to pieces by a ruthless concentration on immediate power advantages. Tolerance, moderation, compassion, freedom for the individual—all these, therefore, were values to which the power calculus was subordinate. These were the proper goals of human endeavor, and only such power strivings as served these goals could be adjudged good.

But we have observed that the relationship between virtue and expediency is precarious. Indeed, in the light of human hopes and fears even the golden rule of "Do unto others" is a classic example of calculating self-interest. So also is the relationship between "good" and "bad" power strivings precarious. If Meinecke went to considerable effort to show that non-power values had a dynamic of their own, he also made an overwhelming case for the thesis that power follows its own rules.

A system of human organization without the power process,

<hr>

[34] "Politische Kultur und Oeffentliche Meinung" in *Probleme des Weltkriegs, op.cit.,* p. 11.

[35] Chapter VIII, above.

however, was unattainable and probably undesirable as well. Not only was the power calculus an apparently necessary spur to the creation of moral and cultural values. It was also an apparently necessary hindrance to the hypertrophy of the power drive. Meinecke subscribed to the thesis that "The pursuit of power is a basic human characteristic, perhaps even an animal drive, which blindly surges forth until it finds external limits."[86] Since human beings are often not wise or strong enough to discipline their own appetites for power, the juxtaposition of opposing power interests was essential to the setting of these limits. History demonstrated that the concern for cultural and ethical values is not in itself sufficient to provide restraints on individuals or on statesmen. The concern for power itself must play a role in the formulation of moral as well as prudent policy. In order to persuade the statesman that the individual must not be made wholly subordinate to the state, it was necessary to buttress ethical remonstrances with practical considerations of the threat of rebellion. And in order to convince him that his state lacks a warrant to be wholly arbitrary in its foreign policy he must be imbued not only with a respect for the cultural and moral values of other states and of humanity as a whole. He must also understand that a state too ruthless in the pursuit of its own ends will attract so many enemies as to bring about its downfall.

New dimensions are added to the problem of self-interest if we recall Meinecke's contention that not only does power create moral values but that moral values also create power—that the society which accords its members moral dignity and freedom enhances its powers of survival.[37] This interplay of power and moral values, each begetting each, was for Meinecke at the center of the problem of politics. Their mutual indispensability at once challenged, admonished, and justified imperfect man. The transformation of the search for power into the discovery of

[86] *Staatsraeson, op.cit.*, p. 5. This thesis, and the conclusions which Meinecke draws from it, find particularly striking parallels in *The Federalist*.

[37] Chapters v, vi, and viii, above.

justice gave to political life the dimensions of drama and beauty. But it was the opposite process, wherein the experience of justice legitimized the demands of power, that was one of the prime reasons why the dramatic tension so often took on the overtones of tragedy.

In "Kultur, Machtpolitik und Militarismus" we saw Meinecke's first sustained endeavor to come to grips with the tragic nature of politics. The unsatisfactory results of his efforts are in significant part due to his failure to stress the darker aspects of that reverse transmutation wherein moral values serve to intensify the quest for power. Here was a source of tragedy in the political drama most tellingly illustrated in the evolution of Meinecke's own attitudes during the war. In his own person he reflected that intertwining of ethical and power purposes which he later portrayed in Gentillet and which made it so difficult to penetrate the thicket of human motivation.

There was no more moving expression of this problem than Meinecke's deeply-felt response in "Die deutsche Freiheit" to the ideological offensive of the Western democracies which reached its peak with the American entry into the war. Conceding, as always, that the German way of life was not beyond criticism, he denied that Germany worshipped only power and was hostile to freedom. There was a German concept of liberty, different but equal if not indeed superior to that preached by the Allies.

The roots of this German idea of liberty he found in the words of Luther: " 'A Christian is a free man over all things and subject to no man and: a Christian is a servant to all things and subject to every man.' " Kant and Fichte, he continued, translated Luther into the secular philosophy which animated the classic period of German letters and the era of the Prussian Reform. "Freedom meant . . . to become free of all bonds of sensuality, to make the spiritual and God-like in us our masters. It meant to let these spiritual forces shape our lives according to the absolutely unambiguous voice of conscience. . . . To become free meant to discard the common human being in order to become a real man. It also meant to strike off old shackles in order to assent to new and far more binding ones. It meant to replace ignoble with honorable servitude. The categorical imperative of Kant required the individual to act in such a way that the norms of his will could serve at the same time as principles of universal legislation. Hence to serve, to subordinate oneself to what one recognizes as rational universal commandments does not degrade, does not enslave, but truly liberates. It means to receive divinity into the individual will. Here we see freedom and unfreedom bound together, not in that usual melancholy union but indivisible, indistinguishable in a supreme expression of spirit."[38]

Now Meinecke applied freedom, so defined, directly to the state. In politics this concept of freedom "exalts the inner voice of the individual to the seat of judgment over that which claims to be a universal law. But then [if the claim is admitted] the actions of the individual are completely subordinated to the law. Hence if I recognize the law of the state in which I find myself to be reasonable and valuable . . . I am obliged to serve it and if necessary to sacrifice myself in that service. Thus the subjects' sentiment for the paternalistic state could develop into an autonomous sense of moral obligation toward the state on the part of human beings who felt themselves to be free." With Stein's reforms, "the state was to rest on the moral freedom and dignity of the citizen and the man and to secure their recognition in all its institutions. This is the real core of our modern idea of political freedom. At the same time it is the spiritual justification of that which our opponents call German servitude; for it both liberates and obligates."[39]

The defense of this German freedom became for Meinecke the central issue of the war at a point where no other goals seemed to him to justify its continuation. In 1916, Meinecke had written that the war had become senseless. But nearly a full year later he was firm in his determination to carry on the strug-

[38] *Die deutsche Freiheit, op.cit.*, pp. 21-22.
[39] *Ibid.*, pp. 22-23.

gle to the bitter end. Confronted by "the enmity of almost the entire world, we stand our ground erect, defiant and free—and resolved to defend German freedom with the last ounce of energy."[40]

Neither a strategic boundary, nor equality on the seas, nor a colonial empire was worth the terrible sacrifices piling up. Only the assumption that basic moral values were at stake could persuade Meinecke—and Meinecke's counterparts in all the warring countries—that still more strenuous efforts must be made. Morality was the most potent of all the arguments to elicit men's consent to stricter regimentation, more massive mobilization, and crueler weapons.

It was the cry for justice which brought the power struggle to its utmost intensity. Conversely, the redoubled exertions which the ideological contest demanded led finally to overexertion and powerlessness. Thus the First World War registered the interaction of power and morality in the largest dimensions and on both the positive and negative ranges. The great state edifices, whose dualism of power concerns and moral and spiritual values led Ranke to call them "thoughts of God,"[41] now exhibited qualities that were rather demoniacal than God-like. The creative relationship of power and morality was replaced by a fearsomely destructive one, and responsible men had lost the ability to control the relationship. Here was the specific meaning of the demonic: one is "possessed," one is no longer free but is driven by events he cannot master.

Little wonder that Meinecke sought more binding controls for the forces which shaped world politics. But it was the supreme irony that the highest ethical ideals to which he gave expression in "Die deutsche Freiheit" had merely served to give added stimulus to the all-out power struggle. Not only did they provide the only rationale for the continuing destruction when all other rationalizations paled before war's fury; their own substantive content harbored a fatal flaw.

Meinecke's eloquent statement of German ideals was a credo and not a description of reality. Meinecke conceded as much in

---

[40] *Ibid.*, p. 14.   [41] *Staatsraeson*, pp. 470-471.

the same essay; it had been more than difficult to "infuse the idea into reality." It was significant that he invoked the Germany of Stein and not of Bismarck in his exposition of the meaning of political freedom, for it had been his constant concern that the era of the Reform and the liberty of the individual for which it stood were being smothered in the modern state with its mighty power apparatus and its culture of the masses.

Even as a credo, however, it was hardly beyond criticism. Was this not the same credo of the Reformers which Meinecke had censured as expecting too much of mortal man? Could one build a political society on the assumption that its members would conduct themselves according to Kant's categorical imperative? Above all, was not Meinecke placing too much confidence in the wisdom of the individual—that same individual whose wisdom was so limited—when he asserted that the state, once "recognized" as "reasonable and valuable" by the individual, could require absolute obedience and self-sacrifice from him? Did this not imply that the individual had sold his freedom to the state? The spontaneous obedience of the individual to the dictates of conscience, that "noble servitude," has its own problematics as a concept. But to posit the same relationship of spontaneous obedience as between the imperfect individual and the imperfect state was to absolutize the political organization and consequently to undercut all restraints on the demonic forces which inhered in it.

Thus Meinecke had personally fallen victim to the tendencies he had warned against both in his prewar investigation of the nation-state and his postwar examination of power and ethics. Indeed, it was his personal experience which was at the root of many of the contradictions which beset his appraisals of international politics in general and of Germany in particular. This should hardly cause surprise, particularly if one accepts Meinecke's own propositions concerning the ubiquity of subjective bias. In any case, Meinecke's own experience exerted a continuing and powerful influence in his attempts to evaluate the nature of *raison d'état*, and it was personal experience, in the final analysis, which led him to an ultimate reevaluation.

CHAPTER X

RAISON D'ÉTAT AND THE PRIMACY
OF THE STATE

In "Kultur, Machtpolitik und Militarismus" Meinecke contended that where there were conflicts of moral duty, the statesman always had to solve the conflict in terms of the *salus populi*. Furthermore, he identified the *salus populi* with the ego of the state.[1] He subsequently reexamined and altered both these judgments. As we have suggested, *Die Idee der Staatsraeson* was the monumental result of his endeavor to strike a new balance between politics and morals.

It has been contended previously that the balance which Meinecke established earlier had amounted to a clearcut primacy of politics. If the statesman's decision must always be in favor of the *salus populi*, understood as the ego of the state, there was no real choice and hence no real tragedy. It was further asserted that just as power dominated the power-morals or power-spirit polarity which Meinecke constructed, so in all the other polarities with which he operated—realism and idealism, nationalism and cosmopolitanism, authority and liberty, state and individual —the power-oriented components of realism, nation, state, and authority always seemed to triumph in practical matters while the ethically-oriented components remained largely abstract and ineffectual admonitions.[2] Such consistent results from the application of the idea of polarity to politics must call into question its conceptual validity.

Moreover, Meinecke himself had pronounced power-politics and war to be hypertrophied and in urgent need of very concrete restraints. His concern that the ideals of individual dignity and liberty and a human community transcending national bound-

[1] Chapter VII, above.
[2] Chapters VI and VII, above.

aries were in danger of total eclipse arose from his recognition that the technology of destruction had vastly improved. It also derived from his belief that irrational anxieties and hatreds were in the ascendant in international politics as inevitable products of the mass state.

If Meinecke's ethical ideals were to be salvaged, it would not do to let them remain glimmering on the boundaries of human experience. They must be solidly built into a system of politics and philosophy in such a way as to make them effective hindrances to power excesses and effective guides for political action dedicated to their realization. Meinecke could not and would not abandon his insistence on the necessary role of power. His recourse was to accept for himself the recommendation he made to the statesmen: "the more dangerous and terrible the consequences which modern civilization tends to impose on actions taken in the name of *raison d'état*, the more untiringly must the statesman seek a unifying bond for his divided sense of responsibility to the state and to the moral law."[3] Meinecke's writing of a history of the idea of *raison d'état* was a heroic attempt to make the sense of duty to the moral law as insistent and immediate as the sense of duty to the state and so to restore vitality and significance to the polarities he had previously emptied of content.

As we have noted, he began his renewed study of the relation of politics and morals with Machiavelli, who was made to symbolize the supreme challenge to the paramountcy of moral law. It is not without interest to detect a hint of self-comparison with Machiavelli in the course of Meinecke's reflections. He described Machiavelli as possessing a profound and passionate idealism alongside his ruthless realism. The Florentine mourned the fate of his fatherland whose downfall he traced to a "decline of moral energies. Thus the real and central problem of his life was to gain a deeper understanding of this collapse, to establish the causes of the rise and decline of peoples and to seek ways

[3] *Staatsraeson, op.cit.,* p. 537.

and means of their regeneration."[4] This was a strikingly accurate statement of Meinecke's own attitudes and undertakings.

The comparison, if any was intended, was valid only in a functional sense. In substantive matters Meinecke had reached a position which profoundly contrasted with Machiavelli's. The culmination of Machiavelli's political thought was the proposition that every other value must bow to the survival of the state: " 'Where the very safety of the fatherland is at stake, there should be no question of reflecting whether a thing is just or unjust, humane or cruel, praiseworthy or shameful. Setting aside every other consideration, one must take only that course of action which will secure the country's life and liberty.' "[5] Here was the *salus populi* argument as Meinecke had presented it in "Kultur, Machtpolitik und Militarismus." But in *Staatsraeson* Meinecke went beyond this position. Like Ranke, he refused "to make the state a God and unconditionally to exalt *raison d'état* to a position superior to morality."[6] On the contrary, the *salus populi*, the state ego, could be satanic as well as God-like. Thus "the statesman must carry both the state and God in his heart if he is to prevent the demon which he cannot wholly exorcise from overwhelming him."[7]

These words concluded Meinecke's study of *raison d'état*. They constituted persuasive evidence that he had finally consigned the state ego to the status of a relative value. Moreover, he pronounced the state not only relative to other values but ambiguous within itself. The state "must strive to live in harmony with the moral law," but "it can never quite reach this goal, for it is fated by the stern necessity of its nature to a constant repetition of its sins."[8]

The nemesis of power is here stated in such a way as to constitute a permanent bar to the worship of the state. In these terms

[4] Introduction to *Der Fuerst*, Berlin, 1923, p. 8. (Volume 8 of the series entitled *Klassiker der Politik*.) Hereafter cited as *Fuerst* Introduction.

[5] Machiavelli, *Discourses*, III, 41, quoted in *Staatsraeson, op.cit.*, pp. 55-56.

[6] *Staatsraeson, op.cit.*, p. 487.

[7] *Ibid.*, p. 542.   [8] *Ibid.*, p. 537.

the statesman cannot automatically place the welfare of the state above every other consideration. Nor can he entertain even as an ideal the concept of a state wholly beneficent in its relation to man's other values. The state is doomed always to remain an imperfect instrument, its power a standing inducement to corruption.

The interest of the state could not function as the end which justified every means because it was itself constantly in need of vindication. Such justification could be meaningful only in terms of the values which the state's nature caused it repeatedly to violate. Individual freedom and the welfare of the human community constituted the ultimate measure of the state's worth, and they were precisely the values which the state again and again subordinated in the name of its survival. No longer, therefore, did Meinecke confront the statesman with an orderly hierarchy of criteria applicable to political decisions. Instead he constructed a set of volatile and ambiguous means-ends relationships in which the statesman seeking moral sanction for his actions could not hope to avoid painful dilemmas and choices that were tragic in the full sense of the word.

What should guide the statesman when faced with this awesome responsibility and task? In *Die Idee der Staatsraeson* Meinecke gave an answer almost as ambiguous as the means-ends relationships which he sought to portray. After all the formulations and reformulations of political wisdom which he traced from Machiavelli's day to his own, Meinecke's final position was that even a morally transfigured *raison d'état* could not be the statesman's final referent. His action must also be judged in terms of a universal moral law transcending the state. But even here there was an ultimate ambiguity which will become apparent as we follow Meinecke's efforts to give the abstract concept of *raison d'état* a concrete significance.

Meinecke's problems with a satisfactory definition of *raison d'état* foreshadowed this final ambiguity. Indeed, he felt obliged to stress that "the complex content of the idea of *raison d'état* defies the narrow limits of conceptual definition."[9] In one perspective *raison d'état* is a mixture of moral and power considerations, "a bridge . . . between *ethos* and *kratos*."[10] In another light the valuing of power above law and morality is the "specific and unambiguous meaning [of] *raison d'état*."[11] In still another and perhaps more comprehensive sense *raison d'état* is "the law governing the movement of the state. It tells the statesman what he must do in order to maintain the state's health and vigor."[12] The implication of determinism in this last definition is then made explicit: the statesman "must" act in harmony with *raison d'état*. "To live in liberty and independence the state must . . . obey the laws dictated by its *raison d'état*." "The meaning of *raison d'état*, concisely stated, . . . is determinism in political conduct."[13] But this determinism, derived from the concept of the "necessities of state," conflicted with the freedom of choice implicit in Meinecke's final position that the statesman is responsible to both the state and the universal moral law.

These apparently contradictory propositions about *raison d'état* suggest the desirability of a closer examination of its nature as Meinecke conceived it. As a preface it should be noted that he remarked upon the circumstance that the phrase "*raison d'état*" had become obsolete and deplored the fact that political science made so little use of it. But "clothed in other terminology, . . . [it] nonetheless continues to exist in fact and theory." The observation that followed was of no little significance: "The power problem, power politics, the idea of the power state— these are the preferred expressions today. This [terminology] is also acceptable, although it does not denote so clearly the essence of the matter, that pulsing life of the state in which there is an intermingling of the natural and the rational and which moves from nature toward spirit."[14]

One can certainly agree that what Meinecke called the newer terminology fails to communicate any suggestion of a spiritual side of political life. It clearly conveys the opposite impression,

[9] *Ibid.*, p. 259.   [10] *Ibid.*, p. 6.   [11] *Ibid.*, pp. 4-5.
[12] *Ibid.*, p. 1.   [13] *Ibid.*, pp. 1-2, 369.   [14] *Ibid.*, p. 511.

namely, that of the state as exclusively an organization of power. Meinecke's reluctant willingness to accept this rephrasing of the ancient problem of politics was perhaps a symbolic concession to the difficulties which beset any attempt to infuse politics with a spiritual and ethical content. As Meinecke wrote, "the natural tendency of *raison d'état* . . . is to restrict itself to reckoning only in terms of tangible advantages to the state's ego. . . . It is perpetually in danger of becoming a mere utilitarian instrument without ethical function. It constantly threatens to retreat from wisdom to mere cunning and to restrain the surface passions only to gratify the more deep-lying and covert passions and egoisms. It can become simply a technique of state; historically seen, such indeed is its origin."[15]

At the very moment, then, when Meinecke implied that *raison d'état* is something more than the selfish calculation of advantages for the state, he asserted that it is precisely this kind of reckoning which is its "natural tendency" and that the origin of the state is to be sought wholly in the realm of self-interest. Certainly the bulk of evidence which Meinecke examined tended to confirm this view. Machiavelli preached it openly. Other thinkers and statesmen might or might not deny it, but the greater part of their actions and rationalizations served as confirmation rather than denial.

Machiavelli stated the case for a conception of *raison d'état* that was both amoral in essence and originated in an ineluctable necessity. The state was a necessity, power was necessary to the state, and in order to secure power it was sometimes necessary to violate the laws of decency and morality. "A prince must also learn how not to be good; this is the demand of necessity which rules the whole of human life."[16] The imperative of state survival might require moral or immoral actions; once the duty to the state was accepted as supreme, the ruler had no choice but to obey.

Meinecke emphasized that Machiavelli did not offer dispensa-

---

[15] *Ibid.*, p. 9.
[16] *Ibid.*, p. 49. (Meinecke's paraphrase of Machiavelli.)

tions for all human sins. Nor did he seek to eliminate the concept of evil. "Good remains good and bad remains bad. Cruelty, deception and faithlessness are not beautified by lending them the robes of virtue."[17] Indeed, Machiavelli urged the prince to be good when he could.[18] Only the stern necessities of state, not personal caprice, nor any other consideration, justified doing evil. Thus good and bad remained considerations to be taken into account; it was simply that they were no longer all-important. "In politics state interest comes before morality. Morality is not denied but . . . it is removed to the realm of secondary [concerns]. . . . This is the great, terribly dangerous and demonic doctrine which Machiavelli preached to the modern state."[19]

Meinecke had good reason to brand the doctrine as dangerous and demonic. As he noted, "There is a profound difference whether one simply commits an act which violates the moral law . . . or whether one justifies the action in the name of an unavoidable 'necessity.' In the first case, the validity and absolute sanctity of the moral law remained unimpaired. . . . Now, however, the super-empirical necessity was breached by an empirical necessity; evil seized a place next to the good, claiming that it was also a good, or at least an indispensable means for the realization of a good. With this the powers of sin which the principles of the Christian ethic had held in check now won a partial victory at the level of principle. The devil invaded God's kingdom. Here was the beginning of that dualism of super-empiric and empiric, of absolute and relative value criteria, which is the source of all the discords of modern culture."[20]

To trace the origin of all the discords of modern culture to the double standard of morality which Machiavelli was in effect the first to preach is no doubt too sweeping a generalization. But one can certainly accept Meinecke's point that the establish-

---

[17] *Fuerst* Introduction, *op.cit.*, p. 6.
[18] *Staatsraeson*, *op.cit.*, pp. 50-51.
[19] *Fuerst* Introduction, *op.cit.*, p. 6.
[20] *Staatsraeson*, *op.cit.*, pp. 49-50.

ment of such a double standard as a political doctrine was a momentous occasion. It was an old, old tradition to preach one thing and practice another. It was something new to make preachments conform to practice, particularly in the period of Renaissance Italy when political practice was peculiarly vicious. "The statesmen themselves may not have learned anything new, but it was new that it was being *taught*. For only after an historical tendency has been conceived as a principle does it achieve its full force and become what one may call an idea."[21]

This was the all-important event—that the idea of utility should be placed on the same level as the idea of the good. Actually, of course, Machiavelli made utility supreme, whatever his contingent concerns for morality. But in either case the principle of the supremacy of moral categories was challenged, and utility and morality contested for the theoretical as well as practical allegiance of men.

While Meinecke identified Machiavelli's absolutization of state utility as the first modern exposition of *raison d'état*, he was careful to point out that Machiavelli was not the inventor of the phrase, which appeared only later in the works of the Archbishop Giovanni della Casa.[22] But della Casa's definition both accurately described Machiavelli's doctrine and eloquently identified its dangers: "If the reasoning which guides the state seeks only utility and advantage in contempt of every other law, where is the difference between tyrants and kings, men and beasts? Today one talks of *Utile Ragion di stato* and so creates two kinds of reason, the one crooked, false and licentious, leading to knavery and spoliation, which is called *Ragion di stato* and to which the government of states is entrusted. The other is simple, direct and steadfast, [but] it is being banished from government and restricted to judicial processes."[23] Meinecke

[21] *Ibid.*, p. 49.

[22] *Ibid.*, p. 59. Meinecke did not accept the thesis that the phrase was in vogue before della Casa's use of it in 1547. See footnote 2 on pp. 58-59.

[23] *Ibid.*, p. 60 (Meinecke's paraphrase).

noted that della Casa fulminated against *raison d'état* for very practical political reasons of his own. But he also stressed the revealing nature of della Casa's words as evidence of the depth of the dichotomy which now plagued thinking about the relation of politics and morals.[24]

Meinecke used Bodin as a prime example of the triumphs which Machiavelli and the idea of *raison d'état* were to celebrate in the camps of their critics. For all of Bodin's condemnations of faithlessness in political action, he could not build his sovereign state without leaving room for the methods of Machiavellianism. He insisted that " 'Good faith is the foundation of all justice. It is the bond which holds together not only states but the whole of human society.' "[25] But he had also asserted that " 'Nothing appears shameful which is connected with the welfare of the state.' "[26] As Meinecke pointed out, success is here made the paramount goal of political action; hence utility is set up as a standard independent of justice. And Bodin was clearly unable to establish a satisfactory relation between the two standards. His rather awkward morally-phrased exceptions to the rule of good faith culminated in his absolution of the state which breaks a treaty containing a promise that is " 'contrary to nature or which is impossible to fulfill.' "[27]

Meinecke cited many other examples besides Bodin to illustrate the struggle between justice and utility. But he was not content to present the contest as one in which the victories that utility attained were the result simply of cool calculation, hypocrisy, or even of failure to recognize the existence of a conflict. The worship of utility, the subordination of all one's actions to political "necessity" could only too often be the product of fanatic instinct which could lead the statesman beyond all rationality and into actions whose results, whether beneficial or harmful to him, he could not control.

Here Meinecke let Boccalini speak in the tones of the Coun-

[24] *Ibid.*
[25] *Ibid.*, p. 79. All quotations from Bodin are taken from the *Republic.*
[26] *Ibid.*, p. 76.   [27] *Ibid.*, p. 79.

ter-Reformation: " 'The interest of the state is like the hounds of Actaeon; it tears at the bowels of its own master. Hell has no terrors for the heart that burns with the passion to rule. The political man indoctrinates himself with the idea that necessity stands above all things. . . . He tramples on all the other goods of earth and heaven. The ambition to rule is a demon which even holy water cannot exorcise.' "[28]

In this perspective utilitarianism and expediency are devoid of all suggestion of the cool and detached calculation and manipulation which Machiavelli recommended to his prince. Machiavelli was conscious of the irrational depths of political action, but he erred in supposing that they could be so handily mastered. He envisioned an unreal *homo politicus* who would remain immune to the corruption which accompanies power and acts of force.

Machiavelli's doctrine of *raison d'état* as the servant of political necessity was nonetheless the thesis which many statesmen felt obliged to affirm and many more felt obliged to practice. It was repeated in the words of Frederick the Great: " 'Princes are slaves to their resources, the interest of the state is their law, and this law is inviolable.' "[29] And its spirit was expressed when Bismarck asserted that " 'It is better to seek salvation via the sewer than to allow oneself to be choked or beaten to death.' "[30]

But few could assert the ego of the state in the matter-of-course tones of Machiavelli. For him the primacy of the state was an incontrovertible thesis. For most of those who followed

[28] *Ibid.*, p. 95. The quotation is from Boccalini's *Ragguagli di Parnaso* (1612-1613).

[29] *Ibid.*, p. 381. The quotation from Frederick is from his *Oeuvres*, 2 xxv.

[30] Quoted in "Bismarck und Gerlach" in *HZ*, vol. 72, 1894, p. 58. It is interesting to note the context in which Meinecke presents this quotation from Bismarck. Meinecke's tone is positively approving: "Bismarck did not shrink from saying [this] to the face of this man [Gerlach] of delicate and over-refined sensibilities." This early almost defiant approval of Bismarck's power politics is in sharp contrast to Meinecke's later position.

him it was in continual warfare with its antithesis. For "the Christian and Germanic Middle Ages had left . . . a legacy of tremendous impact to the modern West, namely, . . . the painful sensitivity to the conflict of *raison d'état* with morality and law, the recurring feeling that a remorseless *raison d'état* was in truth a sin against God and divine norms. . . ."[31] Certainly Machiavelli's own advice that the ruler should support religion even if that religion be false demonstrated the capacity of *raison d'état* to manipulate even God in the name of the state. And he found an abundance of imitators. Campanella vividly portrayed them in his observations on Europe's religious struggle: " 'No one believes the Bible or the Koran, or the gospel or Luther or the Pope unless he finds it useful to do so.' 'Almost all princes are Machiavellian politicians and use religion merely as part of the art of governing.' "[32] Pope Urban VIII furnished dramatic proof of Campanella's thesis when he attacked the Catholic Powers in the midst of their struggle with Gustavus Adolphus.[33]

Johann Kessler, that obscure but imaginative political counselor whose political recipes have already been noted,[34] also confirmed Campanella's charge by identifying "God himself as a 'Direktor' of *raison d'état*. . . . He went to the fantastic length of speculating about the 'angels of state' which God could have assigned . . . to each government." And Kessler entertained all these ideas at the same time as he denounced the irreligion and sinfulness of Machiavelli. As Meinecke remarked, "What all could one not extract from the belief inculcated by Luther that the divine will was both all-powerful and absolutely unknowable?"[35]

Despite all the casuistry which pressed the divine will into the service of *raison d'état*, the struggle which Machiavelli precipitated in the Western conscience was undeniable. Frederick the Great was Meinecke's supreme illustration of the conflict

[31] *Staatsraeson, op.cit.*, p. 36.   [32] *Ibid.*, p. 123.
[33] *Ibid.*, pp. 86-87.   [34] Chapter IX, above.
[35] *Staatsraeson, op.cit.*, p. 171.

precisely because Frederick felt the overwhelming potency of the state's interest and was not content with rationalizations which attempted to belittle its significance or contrariwise to identify it with God's will. "If any man of the eighteenth century had the calling and the force to . . . impose upon *raison d'état* the goal and judgment of universal human reason [and morality] it was he. One can say that he devoted his entire life to this task."[36]

But it was Meinecke's conclusion that Frederick failed to achieve his objective. Frederick's early attacks on Machiavelli and his subsequent retractions, his conception of himself as the "first servant of his people," and his conviction of his own indispensability all testified to a personality in conflict with itself. This was indeed Meinecke's thesis when he asserted that Frederick's resolution to be a scoundrel in the name of the state (*soyons donc fourbes*) was taken in a mood of "profoundest contempt for the world which forced him to it."[37]

The two worlds of politics and morals lived together but remained apart in Frederick's personality. The philosopher condemned what the politician felt he had to do. " 'I hope,' " Frederick wrote, " 'that the future generations for whom I write will distinguish the philosopher from the prince in me, the decent human being from the politician. I must confess that it is very difficult to preserve one's decency and purity when one is caught up in the great political whirlpool of Europe. One sees oneself constantly in danger of being betrayed by one's allies, deserted by one's friends, overwhelmed by jealousy and envy, so that finally one . . . is forced to make the terrible decision either to sacrifice one's people or one's word.' "[38]

Frederick consciously decided to sacrifice the latter whenever the "welfare of the people" (as conceived by him) demanded it. "The statesman had primacy over the philosopher,"[39] and the

[36] *Ibid.*, p. 344.   [37] *Ibid.*, p. 377.

[38] *Ibid.* The quotation from Frederick is taken from the *Avant-propos* to his *Histoire de mon temps* (1743).

[39] *Ibid.*, p. 346. Cf. also p. 361.

· 241 ·

balance between politics and morals which Frederick struck within himself reflects with considerable accuracy the balance which Machiavelli had prescribed for all princes. But the difference between Frederick and Machiavelli was that "painful sensitivity to the conflict of *raison d'état* with morality and law." "In his rage and despair during his seven-year struggle for survival he once cried out: 'The only standard by which the citizen ought to judge the actions of politicians is according to their significance for the good of humanity in terms of public tranquillity, freedom and peace. When I start from this principle, all talk of power, force and greatness no longer moves me.'"[40]

It should be noted that Frederick spoke these words in a moment of despair rather than of triumph. Moreover, Meinecke observed that Frederick was not above expressing such sentiments for their public effect. But he also cited Frederick's many similar statements in contending that this lament was both characteristic and sincere. Thus Frederick remained for Meinecke the great archetype of the ruler who passionately desired to serve the humanitarian ideal but who was forced by inexorable necessity to follow the amoral dictates of *raison d'état*.[41]

In such a perspective, Frederick presented a dramatic example of the profundity and persistence of the challenge which Machiavelli had leveled at the European world. Meinecke refused to follow Ranke in attempting to explain away Machiavelli in terms of the corruptions of the period in which he lived. Ranke's most characteristic conception of Machiavelli was that of a bold thinker who sought the salvation of his fatherland and " 'in its desperate situation . . . was daring enough to prescribe poison.' "[42] It is true that Ranke was trying to rescue Machiavelli from those shallow critics who publicly attacked his teachings and covertly followed them or who had never felt

[40] *Ibid.*, p. 423. The quotation is from Frederick's *Lettre d'un Suisse à un Génois* (1759/1760). (*Oeuvres* 15, p. 143.)

[41] *Ibid.*, p. 424.

[42] *Ibid.*, pp. 473-474. Meinecke noted that in his late years Ranke became more critical of Machiavelli than was apparent in the historicising judgment which he made in 1824.

the pull of power. But Ranke was in rather shallow water himself in attempting to take the curse off Machiavelli by quarantining him in the Italy of the Renaissance.

Meinecke criticized Ranke for having gone too far in stressing the historicity of Machiavelli's doctrines. No less than Ranke, he believed that the path to both historical understanding and authentic moral judgment demanded that the individual and the institution be seen in their historical contexts. Meinecke agreed that Machiavelli's teachings were certainly designed for a specific time and purpose. But he argued that "their content . . . went far beyond the momentary purpose and confronted the reader, whether he approached the book in an historic or unhistoric manner, with the universal problem of *raison d'état* and particularly [with the problem] . . . of necessity in political conduct. His readers in earlier centuries, unschooled in historical thinking, were by no means so wrong in attributing such a universal significance and content to Machiavelli's observations."[43]

Ranke's reluctance to admit the timeless elements in Machiavelli's thought was part of his general tendency to see light rather than shadow in the power struggles of history. For this Meinecke was now ready to criticize Ranke in a way which had not been possible for him in the halcyon days of the prewar era. On occasion Ranke condemned the use of Machiavellian methods or often simply avoided judgment. Then again he had argued along Hegelian lines (and to this extent embraced Machiavellianism) that good results often had their origins in bad actions. Still again he rejected the doctrine of ends justifying means. And suspended above all these conflicting points of view was the proposition that power and morality were generally close allies: " 'You can name very few important wars which cannot be

---

[43] *Ibid.*, p. 474. Meinecke also stressed that Machiavelli's prescriptions were not restricted simply to princely states but applied to all forms of government, denying that there was any fundamental difference between the philosophy of the *Prince* and that animating the *Discourses*. Cf. *ibid.*, p. 54. Cf. also *Fuerst* Introduction, *op.cit.*, pp. 3 and 6.

shown to have resulted in the victory of true moral energy.' "[44]

We have already seen that Meinecke could not fully accept Ranke's optimism even before the war and even when he still thought that he ascertained a "gradual ascent" in the processes of power.[45] But in the light of the war experience he became understandably more sensitive to any tendencies to identify morality and success. Meinecke's critical attitude toward the war policies and peace aims of all the belligerents as well as his bitter feelings regarding Germany's defeat combined to render Ranke's almost trustful attitude toward power politics intolerable for him.

Ranke too saw history in terms of polarities, but his polar opposites in the final analysis were good and evil.[46] As such, they were absolutes; it was impossible to see a relative worth in each of the polar components. Hence there was an over-whelmingly strong tendency for the devout Christian and optimist in Ranke to see the triumphs of the good in each particular conflict. The more skeptical and disillusioned Meinecke could not adopt this view without conceding that the German defeat in 1918 might be due to the superior morality of the Allies. This he was obviously not prepared to do, despite all his criticisms of Imperial Germany.

There is no question that Meinecke's preferences and prejudices played an important role in the more somber view which he adopted toward world politics after 1918. Indeed, Meinecke admitted as much in the concluding paragraphs of his study of *raison d'état*. In reply to Benedetto Croce's restatement of the Ranke position (" 'Upon what other grounds is a war ever undertaken than to achieve a fuller, worthier, more exalted and powerful life? All of us, victors and vanquished, are experienc-

[44] *Ibid.*, pp. 474-480. The Ranke quotation is from his "Politisches Gespraech" (1836).

[45] Chapter v, above.

[46] Thus Ranke referred to the supreme conflict of history as one between Ormudz and Ahriman, the Persian gods of good and evil. Cf. *Staatsraeson, op.cit.*, p. 478.

ing a richer spiritual life than ever we did before the war.' ") Meinecke answered that "We, the vanquished, are supremely aware of the truth of this assertion, but with a sense of profound inner turmoil. We also perceive more clearly than do . . . the victors, however, the terrible antinomy between the ideals of moral reason and the actual processes and causal relationships of history. [Just] because we stand nearer to the abyss than they, we can perhaps see more clearly the danger of this specific moment of history, namely, that the curse of war and power politics threatens to overwhelm the blessings they are capable of bringing."[47]

With these words Meinecke both avoided and transcended the issue of which side had displayed the superior moral energy in the war. What is important to note is that he was willing to concede that political disaster for Germany did not necessarily mean spiritual disaster. The position which he had taken long ago—the refusal to posit an absolute identity between state and culture[48]—now served him in good stead and enabled him to look upon German powerlessness with a degree of objectivity. And, as we have contended earlier, the degree was considerably greater than most of his colleagues were able to achieve.

Above all, it was the special quality of Meinecke's dualistic philosophy which gave him a sense of stability in the postwar chaos of German political life. Unlike Ranke's polar conflict between the absolutes of good and evil, the polarities with which Meinecke operated employed concepts of relative value. At the antipodes of "state" and "nation" stood "individual" and "humanity." In prewar times and during the war Meinecke's position that both elements in these polar relationships had positive and negative connotations spurred him to criticism of the existing regime and immunized him to the extremes of nationalism. Whatever his emphases and leanings, he was never prepared consciously to absolutize any of the values in his polarities. State,

[47] *Ibid.*, pp. 540-541.
[48] Chapter VI, above. Cf. Also *Erhebung, op.cit.*, pp. 8-11.

nationalism, authority—none of them could be meaningful or acceptable except in terms of the individual, of cosmopolitanism, of liberty. So now after the destruction of Germany's power Meinecke could find consolation in the hope that those individualist and cosmopolitan values which had suffered from neglect would better flourish. Thus Meinecke progressively freed himself from the Rankian tendency to assert the consistent triumph of one of the polar elements as a means of retaining faith in the meaning and justice of history.

Consequently Meinecke broke with Ranke at two levels. At the level of theory he criticized Ranke for superimposing on his dualistic thesis of eternal conflict between good and evil a monistic assumption that the victories would always go to the good.[49] This criticism was clearly self-criticism, as Meinecke had often come close to destroying any true dualism in the polarities he constructed precisely because of his earlier tendency to assign all the important victories to one side only. At the level of substantive issues, Meinecke also broke with Ranke and refused to accept his "optimistic, not to say sunny, conception of the power problem and of the pitfalls of *raison d'état*."[50] This, too, was self-criticism in part.

The whole range of Meinecke's political thought was involved in the reappraisal and revisions to which he was subjecting his earlier ideas. But the framework in which he set his reconsiderations made it apparent that he was most concerned with all the problems revolving around sovereignty and the use of force in international politics. Reserving a fuller discussion until later, we should note here that this focus served to perpetuate what we have argued was Meinecke's overemphasis on the role of foreign policy in the life of states.

In any case, one can agree with Meinecke that *raison d'état* and international law and order were natural competitors. "International law," Meinecke observed, "seeks to narrow the sphere of *raison d'état* and to impose upon it as much of the impress

---

[49] *Staatsraeson, op.cit.*, p. 478.
[50] *Ibid.*

of law as possible. But *raison d'état* sets up resistances and very often uses, or rather, misuses, law as a means to its own egotistic ends. In this way it continually undermines the foundations in the building of which international law spends so much effort."[51]

The evidence which Meinecke marshalled to support this contention was overwhelming. It took the form primarily of a recitation of all the rationalizations which men found to justify the breaking of international agreements. Perhaps nothing else symbolized so forcefully the lack of trust and consequently of community beyond the confines of the state. As Meinecke probed the thoughts of Bodin, Botero, Boccalini, Spinoza, Hobbes, Pufendorf, Frederick, Fichte, even Goethe, the egotism of *raison d'état* sounded a defiant refrain. All had to adhere, willingly or unwillingly, openly or covertly, to Machiavelli's thesis that neither the pledged word nor treaty obligations need be honored if the safety of the state demands otherwise.[52]

As we saw, Bodin, who had reduced his loopholes for treaty breakers to an absolute minimum, asserted that good faith was the basis of all justice and community. It was precisely the absence of good faith in relations among states that made justice and a sense of duty and community almost impossible to achieve. All these values, as well as formal international law itself, were being constantly corroded by the exigencies of *raison d'état*.

Meinecke had long held to a position in common with Hegel

[51] *Ibid.*, p. 260. Meinecke's discussion here is part of his brief critique of Grotius. Meinecke cited Grotius' statement that he did not intend to consider the problem of expediency in his treatment of law as evidence of Grotius' inability to deal with the challenge of *raison d'état* and of the consequent unreality of his legal structure (pp. 260-261).

[52] Cf. *ibid.*, pp. 79, 85, 95, 265, 272-273, 287, 371-373, 462-463. Meinecke cited Goethe's reflections on the problem of Polish partition: "'I consider myself a little above the ordinary platitudes of moralizing politicians. I shall say it openly: no king honors his word. He cannot do so: he must always bow to the commands of circumstance. . . . For us poor Philistines the opposite kind of conduct is a duty; not so for the mighty of this earth.'" (*Goethes Unterhaltungen mit dem Kanzler F. von Mueller*, 3rd edition, p. 191.)

[53] *Ibid.*, p. 19.

that law could not be imposed upon the states because there was no magistrate to act as law-giver and arbiter. "Why," he now asked, "cannot the states themselves, in the light of their own properly understood interests and in concert with ethical motivations, reach voluntary agreement to circumscribe the methods of power politics, to observe law and morality, and to develop the institutions of international law and the League of Nations to full and satisfactory effectiveness? The answer is that no state trusts the other. Each state is deeply convinced that the other will not observe the agreed rules in all cases and without exception but will under certain circumstances surely be guided by its natural egotism. And the first dereliction . . . would cause the undertaking to collapse and would destroy the credit of an ethical system of politics. . . . [All the other states] would feel entitled to claim dispensation from the norms of morality in accord with the proposition *à corsaire corsaire et demi*—and the old, old game would begin anew."[53]

À corsaire corsaire et demi—this had been Meinecke's response at the height of the wartime struggle with Britain's naval power. Could this phrase, born of the extremities of enmity and war, serve as the basic rule of the game of international politics? The abstract and ineffectual barriers which Meinecke erected against the state ego in the prewar years indicated that he might then have been content to answer in the affirmative. Now, however, he had called for concrete restraints: "The burning necessity of the time demands . . . those curbs on *raison d'état* that have been so vainly sought throughout the centuries."[54]

Meinecke's skepticism toward the League of Nations has already been remarked. Yet he returned to the League once more to suggest that it constituted an authentic expression of the "burning necessity." Could it also serve as an effective response to that necessity? Here Meinecke modified his skepticism, but only to the point of conceding that the League could function

[53] *Ibid.*, p. 19. [54] *Ibid.*, p. 541.

as "an approach to an unattainable ideal." One must not expect a great deal from the League, for "The natural forces of history will see to it that peace on earth will not so soon come about. . . ." But in representing the idea of the rejection of power politics, the League was perhaps a necessary antithesis to the idea of *raison d'état*. It could help to drive home the admonition that "there is no warrant for buttressing [the natural forces of history] by a doctrine which glorifies power struggles and war and thus only serves to assure that statesmen will be driven to the uses of Machiavellianism."[55]

It is clear, however, that Meinecke could not and did not regard the League as the most effective answer to the quest for restraints on power politics. As the whole spirit and substance of *Staatsraeson* testifies, he was seeking out the basis for the necessary controls on state egotism in the concept of *raison d'état* itself. Consequently, it becomes necessary at this point to attempt a summation of the meaning which Meinecke gave to the concept.

First of all, it should be recalled that Meinecke did not conceive of political activity and its expression in the state as naked ego. He sifted the evidence provided by four centuries of European political thought not simply to document the omnipresence of self-interest in political action. His ardent wish to see the state become a symbiosis of power and culture spurred him to seek at the same time for evidence of ethical and other non-power motivations. In essence, therefore, the objective of his endeavors was precisely the same in the postwar as in the prewar years—to discover the path to a political system in which power and spirit could live harmoniously together. The difference was that Meinecke felt he had been too facile in positing such a harmony in *Weltbuergertum* and his other prewar writings. As a result, he attempted in *Staatsraeson* to face every conceivable difficulty in the way of a satisfactory and creative balance between power and spirit.

Thus while he was willing to stress the idealism of Machia-

[55] *Ibid.*

velli's passionate concern for the regeneration of Italy and of corrupted peoples generally,[56] Meinecke's final judgment was that the ruthless methods of unadorned Machiavellianism would inevitably destroy the ideal they might be intended to serve. His verdict on Hegel was the same. He did not contest Hegel's sincerity when the latter asserted that national culture and not national power was the supreme purpose of the state. But Hegel's explanation of evil as the cunning of reason, his equation of the real to the right, was fatally injurious to his supreme goal. "This kind of theodicy and this uncommon optimism . . . carried with it the grave danger that moral sensibilities might be dulled and the excesses of power politics etherealized."[57] On the other hand, when dealing with those thinkers like Bodin who refused to sanction power politics in the name of high ideals and who sought to build political structures without the aid of *raison d'état*, it was Meinecke's purpose to expose the glint of power and self-interest shining darkly through the network of legal and moral relationships.

In this context it is understandable that Meinecke should find it a particularly intriguing task to investigate the relations of power considerations and moral ideas in a ruler like Frederick the Great. Frederick's attempt to sacrifice his personal ego to the welfare of the state simply succeeded in vastly enlarging the sphere of operations of the personal ego: "Thus the spirit of stern and pure *raison d'état* came to govern him—certainly not in the sense of the abstract and impersonal expertise of a technician . . . but imbued and fused with the will to life of a proud personality who recognized in this task [of governing] the foreordained way of life for himself and the opportunity to realize values which were in fact supremely personal."[58]

But all the ironies of power could not efface the reality that

[56] *Ibid.*, pp. 52-55, and *Fuerst* Introduction, *op.cit.*, pp. 8, 14.

[57] *Staatsraeson, op.cit.*, pp. 457-459. Cf. pp. 467-468 for a similar assessment of Fichte's thought.

[58] *Ibid.*, p. 351. Meinecke cites Frederick's resolve to *gouverner par lui-même* as one of the many ironies which attended Frederick's devotion to the state. Cf. p. 363.

power considerations and moral achievements were often rooted together. Indeed, as has been suggested in the previous chapter, this was perhaps the final irony. The ruler who heeded Machiavelli's advice that self-interest required respect for long-established laws and customs was clearly strengthening the norms of moderation and tolerance, whatever his intent.[59] *Raison d'état* had in fact been a mighty force promoting religious tolerance in the emerging nation-state of the seventeenth century. At the same time it served as the agent of change, breaking down medieval privileges in the name of centralized and more rational political and economic organization.[60] Foreign wars could and did bring unity and peace at home; absolute monarchs brought the curse of feudal and civil war under control.[61] And we have seen how often Meinecke was able to link power requirements abroad with internal reform and liberalization of the state.

Thus in reverting to the example of Frederick once more, Meinecke's readiness to concede the role of ego in Frederick's political ideals was matched by his insistence that the discipline to which Frederick subjected himself was a moral achievement of very considerable proportions. Frederick's famous directive which forbade his ministers or family to ransom him with money or by any sacrifice of Prussian interests should he be taken prisoner of war was a dramatic expression of his disregard of self.[62]

This subordination of the person of the ruler to the welfare of the state was the very foundation of *raison d'état*. Frederick's

[59] *Ibid.*, p. 55. Meinecke quoted Machiavelli's warning that "Princes should realize that they begin to lose the state the moment they begin to violate laws, institutions and customs under which people have lived for a long time." (*Discourses* III, 5.)

[60] *Staatsraeson, op.cit.*, pp. 159-160.

[61] "Since the feudal and class obstinacy of the nobility was broken, the internal life of states and peoples throughout the larger part of the Continent was calmer and more orderly than ever. . . . Absolutism was nearly at its zenith, and it could trace [its strength] in very considerable measure to the mighty power struggles abroad which diverted and absorbed the surplus energies and ambitions of the nobles." (*Ibid.*, p. 310.)

[62] *Ibid.*, p. 352.

resolve to be the "first servant of his people" and to "regard his subjects not only as his peers but in certain respects as his masters"[63] symbolized the natural community of interest between rulers and ruled. "People allow themselves to be ruled because they receive compensations in return. At the same time their own latent will to life and power nourishes that of the ruler. Rulers and ruled thus become joined by a common bond—the basic human need for community. Once power is gained over a people . . . it must be organized. As power is organized it becomes an autonomous entity, a super-individual thing which one must . . . tend and serve. And he who has sought and striven for it is first in line of service. The ruler is transformed into the servant of his own power. The objectives of power begin to restrict personal caprice, and the hour of *raison d'état* has struck."[64]

From this point, *raison d'état* must develop still further. It had been a central thesis of Meinecke's prewar thought that the ethical and cultural values which the state embodied are the final justification of the egotism which the state displays in attending to its security and its power, particularly in the realm of foreign affairs.[65] For this reason the character of Frederick was doubly congenial to Meinecke, for Frederick's ideal was "not simply a powerful state but a state of high culture (*Kulturstaat*) as well."[66] Thus the Prussian king could again serve as model for one of the series of generalizations with which Meinecke built his concept of *raison d'état*. The ruler "serves a higher object which towers far above the individual life; no longer does one serve himself alone. This is the decisive juncture where a crystallization of higher forms commences. This is the moment where that which was at first regarded merely as necessary and expedient begins to be perceived also as something beautiful and good. The state emerges as a moral institution for the fur-

---

[63] *Ibid.*, p. 350. Meinecke's paraphrase of statements from Frederick's *Refutation.* (*Oeuvres*, 8, pp. 168 and 218.)

[64] *Ibid.*, p. 12.

[65] Chapter IV, above.   [66] *Staatsraeson, op.cit.*, p. 353.

therance of the highest goals of life. . . . In imperceptible transitions the *raison d'état* of the rulers is thus refined and ennobled and becomes a connecting link between *kratos* and *ethos.*"[67]

As we have seen, however, Meinecke was profoundly disturbed by the wartime corruption of the belligerent states as cultural and ethical personalities. Hence the whole thesis that state egotism is justified by the values it serves was brought into question. The war experience suggested an antithesis which Meinecke felt obliged to consider but was reluctant to embrace: the power struggles of the state are destroying the ethical and cultural values that are the state's ultimate justification. His response was to seek a synthesis which necessarily had to go beyond a mere verification of the presence of non-power values built into and to a certain extent dependent on the power organization of the state.

Here Frederick could no longer serve as a model on which to build but only as a caveat against the assumption that the presence of moral ends justifies immoral means or guarantees that the immoral means will be held in check. Indeed, if Frederick's own ego was given freer reign in the kind of state he envisioned, so was the ego of the state itself presented with new realms to conquer. Frederick's subordination of dynastic concerns to the humanitarian goal of making his people's happiness the chief aim of the state "did indeed establish a link between the old power-state and the universal humanitarianism . . . of the Enlightenment. But it also sharpened up the weapons of the power state in that it scraped away the rust of . . . non-utilitarian personal-dynastic considerations. Furthermore, while it imposed upon the power-holder new and more rigorous duties toward the state as a whole, for this very reason it strengthened his belief in his good right to use the instruments of power, to draw the sword, to utilize all the large and small tricks of statecraft."[68]

Here was evidence enough that the state's relation to cultural and ethical values is at best an ambivalent one. In view of

[67] *Ibid.*, p. 13.
[68] *Staatsraeson, op.cit.*, pp. 352-355.

this ambivalence, all optimism in regard to the political process and the workings of *raison d'état* is out of place.[69] If the statesman can make an authentic claim to be serving cultural and moral values, he must also recognize that in the course of his service he will also inevitably subordinate and damage such values. What should guide the statesman who finds himself in this unstable polarity of power and ethic? At one level Meinecke could only answer that *raison d'état* must continue to be the statesman's guide, but "a purified and truly wise *raison d'état*."[70]

It was Meinecke's contention that only when *raison d'état* transcends the stage of mere power deliberations and embraces "some kind of spiritual and moral values . . . [can it] realize its highest potential."[71] One of the moral values which he intended *raison d'état* to embrace was clearly an understanding of its own fallibility and limitations: "This and nothing else is the result we have arrived at after having followed the problem of *raison d'état* through the centuries—to recognize the natural [forces] as given, to be conscious of the dark substructure which they represent but to build onto it those [higher] forms which the autonomous spirit of man . . . demands; to understand that the natural forces will again and again rise up and destroy the works of culture but at the same time to realize that the process will provide ever new revelations of the world of the spirit."[72]

The incompleteness and fragility of man's works, the ambiguity of his values, and the subjectivity of his reasoning— these were the truths which *raison d'état* must incorporate. Such a *raison d'état* could not be reconciled with the ethereal character which so much of nineteenth-century German thought had conferred upon it. Hence Meinecke's reexamination of those thinkers who had contributed so powerfully to his own prewar

---

[69] In his treatment of Grotius, Meinecke observed that there was precious little compatibility between the "theory and practice of *raison d'état* and . . . the optimistic notions which Grotius . . . entertained of the nature of men and states." (*Ibid.*, p. 263.)

[70] *Ibid.*, p. 537.   [71] *Ibid.*, p. 269.

[72] *Ibid.*, pp. 521-522.

thought-structure—Fichte, Hegel, Ranke—went beyond criticism to outright refutation.

Fichte had attempted to justify the ruler who followed the precepts of *raison d'état* by clothing him in a higher morality different from the moral norms applicable to the private individual. As Meinecke noted, such a proposition resembled Frederick's doctrine that the prince, as an agent of his people, could break his word with impunity if the welfare of his people demanded it.[73] The moral law of self-sacrifice to the principle of truth and good faith to which the individual was subject would not apply to the ruler. For if the ruler observed the law, he risked sacrificing not only himself but his people as well.

On this basis Fichte made his case for the theory that the ruler practiced a higher morality. Meinecke was unwilling that the ruler should have such scope. He was too conscious of the ease with which personal motives of the ruler or the special interests of particular groups could usurp the state's interest. "The state's advantage is . . . always somehow related to advantages for the rulers."[74] How distinguish with accuracy the extent to which personal or other sub-state interests determine a particular action in the name of the state?[75]

With this question Meinecke exploded the whole theory in which he had invoked the concept of *salus populi* to justify the free play of state ego. The *salus populi* was an elusive commodity; only too often "the state served not the general welfare but the welfare of the rulers."[76] Concede the ruling groups a higher morality and there could be no appeal when they misused the power of the state for their own purposes. Hence Meinecke insisted that the state must not be regarded as practicing a higher morality. Rather, it must be seen from the point of view of a general system of ethics in which every human institu-

---

[73] *Ibid.*, pp. 383-384, 465-466. Spinoza also adhered to this point of view. Cf. pp. 272-273.

[74] *Ibid.*, p. 9.

[75] Cf. *Ibid.*, pp. 8, 12-13. Cf. also *Nach der Revolution, op.cit.*, pp. 19-24, for an analysis of the social structure of the Prussian state.

[76] *Staatsraeson, op.cit.*, p. 429.

tion and individual human being is granted a moral right to behavior which will secure its own well-being, if such behavior
also "redeems the spiritual component in it."[77]

Such an ethic at least succeeds in bringing the state down to
a level where its claim to special dispensation is no better than
that of other human institutions. In this perspective the needs
of the state cannot be deemed automatically to override other
needs and values. One is compelled to subject the acts of the
state to a skeptical appraisal wholly foreign to a philosophy
which exalted the state into an ethical realm transcending that
of ordinary mortals.

On the other hand, there was still no way of passing definitive
moral judgment on acts of state. Indeed, the contention that the
ethics of the state and the ethics of non-state organizations or
individuals are but different expressions of the principle of individuality could lead to a moral chaos in which all sense of a
hierarchy of norms was destroyed, in which every human action
could be excused on the grounds that it conformed to an ethic
peculiar to the individual or institutional actor.

This relativistic result was obviously unconducive to the establishment of effective restraints on power politics. The Hegelian
system could only be even less effectual. Hegel's identification
of the real with the rational and the rational with the right promoted a relativism of moral values not on the basis that each
actor had his own unique ethic but that all the world's actors
were but instruments for the realization of the world spirit. With
this thesis Hegel posited a determinism which had no place for
moral choice or moral judgment. How could any individual or
institution be held accountable for acts which were but expressions of the will of the world spirit? "All, all serves the progressive self-realization of divine reason whose cunning it is to
employ evil itself . . . for its own purposes."[78]

A philosophical system which fused reality and norm, which
settled the general conflict of "is" and "ought" in human con-

[77] *Ibid.*, pp. 533-535.
[78] *Ibid.*, pp. 434-435.

duct by eliminating it, had no trouble in solving the specific problem of Machiavellianism in political action. It merely denied that the doctrines of Machiavelli were in any way incompatible with the realization of moral values. On the contrary, the ubiquity of Machiavellian practices in the conduct of states only stressed their necessity. "Machiavellianism, which had previously simply existed alongside the [various] moral cosmologies which men constructed, was now organically united to an idealistic philosophy of life which embraced and affirmed all the moral values." Wryly, Meinecke observed that "What happened here was almost like the legitimization of a bastard."[79]

In his extensive treatment of Hegel in *Staatsraeson*, Meinecke paid tribute to the insights which the Hegelian philosophy achieved and in general permitted the eloquent shortcomings to speak for themselves. Finally, he dismissed it with the observation that as a "body of integrated doctrine it could not long endure."[80] But later he found the opportunity to state his position in highly polemical terms which left no doubt as to the emphatic nature of his distaste for Hegelian concepts. In *Staatsraeson* he had cited with approval Ranke's position that it was "a dangerous undertaking to postulate that 'one may be justified in doing wrong to another in the name of a world historical mission.' " For this he was attacked by a neo-Hegelian philosopher who asserted that Meinecke was backsliding into an outmoded dualistic ethic and who countered with the familiar thesis that "the state, . . . as the historical and legal expression of the nation, is a moral being; 'all that it undertakes in order to preserve itself and the nation is morally justified . . . before the judgment seat of history and reason.' "[81]

"This," Meinecke responded, "is what transcending obsolete dualism looks like. I call it a debauching of historical reality. The state is not and never was an exclusively moral being; . . .

[79] *Ibid.*, p. 435.   [80] *Ibid.*, p. 458.
[81] Review of Julius Binder's *Staatsraison und Sittlichkeit* (Berlin, 1929) in *HZ*, 140, 1929, p. 566. The passage in single quotation marks is from Binder's text.

it has an elemental and material basis which again and again betrays all attempts to refine [its nature]. In the light of this recognition all high-flying identity-philosophy leaves me unmoved. Certainly there are situations where the statesman may feel morally justified when he transgresses the limits of morality in order to realize the historic mission of his state. Nevertheless there is always a conflict of duties in any such action. Hegelian doctrines may soothe some few with the belief that such a conflict does not exist. But the natural moral sensibilities of most people will not be lulled by their dialectics. [Every] more discriminating judgment will regard a violation of universal moral law by the statesman acting in the name of state necessity as a decision between two colliding ethical duties, as a tragic and tragically guilty undertaking."[82]

Thus Meinecke stood with Ranke in refusing to identify reality with morality. But we have already seen that Ranke's final position was also unsatisfactory to him. Ranke declined to sanction self-interest and power considerations as expressions of divine will, but in the outcomes of individual power struggles in history he tended to see God's will for good prevailing. Thus, as we have already observed, a kind of monistic identity philosophy over-arched Ranke's original separation of norm and reality. "It is clear," Meinecke observed, "that this concealed and unstable dualism could not be the ultimate solution of the problem."[83]

There were two fundamental recognitions which Meinecke deemed necessary in order that the full significance of *raison d'état* be understood. The first was that conduct in accordance with *raison d'état* would never be able to escape guilt. The second was that political imperatives must be given their due: "There are situations which cannot be solved without guilt, but they must be solved."[84] Thus he demanded acknowledg-

---

[82] *Ibid.*   [83] *Staatsraeson, op.cit.,* p. 487.

[84] This formulation was used by Meinecke at a much later date than we are here discussing, but it is typical of earlier propositions. It is taken from the author's notes on seminar discussions which Meinecke con-

ment that *raison d'état* could never be perfectly moral, and he rejected any philosophy which failed to incorporate this recognition.

The imperfections of human understanding and conduct upon whose acknowledgment Meinecke insisted were to be found not only in the realm of morality. Man's reason, too, was incomplete and unreliable. Any conceptualization of *raison d'état* which failed to take this into account was bound to lead the statesman astray. Meinecke assembled data in abundance to support his thesis. Again and again history demonstrated how passion beclouds judgment and even deceives men as to their own motives. Campanella denounced Machiavelli at the same time as he practiced his doctrines and in such a way that confusion rather than hypocrisy seemed to be the dominant note.[85] We have already seen how subtly Frederick's ego and prejudices could insinuate themselves into what he supposed were wholly rational calculations.

The shortcomings of human reason are most apparent in those situations where men are most anxious that it should be flawless. Here Meinecke pointed to prewar policies of Imperial Germany as outstanding examples. Buelow and Holstein, he observed, wanted to act in accordance with unadulterated *raison d'état*. But they were so convinced of the rationality of a continuing conflict between British and Russian interests that they did not foresee the possibilities of an alliance. He traced their failure to a theoretical kind of reasoning which could "dominate the thoughts of those who considered themselves cool-headed realists unencumbered by doctrines—but whose own realism became doctrinaire."[86] The fleet-building program "was a further

---

ducted and which the author attended during 1948 and 1949. The present statement was made in connection with an examination of the ideas of the nineteenth-century German historian Vischer on January 8, 1949.

[85] *Staatsraeson, op.cit.*, pp. 128-129.

[86] *Geschichte des deutsch-englischen Buendnisproblems*, Munich, 1927, p. 264. Hereafter cited as *Buendnisproblem*. Meinecke also made the point in *Staatsraeson, op.cit.*, p. 401, footnote 1.

instance of a false power politics which made still another doctrine out of a crude concept of power." And Bismarck's considerations concerning German interest in the continued existence of Austria-Hungary were allowed "to rigidify into a dogma which refused to see the pathological symptoms of the Habsburg state."[87]

It was Frederick, however, who again provided Meinecke with his most dramatic example. Frederick's objective was to calculate political activity in terms of state interest unobscured by other considerations. It was on this basis that he postulated an "eternal" hostility between France and Austria because the former's richest conquests had been the latter's provinces, and because it was in the French interest to support Prussia as a rival to Austria in Germany. Consequently, he felt safe in signing the Convention of Westminster with France's British enemy. But while French interest might have required another course, French anger at Frederick's presumptuousness touched off the diplomatic revolution in which France allied itself to Austria. "Passions triumphed over interest . . . it was the shipwreck of political rationalism which Machiavelli had originated and which now had become too sure of itself in the atmosphere of the Enlightenment. As soon as the theory of the interests of state became a doctrine it was in danger of overestimating the rational in politics and underestimating the irrational. The necessity of continuous consideration of both was in fact its peculiar task and difficulty. Inherent in this polarity was its tragedy. Required to achieve the highest degree of exactitude, the striving itself could cause error."[88]

The problematic nature of human rationality gave Meinecke still other grounds on which to press his criticism of Hegel. Returning to his rebuttal of Binder, we find him insisting that "The 'judgment seat of history and reason' which allegedly absolves [the statesman] . . . is a very precarious and insecure tribunal that judges very differently at different times and places. I do

[87] *Ibid.*   [88] *Staatsraeson, op.cit.*, pp. 397-401.

not mean, of course, to deny that the statesman must feel himself responsible before history and reason—but it is in his own conscience that this dialogue with history and reason takes place. And however hard he should and must endeavor to discover their objective verdict, he still cannot free himself from the fetters of his own subjectivity."[89]

Here Meinecke made it abundantly clear that there was no room in his concept of *raison d'état* for the *homo politicus* whose actions could be calculated in terms of pure self-interest and power considerations. *Raison d'état* could never be wholly rational. In this perspective it is ironic but not surprising that Meinecke himself yielded on occasion to *homo politicus* reasoning. His contention that the Anglo-American victors of the First World War would "under no circumstances jettison their enormous power in the name of good will and sentiment"[90] was an object lesson in the errors inherent in too "realistic" a reckoning.

Meinecke's own derelictions do not detract from the sincerity of his quest for a *raison d'état* that would reckon with human ambiguities and subjectivities. He meant *raison d'état* to be a guide to practical action in a world in which the essential subjectivity of every individual always prevents perfect objectivity. He would hardly make the claim that his own subjectivity was always under control.

Human passion must be reckoned into the political equation. After his bitter experience in the Seven Years War, Frederick the Great learned—or as Meinecke contended, relearned—this lesson. Thus Meinecke could cite Frederick's reflections in his *Political Testament of 1768*: " 'A frequently deceptive art of conjecture serves as the basis for most political designs. One

[89] Review of Binder's *Staatsraeson und Sittlichkeit, HZ, op.cit.*, pp. 566-567.

[90] *Supra*, p. 210. Meinecke later conceded that this early postwar judgment was in error and asserted that an "Anglo-Saxon diarchy" would develop only slowly. Also, he later felt that an Anglo-American hegemony would be preferable to the chaotic state of world affairs which prevailed in its stead. Cf. "Geschichtliche Betrachtungen zur Weltlage," *Deutsche Allgemeine Zeitung*, April 12, 1922.

uses the most reliable knowledge available as a starting point, proceeds to combine it with things which are only incompletely known, and then makes the most accurate conclusions possible. . . . I shall give an example. Russia desires to win over the Danish King. It promises him Holstein-Gottorp . . . and hopes thus to gain his eternal allegiance. But the King of Denmark is frivolous. How can one foresee all the things which will get into his young head? The favorites, the mistresses and ministers who will dominate his spirit and who will offer him advantages from another power which appear to him greater than those which Russia offers—will they not bring him to reverse himself? A similar uncertainty, though each time in a different form, prevails in all the operations of foreign policy, so that in great alliances the result is often the opposite from what was planned.' "[91]

But Meinecke's concern with the role of passion and subjective bias in political action went far beyond a simple exhortation to calculate the irrational as well as the rational. He did not deal with the irrational merely as something to be cancelled out by dint of more subtle rationality. We saw earlier that Meinecke refused to treat diversity as simply a necessary evil and instead regarded it as a value in itself. So now did he appraise irrationality. *Raison d'état* demanded a high degree of detachment; it demanded that the statesman display "coolness and rationality in his endeavor to identify the interests of the state and free himself from all emotional superfluities. . . . But the elimination of emotional motivations cannot and ought not to be complete, precisely because an elemental impulse to power must reside within the statesman himself. . . . Without it he could ill perform his task."[92]

The profundity of Meinecke's conviction on this score is illustrated by his use of precisely the same polarity of subjective and objective knowledge in his reflections on the writing of history. Agreeing that the law of pure science applies to the political historian, Meinecke conceded that "he can achieve the

---

[91] Quoted in *Staatsraeson, op.cit.*, pp. 402-403.
[92] *Ibid.*, pp. 7-8.

highest goals of his own profession only if he does not allow the mirror of his contemplation to be clouded by the preferences of practical politics. In Ranke's words, he knows . . . that he ought to 'erase his own personality.' Yet he cannot succeed. Indeed, he dare not even wish for complete success because he would thereby be deprived of a source of understanding. Here one sees one of the profound antinomies that run through our lives. Only by living the things one wishes to understand can one grasp their essence. But living them necessarily means living them with purpose. Without such participation by the total personality, the world of action and particularly the world of political action cannot be mastered intellectually and brought into scientific form. No political history of stature and significance has ever been written without a certain element of will and desire on the part of the historian. It is the function of the law of pure contemplation to hold this element of will within limits and to prevent it from dominating. But no conceptual theory can prescribe where and how these limits are to be drawn; tact and self-discipline are the only answers here."[93]

These words were a central part of the credo of historicism which Meinecke was later to develop into *Die Entstehung des Historismus*, his final major work. At the same time they demonstrated why he was so concerned with the relationship of politics and history as to have planned a history of this relationship before the idea of *raison d'état* became supremely important to him. Most important for our purposes, they presented in unmistakable language the thesis that the irrational was not only inevitable but also necessary in any wise conception of life or of *raison d'état*.

Indeed, only by virtue of the irrational can *raison d'état* achieve its fullest flowering. It can "gain an ethical content if it embraces the spiritual-moral welfare of a . . . people. But that

[93] *Vom geschichtlichen Sinn, op.cit.*, pp. 23-24. This quotation is taken from "Ranke's Politisches Gespraech," which, it should be noted, was first published in 1924 and was therefore written at approximately the same time that *Staatsraeson* was being completed.

is not possible without the infusion of new motives, without the presence of warmer and deeper stirrings of the heart, without an inner élan." Or again: "That which is merely expedient, which is simply egotism, be it ever so rational and well-understood, is not adequate to serve as an enduring bond for the great human associations. Some sort of sense for transcendant moral and spiritual values must enter the theory and practice of *raison d'état* if it is to attain its supreme expression."[94]

We need only recall the theses which Meinecke advanced long before the war in order to understand that in the duality of rationality and irrationality we have another of those underlying continuities which spanned and united Meinecke's prewar and postwar thought. He had described the men of the Prussian Reform as often thinking beyond the confines of the real state and "soaring beyond the real and the possible. As the liberators of their country they . . . did not practice a policy of pure realism. But it was nonetheless a policy which finally achieved far greater results than one could expect from a *Realpolitik* which contented itself only with the possible."[95]

Meinecke did not intend that these words should constitute a case against realism in politics. On the contrary, they were written at the time when he was developing his powerful case for political realism in *Weltbuergertum und Nationalstaat.*[96] Yet they expressed the undeniable paradox we noted earlier—that the men of the Reform who did most to revivify the Prussian state were also the most ready to sacrifice it to the universal values of humanity and freedom.[97] Precisely the same paradox persisted in Meinecke's conceptualization of *raison d'état.* Not only did *raison d'état* require a unique combination of cool realism and hot desire but also a warm idealism whose inspiration lay beyond *raison d'état.*

From what has been said so far, it should be evident that Mei-

[94] *Staatsraeson, op.cit.,* pp. 8 and 269.
[95] *Erhebung, op.cit.,* p. 187. Cf. also *Boyen,* II, *op.cit.,* p. 594.
[96] In the summer of 1905. Cf. *Erinnerungen, op.cit.,* pp. 40-42 and 44.
[97] Chapter IV, above.

necke's basic theoretical proposition is that politics is more than the art of the possible. All the subjective values, the selfish biases, the moral fervor which he declared to be inevitable, necessary, and desirable components of *raison d'état* clearly ruled out the feasibility of a policy perfectly adjusted to the possible. The coexistence within a single matrix of rational and irrational, good and bad, refuted all contentions that human beings could create political systems with rationality or morality guaranteed.

Hence *raison d'état* was a guide to both practical and moral action in a world devoid of perfect objectivity or perfect altruism. It was geared to the possible in that it recognized the limitations under which it operated and tried to adjust for these limitations. Its premise was that human values were created and maintained only in the form of concrete individualities which were inevitably and eternally earth-bound. Thus one could not expect it to derive ethical norms from the environment wherein it operated which could claim greater intrinsic validity than the norms of its own individual form: "the best state . . . is not a realization of universally valid principles but the highest and fullest realization of the life-principle of the particular individuality."[98]

Still, the reliance on the individual ethic, as we have noted before, threatened to leave the statesman with a chaos of contending rights and to lead him into a relativism which could provide no effective restraints on *raison d'état* other than that of power and countervailing power. This kind of restraint was necessary but not sufficient. Therefore *raison d'état* must bear within it a sense of its own incompleteness. As a rational concept it must concede its own fallibility and as a moral concept its own relativity. The insight that one could not order all life

---

[98] *Staatsraeson, op.cit.,* p. 278. A striking parallel to this position in the realm of general philosophy will be found in *Schiller und der Individualitaetsgedanke,* Berlin, 1937, p. 1: In a letter of Schiller's (January 4, 1796) Humboldt is quoted as saying that " 'the education of the individual consists not simply in the vague endeavor to reach an absolute and universal ideal but rather in the purest possible representation and development of his individuality.' "

in terms of the norms of *raison d'état*, that one must leave room for those areas of life beyond its ken, was the surest warranty of self-restraint. And Meinecke, as we have seen, found the most effective symbol of these limitations in his admonition to the statesman to carry both God and the state in his heart.

These words enjoined the statesman to seek norms for his conduct which were exterior to the state. He must not restrict himself to asking what is possible for the state's peculiar, earthbound individuality. He must ask what the moral law requires, he "must seek a unifying bond for his divided sense of responsibility to the state and to the moral law." He must not expect too much of the state, and so he must attempt to adjust the dictates of the universal moral law to the individual ethic of the state, to reconcile the desirable with the possible. But the statesman must not permit the state to expect too much of him, either. The individual ethic of the state "which seeks to assert itself alongside the universal [ethic] . . . is never a pure ethic but always bound in essence to egotistic and natural components—to the need for power."[99] Thus *raison d'éat*, which in its highest form expresses this ethic, is one of the "too many things in which God and the devil are joined together."[100]

Raison d'état, the *salus populi*, the welfare of the state, cannot be the statesman's only referent. If his service to the state is "at the cost of the universal moral law, as so often happens, then [he has incurred] a tragic guilt . . . which must be judged in strict accordance with the moral law."[101] But how much guilt could a statesman take upon himself? Meinecke suggested that the answer lay within the personality of the statesman himself: "The way in which the statesman personally resolves the conflict between moral law and state interest within himself determines whether or not one may call his decision for the state's interest a moral act, whether, as Ranke said, the hero is justified in his own mind. But even then tragic guilt remains."[102]

Here the final ambiguity in Meinecke's concept of *raison*

[99] *Ibid.*, p. 534.   [100] *Ibid.*, p. 542.   [101] *Ibid.*, p. 534.
[102] *Ibid.*, p. 535.

d'état is revealed. He makes the implicit assumption that the statesman will always make the decision "for the state's interest." He never considers the relative morality or immorality of a decision against the state's interest. In "Kultur, Machtpolitik und Militarismus" this assumption was explicit "The statesman can act only in accordance with the principle: *salus populi suprema lex esto.*" In *Staatsraeson*, one might be tempted to say, the only difference was that the explicit assumption receded to the realm of the implicit.

But such a judgment would be misleading. While the concept of *raison d'état* clearly had a personal fascination for Meinecke, he poured the resources of a lifetime of scholarship into a search for effective restraints on its operations, not into an advertisement of its magnificence. And he succeeded in finding the basis for such restraints when he insisted that the statesman must serve God as well as the inevitably subjective and morally ambiguous *salus populi*. If in *Staatsraeson* this basis still seemed insecure in comparison with the imperious and subtle demands of the state ego, it was strong enough to persist and grow stronger. For it was the basis which sustained Meinecke when he broke with the state and nation to which he was so intimately bound. In *Staatsraeson* Meinecke's failure to consider the significance of conduct in which the statesman turned his back on the state was indicative of the tremendous value which he continued to place on nation and state. The inner freedom with which he rejected the *raison d'état* of National Socialist Germany spoke eloquently of the still higher value he placed upon the observance of the moral law.

CHAPTER XI

THE PRIMACY OF THE INDIVIDUAL

MEINECKE began his study of *raison d'état* with the assertion that it was the inexorable law of the state's existence; the statesman had no choice but to obey.[1] His conclusion was different. He warned that the statesman must acknowledge two masters: that he must serve both God and the state. It was this relativization of *raison d'état* and the state which henceforth accented Meinecke's political thinking. The character of an absolute which he had imputed to them in his original proposition continued to exercise a distracting influence. But the consequences which flowed from his final position in *Staatsraeson* were given more and more unequivocal expression.

In *Staatsraeson* itself Meinecke declared the idea of *raison d'état* to be in a state of crisis and that in the contemporary world it confronted forces which it could no longer quite master.[2] An unlucky trinity of militarism, nationalism, and capitalism had provided it with such an abundance of power that its own freedom of movement began to be a disadvantage. The multitude of men and weapons which universal military service and capitalist technology provided was charged with the dynamics of national convictions. The war machines thereby created had proved so destructive in practice that not only the justice but also the utility of violence was called into question. "War in general, that ultimate and most powerful instrument of *raison d'état* . . . had become a demonic force which mocked all restraints. . . . The passions and ambitions of nations united with the new and seductive implements of war to create a pernicious atmosphere in which a lucid and prudent statecraft could no longer flourish."[3]

---

[1] *Staatsraeson, op.cit.*, pp. 1-2. [2] *Ibid.*, p. 529.
[3] *Ibid.*, p. 527. Meinecke had foreshadowed these pessimistic observa-

Modern civilization, which was both cause and effect of the forces of militarism, nationalism, and capitalism, had become so complex and sensitive a mechanism that only with great difficulty could it survive the hammer blows of war. In the realm of international politics, where interests jostled and interlocked with one another, the consequences of any foreign policy became more and more difficult to calculate. Even if statesmen had been always masters of their art, the pressures which an aroused and perhaps irrational public opinion could exercise raised the question whether rational men would be permitted to remain at the helm.[4]

For these reasons Meinecke feared that *raison d'état*, understood as a reasonable—if not completely rational—guide to the security and welfare of the state, faced historical oblivion. But he was not willing to concede that such fears would inevitably be realized. Nor would he seek private solace in looking backward and longing for a vanished era when social, economic, and technological forces were less massive in their impact. "On the contrary, all fruitful thought had to address itself to the question of how one could meet . . . an elemental and unavoidable fate with the tools of reason, how one could mold nature by means of spirit—uncertain whether success was possible, but nonetheless undaunted." And then followed the words which revealed why Meinecke had called Machiavelli's political doctrines great as well as terrible: "It was the ancient struggle of freedom and necessity, of *virtù* and *fortuna*, which Western man now had to carry on in the mightiest dimensions."[5]

Thus the image of Machiavelli reappeared in the ultimate evaluation of *raison d'état* as an admonition that the new and terrifying challenges to political skill were only different versions of the eternal problematic of the state. It warned that any schemes for its permanent solution were likely to be misleading, and it

---

tions in "Staatskunst und Leidenschaften" (1916) in *Probleme des Weltkriegs, op.cit.*

[4] *Staatsraeson, op.cit.*, pp. 517-519.　　[5] *Ibid.*, p. 521.

more than outweighed the ambiguous words with which Meinecke welcomed the League of Nations. All the empiricism, all the skepticism, and all the courage of Machiavelli's spirit would be needed to master the ominous problems of contemporary international relations. But the mighty conflicts arising from them reinforced Meinecke's insistence that these qualities be balanced by a distinctly un-Machiavellian sensitivity of conscience and a conviction that the state could not claim the statesman's sole allegiance.

Restraints on the arbitrary will of the state were imperative, and Meinecke was prepared to accept and encourage any contributions which international law and organization might make to this end. But the diversity of human groups and the absence of trust among them were as undeniably factors of international relations in the world of the 1920's as they had been when Meinecke identified them as first principles of political organization in *Weltbuergertum und Nationalstaat*. Regulatory laws and institutions, therefore, could only be fragmentary and incomplete unless they issued from an imperial authority. Meinecke's old fear that a world state could only be a world tyranny was expressed once again when he observed in regard to the League that it "demanded sacrifices of sovereignty from its members which were tolerable only if all were animated by the same community spirit. . . . But how is this to be guaranteed; that is, who shall watch over [the community]? If the greatest Power assumes this task, the League is immediately in danger of degenerating into a vehicle of that Power's . . . interests."[6]

In the absence of stronger bonds among the states, the most reliable source of restraints Meinecke saw now as always in the personality of the enlightened statesman. And the measure of his enlightenment would be his freedom from stereotypes and preconceptions concerning the nature and scope of his functions and his obligations. The well-spring of this freedom was located in that sense of "divided responsibility to the state and to the moral law" which Meinecke demanded of the statesman.

[6] *Ibid.*, pp. 539-540.

In this context it is proper to inquire into the fate of Meinecke's own preconceptions regarding political organization. His relativizing statesman could hardly manifest the same attitudes which Meinecke himself had displayed in the less problematic past. What were the roles of the state and the nation in the situation created by the greater immediacy of the moral law in Meinecke's thought structure? How much validity could one still ascribe to such a fundamental axiom of Meinecke's political theory as the primacy of foreign policy?

As far as the idea of nationality is concerned, we have already seen Meinecke loosen the bonds which he had forged between state and nation when he subscribed to the idea of the primacy of the state and urged the Slavs of Central and Eastern Europe not to insist on the nation-state as the only political form worth achieving.[7] Simultaneously with the development of this position, stemming from considerations of wartime expediency, came the renewed emphasis on the larger community of Western culture, embracing and nourishing the individual nationalities, which rebuked a narrow and self-centered nationalism.[8] Thus opportunistic motives and enduring cultural and ethical principles united to help extricate Meinecke from a situation in which, for all practical purposes, he had absolutized the nation-state.

In his postwar efforts at reappraisal, Meinecke was forthright in pointing to the basic causes which led him to exalt the nation-state to the status of a value transcending all others. The causes were matters of will and not of intellect. The nation-state was "so precious to the Germans because it had been achieved at the price of so much struggle and bitter sacrifice."[9] What had cost so much to possess must be prized beyond all other goods. "In short," Meinecke wrote in another postwar article on the same theme, "even we historians, whose calling it is to be sensi-

---

[7] Chapter VIII, above.

[8] *Ibid.*

[9]"Die Lage der Geisteswissenschaften in Deutschland," *Lunds Dagbladet*, December 24, 1922.

tive to the truth that all things change, paid little heed to the admonition that 'All earth's goods are illusory.' "[10]

Meinecke's whole intellectual development up to the war years reinforced his political preferences. The relativizing tendencies of historical and political thought to which he himself had mightily contributed only served to give an added fillip to that "spontaneous longing of men for firm and secure ideals. Thus in Germany particularly the historical sciences held fast to the idea of a unified nation-state. . . . And not only the idea itself but also the specific manner in which Bismarck realized it was in a certain way . . . absolutized."[11]

As we have noted before, Meinecke attempted to distinguish between the idea of nationality and nationalism, denouncing the latter as a degenerate outgrowth of the former. But it was precisely the absolutization of the nation-state, to which Meinecke himself pleaded guilty, that made the idea into an ism. Thus it was again an admitted self-criticism when Meinecke wrote of the "war guilt of nationalism." National pride, Meinecke suggested, held Germany back from urging acceptance of the Serbian answer to Austria's ultimatum in 1914 and then working for an Anglo-German détente. Again it was nationalism which prevented the monarchies of Austria, Germany, and Russia from making peace in time. And it was nationalism which made the victor powers press on until Europe was tottering. "Nationalism is the demon which pushed the World War beyond the limits of traditional warfare and statecraft and made it into a war of annihilation. Thus it became the ruin of Europe."[12]

When he looked at the developments which ended in a prostrate Germany, Meinecke was moved to observe that "our national consciousness again began to be unpolitical and to put sentiment ahead of the . . . interest of the state. We became un-

[10] *Nach der Revolution, op.cit.*, p. 55.

[11] "Die Lage der Geisteswissenschaften in Deutschland," *Lunds Dagbladet, op.cit.*

[12] Die Kriegsschuld des Nationalismus," *Neue Freie Presse* (Vienna) July 27, 1924.

political because of a mistaken understanding of politics, because of desires which were very understandable and natural but which were blind and undisciplined."[13]

Here was evidence enough that Meinecke recognized that the nation-state could become an enemy of a viable and creative political system, that it could no longer be touted as the ideal political community. Meinecke's own political conduct and the general philosophical principles to which he gave ever greater emphasis in the years after the publication of *Staatsraeson* furnished further and incontrovertible evidence that he recognized the historicity and thus the relativity of the national idea. Thus as he watched the noxious growth of National Socialist Germany from the vantage point of his enforced retirement, he recorded and shared Goethe's concern that notwithstanding the indispensable role which it had played in cultural development, the nation might prove to be a blind alley from which the spirit of creation could neither advance nor retreat. Only the idea of a national individuality developing in and gaining from relationships with other nationalities offered hope that such a blind alley could be avoided. It was for this reason that Meinecke, in candidly anti-Nazi language, called Goethe's concept of nationality, which stressed such interrelationships, superior to the romantic doctrine of the folk-spirit that explained the personality of the nation wholly in terms of inborn or inbred tendencies of the people.[14]

Despite the fact that Meinecke ultimately went beyond the nation as the final referent for political decision, his earlier commitment to the nation-state had been too far-reaching to permit a detailed reexamination and reconstruction of his position. In the wake of the First World War, at the very time when he conceded that the nation-state had been overvalued by those seeking firm and fast ideals in a world of relativity, he reaffirmed his commitment to it. "Germany's collapse . . . did not destroy for

[13] *Nach der Revolution, op.cit.*, p. 57.
[14] *Historismus, op.cit.*, pp. 572-574. Cf. also p. 511.

us the value of the national state; on the contrary, it became even more deeply anchored in our hearts."[15]

Moreover, the history of the interwar years, if it continued to demonstrate the evils of nationalism in abundance, also made it clear that nation-states persisted as the most important sources of political decisions. The fate of the individual was bound, to an even greater degree than before the war, to that of his nation. The all too apparent inadequacies of the League of Nations only seemed to reaffirm the contention of Ranke to which Meinecke had long ago subscribed: "the great state individualities are the central carriers of political history."[16]

The identification of nation and state, for which Meinecke had striven so untiringly, was realized beyond his expectations. The cosmopolitan idea of the world community was all but snuffed out by the multiplicity of nation-states each claiming supreme allegiance. National sentiment was indubitably anchored more deeply in the heart, but the disasters which it brought with it raised the question whether it might not indeed be a blind alley from which there was no exit. Thus Meinecke was moved to confess that the humbling of the German nation-state which followed so closely on its period of glory was an experience which "has shattered the unqualified faith in the reason and sense of modern historical development and has produced a skeptical pessimism."[17]

Henceforth Meinecke's thought was dominated by the problematics of the nation-state as a political community, but he was unable to suggest an alternative. Even when he reflected on the ultimate degeneracy of the national idea in Hitler's Germany he could not assign nationalism to historical oblivion. Could one find the over-all diagnosis in the famous phrase of Grillparzer—"Humanity–nationality–bestiality?" Were these words an ac-

[15] "Die Lage der Geisteswissenschaften in Deutschland," *Lunds Dagbladet, op.cit.*

[16] *Preussen und Deutschland, op.cit.*, p. 373.

[17] "Die Lage der Geisteswissenschaften in Deutschland," *Lunds Dagbladet, op.cit.*

curate description of the progress of German history from Goethe to Hitler? Despite all his criticism of the extreme forms which nationalism had taken, Meinecke was unwilling to see more than a limited validity in Grillparzer's words. "They only suggested the more general outlines of a development which led from the culture of the few to the unculture of the many."[18] Here Meinecke's censure was aimed more at democracy than at nationalism.

Indeed, in his appraisal of the Hitler era Meinecke identified nationalism and socialism as "the two great waves of the nineteenth century" whose fusion was and continued to be altogether desirable, if not in the terrible and unnatural union which Hitler effected.[19] But at the same time he saw post-Hitler Germany's political future not primarily as a national unit but as an integral part of a larger supra-national federal structure. "Only as a member of a future . . . federation of Central and Western European peoples" could Germany expect once again to lead a creative political life. And even this European federation he saw "under the hegemony of the victor powers."[20]

These piecemeal and contradictory reflections on the significance and prospects of the national idea reveal how far removed Meinecke was from the confident assumption in *Weltbuergertum und Nationalstaat* that no human community had a better claim to the title of "man writ large." They also revealed how difficult he found it to discover a satisfactory surrogate.

Under the impact of events since 1945, Meinecke laid increasing stress on the idea of European integration. Now he found a hearing from his compatriots which was wholly denied him when he warned of the dangers of nationalism in the bitter atmosphere of Weimar and Hitler Germany. Still, when he called for a United States of Europe and demanded that the *raison d'état* of the individual nation-states be merged into a common *raison d'état* of Europe, he acknowledged the profound difficul-

[18] *Katastrophe, op.cit.*, pp. 82-83.
[19] *Ibid.*, pp. 9-18, and 163-164.
[20] *Ibid.*, p. 161.

ties attending such a merger and could only argue that the prospects were not hopeless.[21] His own personality and time did not permit Meinecke to undertake a systematic search for a political framework superseding the nation-state. If this is a criticism, then it must apply to the whole of the contemporary world which is still torn by the fact that nationalism continues to be a phenomenon engendering both hope and despair.

It was an even more difficult task for Meinecke to achieve a measure of perspective in regard to the state. We have already noted in the previous chapter the final ambiguity in his attitude toward the state as he expressed it in *Staatsraeson*. His implicit assumption that the statesman would serve the state's interest regardless of the measure of personal guilt he might thereby incur told eloquently of the reverent light in which Meinecke saw the state. This was hardly surprising in view of the role which he had assigned it as protector and cultivator of cultural values. It is even less surprising if one considers the hundred years of tradition in German political thought which preceded him, a tradition accurately described in the words of Ernst Troeltsch: ". . . it is a characteristic of German history since Hegel and Ranke . . . to regard the state and its power as the measure as well as the center of all values. . . ."[22] Even though Meinecke broke with the tradition, he could not deny his heritage. And even though Hegel and the Hegelian state were the objects of his stern criticism, he was closer to them than he might have wanted to concede.[23]

Finally, Meinecke's reverence for the state becomes less surprising still in view of the fact that much of his case for the indispensability of the state is clearly incontrovertible. The state is in fact a necessity for the preservation and dissemination of

[21] "Ein ernstes Wort," *Der Kurier*, December 31, 1949.

[22] Ernst Troeltsch, *Der Historismus und seine Probleme, Gesammelte Schriften*, vol. III, Tuebingen, 1922, p. 163.

[23] While Meinecke always stressed the difference between the political thought of Hegel and Ranke, he was often moved to comment on the similarity of some of their positions. Cf. *Staatsraeson, op.cit.*, pp. 471, 476-477, 479, 483-484, and 487.

cultural values. It does indeed have a civilizing function which cannot be performed in its absence. And these functions have not been and cannot be performed by an abstract ideal of political organization but only by concrete states with all their advantages and limitations as they have developed in history. Considerations such as these moved Burke to define the state as an unbreakable contract between the living, the dead, and those yet to be born and made Meinecke feel closer to Burke than to almost any other non-German political thinker.[24] It was Meinecke's tragedy that he lived at a time and in a state in which the contract had to be broken if the integrity of cultural values and personal honor were to prevail.

If one had to sum up Meinecke's political thought in a phrase it might be said that he sought to preserve the state contract by every means except an irremedial loss of personal integrity. This at once indicates the irreducible paradox of Meinecke's deep-rooted conservatism and his ultimate commitment to the liberal principle of the unencumbered individual conscience. It also provides some measure of the pain and horror which Germany's embrace of National Socialism held for him.

Meinecke sought to infuse cultural and ethical values into the state in order to make the necessary political contract tolerable to the individual conscience. And yet he was plagued by his own assumption that power was the first requirement of the state. As we have seen earlier, it was one of Meinecke's basic propositions that one could turn to the pursuit of other aims only after power had been secured. The corollary was that in case the power basis was threatened, non-power values would have to assume secondary roles for the duration of the renewed struggle for power.[25]

The same propositions were present in *Staatsraeson*. "Power," Meinecke wrote, "will always be part of the state's essence. But it does not comprise the whole of this essence. Law, morality

---

[24] Cf. Meinecke's discussion of Burke in *Weltbuergertum, op.cit.*, pp. 133-141 and *Historismus, op.cit.*, pp. 272-287.

[25] Chapter v, above.

and religion are also integral parts." And then came the crucial qualification: "At least they demand their place as soon as the state has fulfilled the first basic injunction to be powerful. . . ." Now Meinecke concluded that "power is certainly the most elementary and the most indispensable and persistent essential of the state, but it is not and does not remain the only one. And *raison d'état,* . . . when it has achieved higher levels of development, cannot limit itself to the realization of this first requisite of power but must endeavor to serve those other forces of life" —and then followed another significant observation—"precisely in order to provide power with deeper and stronger foundations and to anchor it in the spirit."[26]

Here again in this intimate fusion of power and non-power values there is an unmistakable tendency to give power the prime position. Although Meinecke criticized Treitschke's famous dictum that the state is power, again power, and still again power, he had difficulty in distinguishing his own position from that of Treitschke.[27] Perhaps one could say that the chief difference was that Treitschke's acceptance of the primacy of power was confident and even joyful while Meinecke's acceptance, even allowing for his fascination with the idea of power, was reluctant.[28] But this would not do justice to Meinecke's ultimate posi-

---

[26] *Staatsraeson, op.cit.,* pp. 496-497.

[27] This may be one reason why Meinecke found it so difficult to subject Treitschke to a thoroughgoing critique and why he felt compelled to defend and explain Treitschke's views. In addition to Meinecke's discussion of Treitschke in *Staatsraeson* (pp. 488-510), see his articles in the *Historische Zeitschrift:* "Heinrich von Treitschke" (obituary) (volume 78, 1897, pp. 111-114), Reviews of Max Cornicelius' edition of *Heinrich von Treitschkes Briefe* (volume 114, 1914, pp. 147-151 and volume 123, 1921, pp. 315-321): and "Treitschke und die Historische Zeitschrift" (volume 150, 1934) reprinted in *Vom geschichtlichen Sinn, op.cit.,* pp. 120-134.

[28] A Nazi attack on Meinecke's attitude toward power is instructive if misleading: "He [Meinecke] is simply afraid of power. To him . . . it is terrifying and cruel, it is the elemental, blind, crude, nature-bound, animalistic, brutal, dangerous, irrational, demonic and incorrigible force which the spirit must first restrain and then make moral. That means

tion, the beginnings of which were already apparent in *Staats-raeson* when he reproved Treitschke for assuming that among the myriad relative truths the historian could at least count on a few absolutes "such as the truth that the state is power."[29]

Meinecke's resistance to the Treitschke doctrine can be derived in the final analysis from his reliance on the Rankian concept that the state joined power and non-power values in an inseparable union. The state was one of the great super-individual personalities which Ranke saw as an original admixture of the "material and spiritual"—" 'not to be derived from any higher principle.' "[30] This formulation implied that neither power nor moral values could claim temporal primacy in the history of the state. It also implied that the thesis which asserts "the state is power" does violence to the true nature of the state.

If this position made it possible for Meinecke to deny the primacy of power, however, we have seen how difficult it was for him to adhere to it consistently. Moreover, if the state was not simply power, the temptation to absolutize it was even greater. The temptation exerted its influence once more at the point of Meinecke's culminating arguments designed to relativize the state. Against his call to put an end to "the false idolatry of the state"[31] stood Meinecke's insistence on its qualitative distinction from other human institutions—a distinction that once again gave it an aura of the absolute. Here he found the qualitative differentiation in the proposition that the violation of the rules of a non-state institution compromised only the trans-

---

to rob power of its specific nature." (Ernst Krieck, "Schoepferisches Epigonentum?" in *Voelkischer Beobachter*, July 14, 1935, p. 5.)

[29] *Staatsraeson, op.cit.,* p. 503. Cf. also Meinecke's reiteration of this charge against Treitschke in *Katastrophe, op.cit.,* pp. 83-84, in which Treitschke is described as having participated in that error of the German spirit which thought it had conquered a metaphysical realm with the concept of *Realpolitik* but which in fact had only succeeded in giving to a very earthy phenomenon "the dignity of the metaphysical."

[30] *Ibid.,* p. 477. The quotation from Ranke is from his "Politisches Gespraech."

[31] *Staatsraeson, op.cit.,* p. 537.

gressor. The norms themselves were unaffected. The state, how-ever, was constantly fated to violate its own norms, for history had demonstrated again and again that violence and the desecra-tion of law and custom had been the state's necessary resort in its quest for security: "It seems, then, that the state must sin. ... This is the terrible and shattering fact of world history: it cannot consummate the civilization of the very human com-munity which encompasses, protects and promotes all the other communities, which thus comprises the richest and most vari-egated cultural content and which therefore should properly set an example for the other communities by the purity of its own being."[32]

These words displayed not only a strongly Hegelian concept of the state as the supreme human community but also a con-fusion about the nature of non-state institutions. On what grounds did Meinecke assume that the church, the club, the business organization never violated their own norms and that these norms remained unadulterated in the face of individual transgressions? Indulgences, exceptions, and special considera-tions are an integral part of the history of any human associa-tion, and their use and limitation play a central role in determin-ing the vitality and durability of the association.

Here Meinecke enmeshed himself in a curious contradiction. As soon as he had given a qualitative distinction to the state, he reduced it again to one of degree by conceding that every human institution was dependent on power. The state differed only in that the other communities were not usually equipped to exercise physical power and were thus more easily moralized and less subject to corruption.[33] This was a perfectly tenable position, but it ruled out the thesis of a qualitative difference. Yet Mei-necke proceeded to derive from this second position the postu-late that the state was unique in its inability to achieve even a theoretically pure set of norms because its *raison d'état* re-peatedly forced it beyond the limits of law and morality. On the

[32] *Ibid.*, pp. 14-15.   [33] *Ibid.*, p. 16.

other hand, Meinecke elsewhere recognized that in every supra-individual community there was a *raison* which could be "cold" and "heartless" toward human values.[34] Clearly the theoretical norms of such communities could not be so essentially different from those of the state. If Meinecke felt obliged to assert that "the state must sin" he might as well have expanded his thought to the proposition that man must sin.

What makes the paradox so puzzling is that Meinecke did in fact make such a proposition by implication when he observed that while *Staatsraeson* sought to show how considerations of power and self-interest tainted all the state's actions, "one can also demonstrate [this process] in all personal conduct. . . ."[35] With these words Meinecke placed all personal and super-personal norms within the same ethical framework. This was precisely his explicit objective in his refusal to subscribe to the "higher morality" concept which he found in Frederick the Great, Fichte, and Hegel: "The doctrine that there is an ethic peculiar to the state . . . is misleading. For it refers to only an isolated expression of a far more universal phenomenon, namely, the conflict between an individual and a universal morality."[36]

Enough has been said to lend support to a criticism of Meinecke's thinking about the state identical with the criticism made in regard to his concept of the nation. The source of all these paradoxes and contradictions was located in Meinecke's own search for an absolute value among the relativities of history. In *Staatsraeson* he saw the state as only one among many supra-individual communities: ". . . the state is an amphibian that lives in both the ethical and natural worlds. And all men and human institutions are also such amphibia."[37] But Meinecke followed Hegel, Ranke, and Treitschke—and Machiavelli—in perceiving the state as the most important of these communities. He wrote of Hegel that "his keen sense of reality recognized [the state] as the mightiest and most efficacious, all-pervading factor in human history. What his empiricism discovered, his

---

[34] *Ibid.*, pp. 507-508.   [35] *Ibid.*, p. 534.   [36] *Ibid.*, p. 533.
[37] *Ibid.*, p. 20.

idealism had to sanction."[38] Meinecke might almost have written this of himself, for in *Staatsraeson* he came close again and again to accepting as a practical solution to historical relativity a heirarchy of values culminating in the state.

The only consideration which prevented Meinecke from seeking final philosophical refuge in an absolutization of the state was his old and deeply-rooted commitment to the dignity of the individual. In *Das Zeitalter der deutschen Erhebung* he had defined the supreme task of civilization as the reconciliation of "the inalienable rights of the individual . . . with the stern and unyielding demands of the . . . egotistic and domineering state."[39] In the same book, as we have noted, he went still further and identified "the inner freedom of the human being [as] the highest of all values."[40] When the crushing pressures of war began to open great fissures in the German state, Meinecke took his stand with those who put internal freedom before external power. In joining the founders of the embattled *Volksbund fuer Freiheit und Vaterland* Meinecke wrote "But before the word Fatherland . . . we have put the word freedom, because only a free Fatherland can give the full measure of happiness to the national community."[41]

Throughout his writings, Meinecke reverted to this position. As the war entered its final year Meinecke voiced his concern that the individual was in danger of losing the status of an end in himself, and he repeated Humboldt's prescient warning directed specifically to the state that "the man must not be sacrificed to the citizen."[42] Meinecke again turned to Humboldt's individualism for support against the state in the almost equally critical year of 1920. "For what he said regarding the dangers with which the state threatens the individual is eternally true. Today every thinking person senses it. There will always be those silent hours when the innermost feelings of the human

[38] *Ibid.*, p. 435. [39] *Erhebung, op.cit.*, p. 125. [40] *Ibid.*, p. 52.
[41] *Um Freiheit und Vaterland, op.cit.*, p. 27.
[42] "Persoenlichkeit und geschichtliche Welt" (January, 1918) reprinted in *Staat und Persoenlichkeit, op.cit.*, p. 17.

being will passionately revolt . . . against the mechanized and mechanizing will of the state, whether it has the characteristics of the authoritarian or the popular state. And the loftiest political idealism will always have to admit that in every state there is an element of the Leviathan."[43]

The note is sounded once again in 1932. "It has never seemed satisfactory to me that the political historian should permit an exaggerated emphasis on technique to cause him to restrict his attention to the state in his probings into historical change and development. This can lead all too easily to a point where the human being is reduced to the status of a mere instrumentality of [the state's] progress. . . . To me the ideal historical method sees the bipolarity [of individual and super-individual] in all historical events and recognizes the creative personality as the primary factor in the development of all super-individual forces, whether political, social or economic."[44]

Shortly after the publication of *Staatsraeson*, Meinecke defined the relationship between state and individual in a way which sustained all of his subsequent political thought: "Next to the commandment to elevate one's own spiritual and moral personality, the moralization and spiritualization of the state in which one lives . . . is the greatest challenge which can be directed to man's [capacity for] ethical conduct. This is true because the state is the most comprehensive and powerful of all life's communities . . . and because the human being striving for fulfillment can breathe freely only in a state which is [also] seeking its consummation."[45]

[43] "Wilhelm von Humboldt und der deutsche Staat" (August, 1920), reprinted in *Staat und Persoenlichkeit, op.cit.*, p. 88.

[44] Foreword to *Staat und Persoenlichkeit, op.cit.* It is worthy of note that in this same foreword, written in 1932, Meinecke expressed the hope that his study would "serve the free state as well as the free personality."

[45] "Kausalitaeten und Werte in der Geschichte" (1925) reprinted in *Staat und Persoenlichkeit, op.cit.*, pp. 51-52. The same idea is expressed in "Treitschke und die Historische Zeitschrift" (1934) reprinted in *Vom geschichtlichen Sinn, op.cit.*, p. 126: "next to the duties which the in-

These were clearly testimonials to the primacy of the individual over the state, and they found their culmination in the structure of Meinecke's final great work, *Die Entstehung des Historismus*. The book was dominated by the spirit of Goethe—a cosmopolitan spirit, highly ambivalent in its attitude toward nation and state and toward historicism itself. It is symbolic of Meinecke's own greatness of spirit that he found the deepest wells of human understanding in a philosophy and a man who could never muster wholehearted enthusiasm for those values which were so close to Meinecke's own heart. He had to transcend many barriers of differing sentiment in order to stand with Goethe on the principle that "the creative human being . . . was the main thing, the creator more precious . . . than the creation."[46] It was this commitment to and identification with the spirit of Goethe which led Meinecke to his ultimate position that placed the individual above the state. In *Weltbuergertum* and *Staatsraeson* Meinecke's intellectual insights and subjective preferences tended to make nation and state absolute and loyalty to them unconditional. With the complete perversion of both in Nazi Germany, the idea of such a loyalty became intolerable for him. Over the years Meinecke's relationship to his state had changed from affirmation to criticism to enmity. This development did not deny Meinecke's thesis of the intimate union between the individual and his political community, but it did demonstrate that the individual could make the crucial decision determining the nature of the union. It was in this sense that the creative human being was superior to the super-personal forces which constituted his heritage and environment.

Meinecke's conclusion that individual human beings must be the judges of their super-individual environments necessarily rested on the assumption that men are capable of transcending those environments. The positing of such a transcendent capacity, in turn, facilitated an ultimate clarification of the cause and

---

dividual soul owes to the divine, it is the supreme and most imperative moral duty to live for one's state and people."

[46] *Historismus, op.cit.*, p. 611.

effect relationship of the individual to the super-individual forces. Nation and state, those super-individual forces to which Meinecke had devoted so much of his thought, had been assigned the qualities of great collective personalities. It was this endowment of the nation-state with the characteristics of a mighty and indivisible personality, the identification of the nation-state as the true macrocosm of individual man, which contributed so profoundly to Meinecke's tendencies to subordinate the individual to the collective and to embrace a deterministic interpretation of human existence.

Nation and state, and culture and religion as well—all these were super-individual personalities animated by a unique spirit and developing according to their own tendencies. This thesis was at the core of Meinecke's concept of historicism and the root of his objection to the universalistic and standardizing doctrines of natural law. We have seen Meinecke succumb to and then resist claims to the absolute loyalty of the individual which the great collective personalities, no less than the abstract doctrines of natural law, tended to assert. But only among the latest of his theoretical writings[47] did he state the explicit philosophical basis for the rejection of absolute commitments. Here Meinecke identified the individual not only as judge but also creator of the super-individual personalities. If the collective individuals evolve according to their own tendencies, they "obviously do not evolve by themselves. . . . They are created by men." Their origin and evolution are products of "the actions of the human being, of the totality of the personalities by which they are supported."[48] If there is a state personality or national character it is a human heritage which is absorbed by individual personalities, conditioning them but also being conditioned by them. The very existence of the super-individual is dependent upon the individual's decision to accept, alter, or reject it. This final clarification of

[47] "Ein Wort ueber geschichtliche Entwicklung," in *Aphorismen und Skizzen zur Geschichte, op.cit.* This essay was written in 1941 or 1942. Cf. p. 92, footnote 2.

[48] *Ibid.*, p. 104.

terms dispelled all semblance of that mysticism in the concept of the collective personality which has plagued so much of political thought and which reached its apogee in Hitler's Germany.

It also revealed the intellectual root of Meinecke's profound abhorrence of the National Socialist state. His subjective antipathy to Nazi methods was joined by an intellectual resistance to the demands of the totalitarian state for absolute obedience and the right to use any means to achieve power. Thus he repudiated the *raison d'état* of the Third Reich and made common cause with those who conspired to destroy it. Of the participants in the conspiracy against Hitler Meinecke wrote, "They have shown the world that there were still forces in the German Army and people that refused to submit like dumb animals, that possessed the courage of martyrdom."[49]

There was a value beyond the state which could not be sacrificed. All the glittering feats of power and foreign policy—even had they proved lasting rather than transient—could not justify "the sacrifice of the sense of decency. . . . What is a man profited, if he shall gain the whole world, and lose his own soul?"[50] These biblical words rejected the primacy of the state. They were the basis of Meinecke's final position that the only possible answer to a state whose necessities had become a moral enormity is treason.

It has become apparent enough that Meinecke developed an intimate relationship between the doctrine of the primacy of the state and the doctrine of the primacy of foreign policy. The explicit rejection of the former was bound to have an impact on his ultimate appraisals of the latter. Since the primacy of foreign policy was so specifically and peculiarly central to Meinecke's thought, it is appropriate that we now inquire into the fate of this doctrine in the final maturing of his political reflections.

As we have seen, Meinecke long assumed that the greatest threat to a state's welfare derived from its external environment.[51] This assumption was expressed again and again in *Staats-*

---

[49] *Katastrophe, op.cit.*, p. 150.
[50] *Ibid.*, p. 152.   [51] Chapter v, above.

raeson. It appeared in such formulations as that which spoke of
the "recognition that power—understood as the capacity for self-
assertion *vis-à-vis* other states—was the first and most essential
property of the state. This was the governing [reality] for all
practical *raison d'état.*"[52]

It also appeared in more complicated form. Meinecke had asserted that the state could not be ethically pure even in theory
because one had to concede the state's right in certain circumstances to violate ethical standards in the pursuit of security.
He saw the great bulk of these violations occurring in the realm
of international politics. Meinecke then proceeded from this un-
objectionable observation to the incautious generalization that
"the compulsive force which leads the state beyond law and
morality . . . is to be found in the external and not in the internal
actions of states. In the internal affairs of the state, *raison d'état*
can coexist harmoniously with law and morality . . . because
no other power contests the state's power."[53]

Meinecke immediately pointed out that the state's power had
not always been unopposed by domestic forces and that every
revolution renews the temptation and opportunity to use violent
and immoral methods in internal politics. But this qualification
was more of an aside than an integral part of his theory of the
state. It was the "temporary deviation" from Ranke's "natural
law" that "the internal constitution and development of the state
are subordinated to the compulsions generated by the struggle
for power and independence in the outside world."[54]

One can here detect a process in which Meinecke has been
led to commit the very act that his critical understanding most
vigorously condemned. He observed the unique circumstances
of his own times before the advent of Hitler and saw the greatest
threat to cultural values in international conflict. And he noted
that at least the victor powers of World War One were immune

[52] *Staatsraeson, op.cit.,* p. 440.

[53] *Ibid.,* p. 17.

[54] Cf. Chapter v, above, and "Ranke's politisches Gespraech" (1924)
in *Vom geschichtlichen Sinn, op.cit.,* p. 30.

to internal revolution. Thus he yielded to the temptation to generalize that Ranke had discovered a natural law in his doctrine that the internal issues of revolution and reaction were secondary to and dependent on the course of world politics.

This is a necessary but not sufficient explanation for Meinecke's long-time acceptance of the primacy of foreign policy. Meinecke was obviously aware, as we have noted, that internal struggles within the state had in the past and could in the future both constitute the state's chief political problem and call forth all the norm-defying qualities of *raison d'état*. Many of his contemporary reflections on the German war effort and subsequent defeat and revolution of 1918 displayed a very intense awareness of the crucial role played by internal political structures in the realm of foreign policy. He could hardly have been more forthright than in his negative response to the proposition that German wartime policy necessarily had to aim toward annexations in the name of security: "The first and most necessary security which Germany needed . . . was security from the revolution that threatened us should the masses lose faith in the necessity of the war. One must test and make safe the foundations of the house before one thinks about adding a tower to it."[55]

We have already seen the vigor with which Meinecke devoted himself to domestic reforms during the war years in the conviction that a change in the internal political balance might be the deciding factor making for victory or defeat. Above all, we saw him slowly developing a position in which foreign policy functioned as the servant and not as the master of domestic

[55] *Nach der Revolution, op.cit.*, p. 133. On the other hand, one can find statements made in the same period in which the primacy of foreign policy is strongly urged. Cf. pp. 25-26 of *Nach der Revolution* in which Meinecke quotes with approval the newly-fallen (July 1918) German foreign Minister Kuehlmann: " 'Revolutions have their origin in errors of foreign policy. When the classes which have been entrusted with national leadership fail to understand their function and are unable to find the way to peace, they lose authority in the eyes of the masses and the whole edifice collapses.' " (Meinecke identified the words as Kuehlmann's only later when he wrote his memoirs. Cf. *Erinnerungen, op.cit.*, p. 251.)

politics.[56] But it was also true that he continued to subscribe to the principle of the primacy of foreign policy long after World War One.[57]

Not until after the Second World War did Meinecke explicitly criticize Ranke's doctrine.[58] Along with shifts of emphasis in his interpretation of the German revolution of 1848, Meinecke called for revisions in the "natural law" which Ranke had discovered "There has been much talk since Ranke of a primacy of foreign policy which is supposed to exercise a formative and dominating influence upon domestic affairs. I believe that this doctrine, while containing an indisputable kernel of truth, today requires revision and certain qualifications. The motives as well as the effects of foreign policy—and particularly whether its success is to be lasting or only temporary—depend to a considerable extent upon the inner coherence and sturdiness of the individual state, upon the type and degree of a common spirit which animates it."[59]

Actually, Meinecke already expressed the substance of this view during the First World War. Why could he not find the same words of criticism for the doctrine then? The evidence points to the answer that Meinecke could not criticize it without questioning profounder values which still retained for him the status of near-absolutes. The idea of the primacy of foreign policy was intimately related to the often confusing distinctions which Meinecke made between state and non-state organizations. Both kinds of distinctions—between the state and non-state organizations and between external and internal politics—resulted from

---

[56] Chapter VIII, above.

[57] Chapter V, above.

[58] Meinecke did speak out during the Hitler period against a misinterpretation of Ranke's position in regard to the primacy of foreign policy. But his defense of Ranke was unconvincing, and at all events he did not call for a revision. Cf. *Aphorismen und Skizzen zur Geschichte, op.cit.,* pp. 79-81.

[59] "The Year 1848 in German History; Reflections on a Centenary" in the *Review of Politics,* vol. 10, October, 1948, p. 489. This article, translated by Hans Rothfels, appeared in Germany as a separate publication under the title *1848: Eine Sekulaerbetrachtung,* Berlin, 1948.

Meinecke's deep-rooted commitment to the nation-state as the ideal political community. *Staatsraeson* was in many respects a far-reaching criticism of the conclusions which Meinecke had reached in *Weltbuergertum und Nationalstaat*. But it did not finally break with the basic supposition that the nation-state represented the culmination of all previous political systems and that it was supreme among all the relative values of the temporal world.

Viewed in this light, the nation-state became "the symbol of an eternal value"[60] whose significance far transcended the aims of other human institutions, including the factions which constituted its own internal body politic. Here again the state emerges as a mighty super-individual personality whose consummate form is found in the nation-state. Once this form was achieved, it was difficult to conceive of the state in any other way than as an indivisible unit. "For that law which requires the assertion of power and of the self, which forces all states to adapt their domestic institutions [to its dictates], is only an effect and emanation of a still higher and more comprehensive reality in the life of states. That is that each state is characterized by a singular and inimitable way of life, that each is a unique spiritual being, an individual with an organizational and creative principle derived from the hidden depths of its own life. . . . Each state seeks to realize its own immanent ideal. In the process it can degenerate, take ill, grow old and expire, but in the interval granted it can only seek to develop its individuality to the limit of its possibilities."[61]

This was Meinecke's description of Rankian political theories, but it is clear that he long found them in harmony with his own innermost convictions. For, he asserted, these concepts of the state provided the basis from which to rebut the idea of natural law he had so long condemned as a fundamental source of error

[60] *Staatsraeson, op.cit.,* p. 13.
[61] "Ranke's politisches Gespraech" in *Vom geschichtlichen Sinn, op.cit.,* p. 31.

in political thinking.[62] Ranke saw each state as a collective individuality combining values of both power and spirit in a unique and irreplaceable expression of life. This was the great philosophical and ethical answer to the natural law doctrine which posited an ideal state to whose constitution all the concrete states were expected to conform.

It was just the claim of universality, the endeavor to impose uniformity on a protean world, which offended Meinecke's profoundest sensibilities as an historian, a political thinker, and a German. Against the abstract norm of an ideal state he pitted the concrete state of reality in the name of empiricism and intellectual honesty. Here he wholeheartedly followed the footsteps of Machiavelli in his preference for dealing with the world as it is rather than the world as it ought to be.

And over against the idea of uniformity Meinecke placed the idea of individuality, "an individualizing rather than a generalizing approach" to human affairs, as he defined historicism.[63] Such an approach, as we have observed, saw truth expressing itself not in generalities but in particulars. To Meinecke this method of viewing history and politics was "one of the greatest revolutions in human thought." "Herder, Goethe, Wilhelm von Humboldt, the Romantics and Ranke are the spiritual fathers of the idea of individuality. . . ."[64]

In view of these sentiments, it is superfluous to say that Meinecke was not prepared to abandon the philosophy of individuality. The concept of individuality was the key idea with which Meinecke operated in his search not only for political understanding but also for the meaning of history as a whole. He was committed to treating all emanations of the principle of individuality, whether personal or superpersonal, as ends in themselves. In the face of such a commitment, as we have noted at

[62] Chapter II, above.

[63] *Historismus, op.cit.,* p. 2.

[64] "Ernst Troeltsch und das Problem des Historismus" (1923) reprinted in *Schaffender Spiegel, op.cit.,* pp. 219 and 221-222. This article was also reprinted in *Staat und Persoenlichkeit, op.cit.*

the outset of this study, any attempt to subsume these individualities into general categories, any attempt to establish typologies, must bring with it enormous difficulties. Above all, to assign them places in a normative hierarchy would be an undertaking whose hazards are best suggested in the admonition to "judge not, that ye be not judged."

Yet the human being must constantly make judgments or be condemned to inanition. To deal successfully with the dilemma posed by the conflicting imperatives of passing and avoiding judgment one must fashion his verdicts with a sense of their inevitable fallibility and temper them with understanding for the thing judged. In order to fulfill these requirements, however, one must not permit his valuations to lie concealed in the substructure of his thought and action but must examine them in the full light of consciousness. We have seen Meinecke register both successes and failures in this supremely difficult endeavor. Now we must observe its relationship to his concept of the primacy of foreign policy in the period before he called for its revision.

Meinecke observed with pride as well as concern that the philosophy of individuality with its attack on natural-law doctrines was for the most part restricted to the German world of ideas. And since it was the essence of this philosophy to perceive individuality and uniqueness as valuable and desirable and not something to be overcome in the name of some abstract normative standard, Meinecke was moved to defend the unique German world of ideas not only because he was part of it but also as a matter of principle.

In his innermost thoughts Meinecke visualized the war of 1914-1918 as a struggle between two great sets of values. Each had its unique worth, but for him the German heritage was clearly superior. Precisely because it implied an absolutization of German culture, however, Meinecke was not fully capable of admitting that this was his root judgment. It disturbed his concept of an international society in which each participant had as good a claim to moral and cultural justification as any other. For the best of reasons, perhaps, Meinecke was here unable and unwilling to remove this basic preference from the wrappings of its subconscious context. Yet his failure to objectify this relationship to his German nationality made his path toward an objective evaluation of politics a still more arduous one.

One need only recall with what passion, idealism, and occasional recklessness Meinecke played his part in the struggle between Germany and the external world. "What an intimate connection there was," Meinecke wrote, between the idea of individuality and "the peculiarly German concept of the state with which we proudly confronted a world in war. And of course it was to be expected that our desire to be different from the rest of the modern civilized world would be anathema to a way of thinking which believed that reason expressed itself in universals and not in individualities."[65]

The supreme challenge to the way of life and thought which Meinecke held dear he saw as emanating from Germany's foreign enemies. It followed that the supreme objective was to "save Germany, because Germany's mortal danger was and is the mortal danger to our spiritual world."[66] The relationship between political structure and cultural value was so intense that one could not be destroyed without imperilling the existence of the other. The great collective individuality, the community of power and spirit, had to be defended as an indivisible unit. The law of its self-assertion in the external world was identical with the "natural law" of the primacy of foreign policy.

Here we are plagued by paradox once again. Meinecke did not find an exact correlation between the welfare of German culture and the preservation of Germany's unique political system. As we noted earlier, however intricate the connection between the two, Meinecke always refused to posit an identity between state and culture.[67] This refusal was only one expression of his basically dualistic philosophy which resisted the Hegelian

[65] *Ibid.*, p. 223.

[66] Meinecke's introduction to a posthumous publication of Ernst Troeltsch's *Spektator-Briefe, op.cit.*, p. v.

[67] Chapter VI and X, above.

synthesis of the real and the ideal. Hence politics and culture were fundamentally autonomous spheres of human life, interdependent and yet independent. "The unknown x," Meinecke wrote, "which at once explains this unity and polarity, we shall leave unsolved, because it is insoluble."[68]

With the coming of National Socialism, however, Meinecke finally exposed the nerve of his deep-rooted preference for his German heritage in a way which defied the proposition of a theoretically insoluble relationship between state and culture. He now was moved to observe with anguish that he could no longer assume a superiority for his own world of ideas. The world of the Western democracies, despite all the criticism he had leveled against it, had demonstrated a hardier resistance to degenerating influences than had the community of power and spirit which had developed in German history. The Third Reich had succeeded in destroying the "freedom of the soul." In the Western democracies, by contrast, "that basic right for which Western Christendom has sacrificed so much to gain, the right of freedom of conscience and of thought, was not subverted."[69]

Meinecke now fused subjective and objective truth at the highest level of which he was capable. He moved beyond the cultural relativism which was intimately related to but not identical with the idea of individuality. Following his own insistence in *Staatsraeson* upon the necessity of regaining faith in an absolute standard among all the relativities of life,[70] he found such a standard in the proposition of Goethe which stood as a challenge to all relativism: "Only man can do the impossible; he distinguishes, chooses and passes judgment."[71]

If Meinecke once made an implicit judgment in favor of his own inheritance, he now explicitly judged against it. However ambiguous, there was a relationship between the Nazi state and

---

[68] *Staatsraeson, op.cit.,* p. 536.

[69] *Katastrophe, op.cit.,* pp. 130-131.

[70] *Staatsraeson, op.cit.,* p. 542.

[71] Quoted in *Katastrophe, op.cit.,* p. 157, and in several of Meinecke's later writings.

the longer range development of German culture both past and future which could not be denied. If Meinecke could not solve the "unknown x" of this relationship, he felt and responded to the impelling need to take a stand against his own state even though he could not foresee the consequences to the values of his culture. His stand was that even though the state's demise may doom a dear way of life, that risk must be taken in preference to a repudiation of the moral law. In making the choice, Meinecke was reexperiencing in his own life that paradox which he noted long ago in the attitude of the men of the Prussian reform, that those who willed most for the state were most ready to sacrifice it.[72]

The transmitter and interpreter of the moral law was "in Dilthey's words, 'that wondrous capacity in us which we call conscience.' "[73] In the fateful year of 1933, Meinecke said of conscience that despite all the subjective forces and values that use its voice it is "always able to set exact limits to mere subjectivity, arbitrariness and still more sinister temptations."[74] Yet it cannot be overlooked that Meinecke had approached conscience with less certainty only a few years earlier when he warned his Hegelian critic against putting too much faith in what his subjective conscience told him.[75]

The two positions could not be logically reconciled. If Meinecke is open to challenge on these grounds, it can only be said that he himself would have conceded the point and referred to his own confession of faith which paralleled that of Goethe: "How that which seems impossible nonetheless becomes possible, how we perceive sin and salvation intertwined and still are able to distinguish between them in moral action and to choose the good—all this will never be completely explained in logical terms. It must be experienced in order to be understood."[76]

[72] Chapters v and vi, above.

[73] "Geschichte und Gegenwart" (1933) reprinted in *Vom geschichtlichen Sinn, op.cit.*, p. 20.

[74] *Ibid.*, p. 21.   [75] Chapter x, above.

[76] *Katastrophe, op.cit.*, p. 157.

"Only faith can offer the consolation that there is a transcendent solution to life and culture that is to us insoluble."[77]

Whatever else may be said, Meinecke's ultimate reliance on conscience confirmed his ultimate reliance on the individual. He accepted the words of his one-time teacher Johann Gustav Droysen " 'Every man finds absolute certainty only in his conscience; it is his truth and the center of his world.' "[78] This acceptance elevated conscience to the position of supreme criterion in terms of which all human values had only relative claims to allegiance. Conscience alone provided that detachment which prevented the human being from selling his freedom in order to satisfy his desire to worship more massive and tangible emanations of the human spirit. Their very tangibility fated them to join together good and evil in an inseparable union. It was the task of the free individual, guided by conscience, to develop their relative potentialities for good. But the moment freedom and conscience are sacrificed the superpersonal value becomes absolute. The individual no longer has control over the fusion of good and evil which is its central characteristic, and it becomes a false god, a demonic force which can destroy both the idolator and the idol.

In the tension between the conscience and the myriad values of life Meinecke found the polarity which could support and give meaning to all the other polarities which he had posited. Like the other polarities, each element was a necessary component of the relationship. It followed that the imperfect institutions which men created had a legitimacy of their own. From this legitimacy they derived a claim upon the loyalty and conscience of the individual that increased in proportion to the extent that the institutions were themselves permeated with the ideals of men of conscience. In this situation there can be no way to avoid that intimate identification of individuals with such relative values as state and nation—and their *raison d'état* —or with those larger but still limited fellowships in culture or

[77] *Staat und Persoenlichkeit, op.cit.,* p. 46.
[78] Quoted in *Vom geschichtlichen Sinn, op.cit.,* pp. 20-21.

religion. These identifications fate human history to be an end-less drama of tragic conflict in which good and evil are mys-teriously joined. But it is the mission of conscience to attempt to distinguish between them. Only the constant endeavor to "distinguish, choose and pass judgment" can prevent human er-ror from destroying human creativity.

This ultimate primacy of the individual conscience enabled Meinecke finally to divest the nation-state of the aura of the absolute which he had conferred upon it. It was not an in-divisible unit. The human conscience with its powers of analysis was the greatest testimony to the synthetic nature of state and nation. The great values of Meinecke's own culture which the national state had once nourished and latterly degraded were now given their final autonomy. Their surest safety lay in posit-ing them truly as "ends in themselves," emancipated from the matrix of political organization whose relationship to them was at best ambivalent. So long as the state gave warrant of its serv-ice to the values of culture the man of conscience would seek to further the symbiosis of power and spirit, both to infuse politics with the idea of the true, the good, and the beautiful and to em-ploy the political society as a primary and ultimately indispensa-ble means for the diffusion of culture. But he must be on his guard not to transmute the symbiotic relationship into one of identity, and he must demand constantly renewed evidence that the symbiosis will continue to be creative. If such evidence is consistently forthcoming, then the individual can count himself the witness of a golden age. When, however, the evidence is negative, then he must have the courage to turn his back on the existing political society and seek to build anew. If Meinecke re-called that in his youth he felt himself to be "both conservative and revolutionary," one can say here that his maturity and old age gave a progressively more profound significance to both quali-ties.

The man of conscience must be both conservative and revolu-tionary. If history provides him with a heritage in which power and justice coexist in harmony, he must seek to conserve it as the most providential context for the development of human freedom. If such a heritage is not vouchsafed him—or if, as in the case of Meinecke's own lifetime, it disintegrates before his eyes—then he must grasp the two-edged weapon of revolution, and so accept the possibility not merely of personal self-sacrifice but also of the martyrdom of the values which have given his personal existence its light and meaning. His hope, which cannot be confused with certainty, will be that even without the fortunate political nexus these super-personal values, these great collective personalities, will persist and develop in new contexts so long as there are creative individuals to apprehend them and give them new life.

Only after achieving this level of insight did Meinecke feel free to revise the doctrine of the primacy of foreign policy. When the experience of the Nazi state brought home to him the realization that the internal enemy "constricts the soul far more than any foreign master can"[79] the primacy of foreign policy had to give way. As we have seen, Meinecke was willing only to revise, not to abandon it. It still functioned for him as a symbol of the undeniable impact of external relationships upon the domestic culture. It also stood witness to the truth that the fate of individual cultures and societies was but part of the greater process embracing all mankind. But insofar as it could also serve as an insidious disguise for the primacy of power as such, it had to be rejected. Despite all the inconsistencies and contradictions which his thought displayed, one can discern the truth in Meinecke's avowal that the primacy of the spirit, and not of power, was the answer "which I unconsciously bore within me . . . through my whole life."[80] The state must first of all be moral. Not every value may be sacrificed merely to perpetuate the state's existence.

Thus we have found Meinecke's moving steadily toward an acceptance of the full consequences of his own theory of individuality which posited the historicity and relativity of all hu-

---

[79] *Katastrophe, op.cit.,* p. 152.
[80] *Erinnerungen, op.cit.,* pp. 284-285.

man values, including nation and state. If they had to be abandoned when their time was done, Meinecke found consolation in the same theory that proclaimed their relativity: "for it is characteristic of the innermost nature of divinity, insofar as we can understand it, that it reveals itself to the human conscience not only in long familiar patterns and precepts; it also appears to us in ever new and unimagined forms."[81]

[81] *Ibid.*, p. 286.

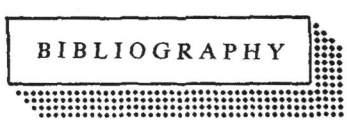

The following bibliography is divided into two main parts. Part I lists writings by Meinecke and Part II writings about him. No claim of completeness can be made for either part, although Part I represents a very comprehensive selection. Insofar as Meinecke's own published works are concerned, only those are included which have directly contributed to the present study of his political ideas. In general, the same limitation has been placed on the listing of published materials in which Meinecke is the subject.

There is a very extensive general bibliography of Meinecke's works prepared by Anne-Marie Reinold and published in the issue of the *Historische Zeitschrift* which was dedicated to the celebration of Meinecke's ninetieth birthday (vol. 174, No. 3, October, 1952, pp. 503-523.)* The Reinold bibliography contains some titles not listed here. At the same time it lacks a number of items which are included in the present bibliography, particularly in section ID. The literature in Part II, of course, has grown considerably since the Reinold bibliography was published.

Walther Hofer's monograph on Meinecke, *Geschichtschreibung und Weltanschauung*, contains a generous listing of writings by Meinecke's contemporaries, both of those who were of his intellectual persuasion and of those who were critics.

PART I[1]

A. BOOKS[2]

Die deutsche Gesellschaften und der Hoffmannsche Bund, J. G. Cottasche Buchhandlung Nachfolger, Stuttgart, 1891.

---

* This bibliography has also been published separately: Anne-Marie Reinold, *Friedrich Meinecke Bibliographie*, Munich, 1952.

[1] Chronological order will be followed within each section of this part.

[2] Publication dates refer to first editions. When a later edition has been used as the basis for page references it will be indicated in parenthesis.

BIBLIOGRAPHY

Das Leben des Generalfeldmarschalls Hermann von Boyen, J. G. Cottasche Buchhandlung Nachfolger (two volumes) Stuttgart, 1896/99.

Das Zeitalter der deutschen Erhebung, Velhagen und Klasing, Bielefeld, 1906. (Fourth edition, Koehler und Amelang, Leipzig, 1941.)

Von Stein zu Bismarck, Verlag Deutsche Buecherei, Berlin, 1907.

Weltbuergertum und Nationalstaat: Studien zur Genesis des deutschen Nationalstaates, R. Oldenbourg, Munich, 1908. (Fourth edition, 1917.)

Radowitz und die deutsche Revolution, E. S. Mittler und Sohn, Berlin, 1913.

Die deutsche Erhebung von 1914, J. G. Cottasche Buchhandlung Nachfolger, Stuttgart, 1914. English translation (in part): *The Warfare of a Nation*, translated by John A. Spalding, Worcester, Massachusetts, 1915.

Probleme des Weltkriegs, R. Oldenbourg, Munich, 1917.

Preussen und Deutschland im 19. und 20. Jahrhundert, R. Oldenbourg, Munich, 1918.

Nach der Revolution, R. Oldenbourg, Munich and Berlin, 1919.

Die Idee der Staatsraeson in der neueren Geschichte, R. Oldenbourg, Munich and Berlin, 1924. English translation: *Machiavellism: The Doctrine of Raison d'État and Its Place in Modern History*, translated by Douglas Scott, New Haven, Connecticut, 1957. This edition contains a general introduction to Meinecke's work by W. Stark.

Geschichte des deutsch-englischen Buendnisproblems, R. Oldenbourg, Munich, 1927.

Staat und Persoenlichkeit, R. Oldenbourg, Berlin, 1933.

Die Entstehung des Historismus, R. Oldenbourg, Munich and Berlin, 1936. (Second edition, Munich, 1946.)

Schiller und der Individualitaetsgedanke, Koehler und Amelang, Leipzig, 1937.

Vom Geschichtlichen Sinn und vom Sinn der Geschichte, Koehler und Amelang, Leipzig, 1939. (Fourth edition, 1942.)

Preussisch-deutsche Gestalten und Probleme, Koehler und Amelang, Leipzig, 1940.

Erlebtes 1862-1901, Koehler und Amelang, Leipzig, 1941.

Aphorismen und Skizzen zur Geschichte, Koehler und Amelang, Leipzig, 1942.

Die deutsche Katastrophe, Eberhard Brockhaus, Wiesbaden, 1946, (Fourth edition, Wiesbaden, 1946.) English translation: *The*

German Catastrophe, translated by Sidney B. Fay, Cambridge, Massachusetts, 1950.

Schaffender Spiegel, K. F. Koehler, Stuttgart, 1948.

Strassburg, Freiburg, Berlin 1901-1919: Erinnerungen, K. F. Koehler, Stuttgart, 1949.

B. ARTICLES AND REVIEWS PUBLISHED IN THE HISTORISCHE ZEITSCHRIFT[1]

"Gerlach und Bismarck," vol. 72, 1894, 44-60.

Heinrich von Sybel (obituary), vol. 75, 1895, 98-104.

"Entgegnung" (auf Lamprecht), vol. 76, 1896, 530ff.

Heinrich von Treitschke (obituary), vol. 77, 1896, 86-90.

"Erwiderung" (auf Lamprecht), vol. 77, 1896, 262ff.

Review of Bruno Gebhardt's *Wilhelm von Humboldt als Staatsmann* (vol. i), vol. 78, 1897, 86-90.

"Entgegnung" (auf Lamprecht), vol. 78, 1897, 334ff.

"Zur Geschichte des Gedankens der preussischen Hegemonie in Deutschland," vol. 82, 1899, 98-104.

Review of Bismarck's *Gedanken und Erinnerungen*, vol. 82, 1899, 282-295.

Review of Bruno Gebhardt's *Wilhelm von Humboldt als Staatsmann* (vol. ii), vol. 85, 1900, 495-501.

"Zur Geschichte Bismarcks," vol. 87, 1901, 22-55.

Review of Hermann von Petersdorff's *Koenig Friedrich Wilhelm IV* and of *Denkwuerdigkeiten des Minister-praesidenten Otto von Manteuffel* (edited by Heinrich von Poschinger), vol. 87, 1901, 499-506.

Review of the Supplement to Bismarck's *Gedanken und Erinnerungen* and of Robert von Keudell's *Fuerst und Fuerstin Bismarck*, vol. 89, 1902, 320-326.

Review of Rudolf Haym's *Aus meinem Leben*, vol. 89, 1902, 317-320.

Review of Alexander Bergengruen's *David Hansemann* and of Anna Caspary's *Ludolf Camphausens Leben*, vol. 92, 1904, 306-309.

Review of the Commentaries of *Ernst Ludwig von Gerlach*, vol. 93, 1904, 488-490.

Review of Hermann Oncken's biography of *Lassalle*, vol. 95, 1905, 97-100.

---

[1] With one or two exceptions, articles which have appeared as reprints in books listed in Section A are not listed separately here. This procedure has also been followed in sections C and D.

Review of Jakob Burckhardt's *Weltgeschichtliche Betrachtungen*, vol. 97, 1906, 557ff.

Review of Paul Hassell's biography of *Josef von Radowitz*, vol. 98, 1907, 180-183.

"Geleitwort zum 100. Bande der Historischen Zeitschrift," vol. 100, 1908, 1-10.

Review of Christoph von Tiedemann's recollections of *Bismarck*, vol. 103, 1909, 378-381.

"Entgegnung" (auf Lamprecht), vol. 104, 1910, 421.

Review of Hermann Oncken's *Rudolf von Bennigsen, ein deutscher liberaler Politiker*, vol. 106, 1911, 190-193.

"Radowitz *de se ipso*," vol. 111, 1913, 133-136.

Review of Max Cornicelius' edition of *Heinrich von Treitschkes Briefe* (vols. I and II), vol. 114, 1914, 47-51.

Karl Lamprecht (obituary), vol. 114, 1914, 696-698.

"Des Kronprinzen Friedrichs Considerations sur l'etat present du corps politiques de l'Europe," vol. 117, 1917, 42-73.

"Luther ueber christliches Gemeinwesen und christlichen Staat," vol. 121, 1920, 1-22.

Review of Philipp Hiltebrandt's *Das europaeische Verhaengnis*, vol. 121, 1920, 118-123.

Review of Carl Schmitt-Dorotic's *Die politische Romantik*, vol. 121, 1920, 292-296.

Review of Max Cornicelius' edition of *Heinrich von Treitschkes Briefe* (vol. III), vol. 123, 1921, 315-321.

"Die Lehre von den Interessen der Staaten im Frankreich Richelieus," vol. 123, 1921, 14-80.

Ernst Troeltsch (obituary), vol. 128, 1923, 185-187.

Fritz Vigener (obituary), vol. 132, 1925, 277-288.

Review of Wilhelm Dilthey's *Leben Schleiermachers* and of the correspondence between *Dilthey und Graf Yorck von Wartenburg*, vol. 130, 1924, 458ff.

Review of Erich Volkmann's *Der Marxismus und das deutsche Heer im Weltkriege*, vol. 132, 1925, 125-129.

Review of Sir Edward Grey's *Twenty-five Years*, vol. 135, 1927, 118-122.

Review of Marianne Weber's biography of *Max Weber*, vol. 135, 1927, 243-245.

Review of Carl Neumann's *Jakob Burckhardt*, vol. 138, 1928, 79-83.

Review of Walter Frank's *Hofprediger Adolf Stoecker und die christlichsoziale Bewegung*, vol. 140, 1929, 151-154.

Review of Gerhard Ritter's *Die Legende von der verschmaehten englischen Freundschaft 1898-1901*, vol. 140, 1929, 404-406.

Review of Julius Binder's *Staatsraison und Sittlichkeit*, vol. 140, 1929, 565-568.

Hans Delbrueck (obituary), vol. 140, 1929, 702-704.

Review of Gustav Wuertenberg's *Goethe und der Historismus* and of Walter Lehmann's *Goethes Geschichtsauffassung in ihren Grundlagen*, vol. 142, 1930, 562-566.

Review of Antonello Gerbi's *La politica del settecento, storia di un' idea*, vol. 142, 1930, 578-582.

Review of Hugo Preller's *Salisbury und die tuerkische Frage im Jahre 1895*, vol. 142, 1930, 587-593.

Review of Rudolf Stadelmann's *Das geschichtliche Selbstbewusstsein der Nation*, vol. 149, 1933, 554-556.

Review of Karl Heussi's *Die Krise des Historismus*, vol. 149, 1934, 303-305.

Review of Koppel S. Pinson's *Pietism as a Factor in the Rise of German Nationalism*, vol. 151, 1935, 116-117.

"Tagebuchdiktate Leopold von Rankes aus dem Jahre 1881," vol. 151, 1935, 332-335.

Review of Walter Frank's *Kaempfende Wissenschaft*, vol. 152, 1935, 101-103.

Review of Alfred Hoche's *Innenaussicht eines Menschenlebens* and of Elly Heuss-Knapp's *Erlebtes aus dem Elsass und dem Reich*, vol. 151, 1934-1935, 596-599.

C. OTHER ARTICLES, SPEECHES AND MISCELLANEOUS WRITINGS

"Liberalism and Nationalism in Germany and Austria" in *The Cambridge Modern History*, vol. XI, New York, 1909, 43-64.

"Ein Appell an die Parteien" in *Der Berliner Dienst* (newsletter for National Liberals), November 29, 1911.

"Ein Blick auf die Weltlage," *Deutsche Volksbote* (Wochenschrift der Nationalliberalen Partei des Grossherzogtums Baden, published in Karlsruhe) January 5, 1913.

"Deutschland und der Weltkrieg," *Das groessere Deutschland*, August 29, 1914, 617-622.

"Der Weltkrieg," *Die neue Rundschau*, Vol. 25, December, 1914, 1615-1627.

"Praeliminarien der Kriegsziele," *Das groessere Deutschland*, July 31, 1915, 1001-1014.

BIBLIOGRAPHY

Antrittsrede, *Sitzungsberichte der preussischen Akademie der Wissenschaften* (Philosophische-Historische Klasse 2), 1915, 496ff.

"Kultur, Machtpolitik und Militarismus" in Otto Hintze *et al.*, *Deutschland und der Weltkrieg*, Berlin and Leipzig, 1915, 616-643.

"Sozialdemokratie und Machtpolitik" in *Die Arbeiterschaft im neuen Deutschland*, Leipzig, 1915, 21-37.

Leopold von Ranke, *Die grossen Maechte* (edited and with an introduction by Friedrich Meinecke), Leipzig, 1916.

Rudolf Kjéllen, *Schweden* (edited and with an introduction by Friedrich Meinecke), Munich and Berlin, 1917.

"Die deutsche Freiheit" in *Die deutsche Freiheit*, Bund deutscher Gelehrter und Kuenstler, Gotha, 1917, 14ff.

Adresse an Herrn Max Lehmann zum fuenfzigjaehrigen Doktorjubilaeum, *Sitzungsberichte der preussischen Akademie der Wissenschaften* (Philosophische-Historische Klasse 2) January 11, 1917, 23-25.

"Zum 18 Januar 1917," *Deutsche Kriegswochenschau*, No. 7, January 21, 1917.

"Kriegsziele Hueben und Drueben," *Deutsche Politik*, vol. 2, June 1917.

Speech of November 14, 1917, printed in *Um Freiheit und Vaterland*, Gotha, 1918, 25-34.

"Vaterlandspartei und deutsche Politik," *Die Hilfe*, no. 47, November 22, 1917.

"Die Ursachen des Deutschenhasses," *Die neue Rundschau*, vol. 29, January, 1918, 13-23.

"Grundfragen deutscher Nationalpolitik," *Die neue Rundschau*, vol. 29, June, 1918, 721-737.

"Zwei Systeme," *Deutsche Politik*, vol. 3, June 7, 1918.

"Verstaendigungsfriede und Heeresleitung," in *Festgabe fuer Adele Gerhard*, June 8, 1918.

Fuer welchen Gueter zog Deutschland 1914 sein Schwert? Schuetzengrabenbuecher fuer das deutsche Volk, Berlin, 1918 (written in September 1918).

"Der Geist von 1813," *Deutsche Kriegswochenschau*, no. 96, October 6, 1918.

"Deutschland und der Friede," *Die Hilfe*, no. 43, October 24, 1918, 506-508.

"Verfassung und Verwaltung der deutschen Republik," *Die neue Rundschau*, vol. 30, January 1919, 1-16.

BIBLIOGRAPHY

"Bemerkungen zum Entwurf der Reichsverfassung," *Deutsche Politik*, vol. 4, nos. 5 and 6, 1919.

"Der 'historische' Anspruch Frankreichs auf das Saargebiet" *Das Saargebiet*, vol. 4, 1919.

"Das preussische-deutsche Problem im Jahre 1921," *Deutsche Nation*, March 1921.

Josef von Radowitz, Schriften und Reden (edited and with an introduction by Friedrich Meinecke), Munich, 1921.

"Volksgemeinschaft," *Der Deutsche* (Berlin) April 8, 1921.

Machiavellis Der Fuerst (vol. 8 in the series *Klassiker der Politik*. Edited and with an introduction by Friedrich Meinecke), Berlin, 1923.

"Hegel und die Anfaenge des deutschen Machtstaatgedankens im 19. Jahrhundert," *Zeitschrift fuer Politik*, vol. 13, no. 3, 1923, 197-213.

"Ueber Spenglers Geschichtsbetrachtung," *Wissen und Leben* (Zurich), vol. 16, April 20, 1923.

"Ein Wort an Frankreich," *Rheinischer Beobachter*, vol. 2, no. 25, 1923, 388-389.

"Wie deine Tage sind, so soll deine Kraft sein," *Die Hilfe*, no. 24, December 15, 1923.

Ernst Troeltsch, *Spektator-Briefe* (with a foreword by Friedrich Meinecke), Tuebingen, 1924.

"Republik, Buergertum und Jugend" in *Die Paulskirche*, Frankfurt (Main), 1925.

"Die Kulturfragen und die Parteien," *Die neue Rundschau*, 1925, 673ff.

Comment on the election of Hindenburg as President of the Weimar Republic. Printed in *Deutsche Einheit* (Hamburg) vol. 7, no. 19, May 9, 1925, 634-635.

"Die deutsche Universitaeten und der heutige Staat," *Recht und Staat in Geschichte und Gegenwart*, vol. 44, 1926, 17-31.

"Heroismus und Demokratie," *Fuehrer-Stimmen* (newsletter of the Demokratischer Zeitungsdienst Berlin), vol. 5, no. 86, October 26, 1926.

"Einige Gedanken ueber Liberalismus," *Wille und Weg* (Berlin), vol. 2, no. 19, January 1, 1927, 441-444.

"Die Weimarer Tagung der Hochschullehrer," *Wille und Weg*, vol. 3, no. 4, May 15, 1927, 77ff.

"Bielfeld als Lehrer der Staatskunst," *Zeitschrift fuer oeffentliches Recht* (Vienna), vol. 6, no. 4, July, 1927, 473-478.

"Zur Geschichte der deutsch-englischen Buendnisverhandlung von 1901," in *Am Webstuhl der Zeit*, eine Erinnerungsgabe Hans Delbrueck . . . dargebracht, edited by Emil Daniels and Paul Ruehlmann, Berlin, 1928, 82-90.

"Kuehlmann und die paepstliche Friedensaktion von 1917," *Sitzungsbericht der preussischen Akademie der Wissenschaften* (Philosophische-Historische Klasse 2) Berlin, 1928, 174-192.

"Petrus Valckeniers Lehre von den Interessen der Staaten" in *Aus Politik und Geschichte: Gedaechtnisschrift fuer Georg von Below*, Berlin, 1928, 146-155.

Speech to the Liberaler Tag im deutschen Reichstag (Berlin, July 1, 1928). (Printed in Dresden, 1928.)

"Zum 18. Januar 1931," *Blaetter der Staatspartei* (Berlin, vol. 1, no. 1, January 5, 1931, 2-5.

"Reichsverfassung und Weltverfassung," *Blaetter des Deutschlandbundes* (Berlin), August 5, 1931, 1-2.

"Keine Fahnenflucht vor der Schlacht," *Deutscher Aufstieg* (Wochenblatt der deutschen Staatspartei), October 30, 1932.

"Bemerkungen ueber Gibbon" in *Reine und angewandte Soziologie: Eine Festgabe fuer Ferdinand Toennies*, Leipzig, 1936.

"A German Calls for Self-Examination," *Christianity and Crisis*, Vol. 5, No. 26, November 26, 1945, 3-4. This is a translation of "Ein Wort zur Selbstbesinnung," published in the *Muenchener Zeitung* in June 1945.

"Ranke und Burckhardt," Berlin, 1948. Published in English in Hans Kohn, *German History: Some New German Views*, Boston, 1954.

"The Year 1848 in German History—Reflections on a Centenary," *Review of Politics*, vol. 10, October 1948, 475-492. (This article, translated by Hans Rothfels, appeared in Germany as a separate publication under the title *1848: Eine Saekularbetrachtung*, Berlin, 1948.)

"Die Stimme des Gewissens" (speech as first rector of the Free University of Berlin at its founding ceremony, November 1948). Published in *Colloquium* (Berlin), vol. 3, no. 1, 1949.

"Irrwege in unserer Geschichte?" *Der Monat*, no. 13, October 1949, 3-6.

"Geschichte und Politik," *Colloquium*, vol. 5, no. 11, 1951.

"Lebenstroester—Betrachtungen ueber zwei Goethesche Gedichte" in *Goethe: Neue Folge des Jahrbuchs der Goethegesellschaft* (Weimar), vol. 16, 1954, 199-212.

BIBLIOGRAPHY

D. *NEWSPAPER ARTICLES*

Vossische Zeitung (Sunday Supplements), November 27 and December 4, 1887, "Willensfreiheit und Geschichtswissenschaft."

Strassburger Post, December 18, 1911, "Die Reichspartei am Oberrhein."

———, January 10, 1912, untitled article.

National-Zeitung (Supplement), January 15, 1912, "Maenner der Wissenschaft ueber die Reichstagswahlen," (Comment).

Breisgauer Zeitung, July 20, 1912, "Zum Hochburgfest der Nationalliberalen Partei."

Strassburger Post, November 8, 1912, "Deutschland und der Balkankrieg."

———, April 25, 1913, "Wehrvorlage und Weltlage."

———, October 28, 1913, "Vor den badischen Stichwahlen."

———, August 5, 1914, "Nibelungentreue?"

Freiburger Zeitung, August 6, 1914, untitled article.

Breisgauer Zeitung, August 9, 1914, "Zur Lage."

Leipziger Tageblatt, January 1, 1915, "Friedensaufgaben."

Frankfurter Zeitung, April 2, 1915, "Preussen und Deutschland."

———, June 12, 1915, "Die Hundertjahrfeier der deutschen Burschenschaft."

Leipziger Tageblatt, October 9, 1915, "Deutschland und die kleinen germanischen Nationen."

———, March 30, 1916, "Unsere Lage."

Zuericher Post, December 18, 1916, "Ein deutscher Demokrat."

Kriegszeitung der Vierten Armee, December 24, 1916, "Und Friede auf Erden."

Koelnische Zeitung, April 29, 1917, "Osterbotschaft, Wahlreform und parlamentarisches Regime."

Vossische Zeitung, May 17, 1917, "Grenzen der Neuorientierung."

Frankfurter Zeitung, September 23, 1917, "Demobilmachung der Geister."

———, October 21, 1917, "Um Elsass-Lothringen."

Koelnische Zeitung, November 14, 1917, "Die Loesung der inneren Krisis."

Frankfurter Zeitung, January 3, 1918, "Der Band zwischen Staat und Massen."

Strassburger Post, February 10, 1918, "Volksbund und Vaterlandspartei."

Dresdener Neueste Nachrichten, August 1, 1918, "Die Forderung der Stunde."

BIBLIOGRAPHY

Dresdener Neueste Nachrichten, September 7, 1918, "Das deutsche Buergertum im Kriege."

Norddeutsche Allgemeine Zeitung, October 27 and November 3, 1918, "Zur nationalen Selbstkritik."

Deutsche Allgemeine Zeitung, November 20 and 30, 1918, "Das alte und das neue Deutschland."

————, December 13, 1918, "Die Forderung der Stunde."

Vossische Zeitung, January 18, 1919, "Hochschullehrer und Parteien."

Deutsche Allgemeine Zeitung, January 19, 1919, "Frankreichs Ansprueche auf das Saargebiet."

————, September 12, 1920, "Der Bund der Erneuerung."

————, January 18, 1921, "Der deutsche Einheitswille."

General-Anzeiger (Frankfurt/Main) March 26, 1921, "Osterbetrachtungen."

Deutsche Allgemeine Zeitung, April 12, 1922, "Geschichtliche Betrachtungen zur Weltlage."

Neue Freie Presse (Vienna), April 16, 1922, "Die Lage des geistigen Deutschlands."

————, June 11, 1922, "Zeichen des politischen Fortschritts in Deutschland."

————, August 6, 1922, "Der Geist der akademischen Jugend in Deutschland; Zur Erklaerung der psychologischen Ursachen des Rathenau-Mordes."

Lunds Dagbladet, December 24, 1922, "Die Lage der Geisteswissenschaften in Deutschland."

Neue Freie Presse, December 24, 1922, "Das Ende der monarchischen Welt."

————, June 17, 1923, "Verzweiflung oder Hoffnung auf Besserung? Das Weltbild der Gegenwart."

————, August 26, 1923, "Duerfen wir hoffen?"

————, April 20, 1924, "Vor den Reichstagswahlen."

————, July 27, 1924, "Die Kriegsschuld des Nationalismus."

————, December 25, 1924, "Schwarz-Rot-Gold und Schwarz-Weiss-Rot."

Berliner Tageblatt, October 14, 1925, "Versailles und Locarno."

Frankfurter Zeitung, November 8, 1925, "Frankreich und Deutschland nach Locarno."

Neue Freie Presse, December 25, 1925, "Der Geist von Locarno."

Hamburger Fremdenblatt, June 15, 1926, "Hochschule und Politik."

Rheinisch-westfalische Zeitung, July 17, 1927, "Die 'Friedensentschliessung' im Lichte 10-jaehriger Erfahrung."

BIBLIOGRAPHY

Neue Freie Presse, June 17, 1928, "Neues Recht und neuer Staat: zum Problem der deutschen Justiz."

Koelnische Zeitung, November 9, 1928, "Das Ende der Monarchie."

———, August 11, 1929, "Ein Tag des Denkens."

———, December 2, 1929, "Mindestmandatzahl fuer die Parteien."

———, August 3, 1930, "Regierung, Parlamentarismus, Staatspartei."

Kolberger Zeitung fuer Pommern, August 29, 1930, "Staatsinteresse ist Volksinteresse."

Koelnische Zeitung, December 21, 1930, "Nationalsozialismus und Buergertum."

———, January 18, 1931, "Das Reich der Zukunft."

Vossische Zeitung, May 1, 1931, "Gedanken ueber Deutschland."

Koelnische Zeitung, January 17, 1932, "Deutschlands Krise."

Stockacher Tageblatt, February 29, 1932, "Waehlt Hindenburg!"

Berliner Tageblatt, March 27, 1932, "Ein Osterwort an die deutsche Jugend."

Vossische Zeitung, July 29, 1932, "Staatsraison."

———, October 12, 1932, "Ein Wort ueber Verfassungsreform."

Saganer Tageblatt, February 22, 1933, "Von Schleicher zu Hitler."

Frankfurter Zeitung, March 28, 1937, "Droysen's Historik."

Der Kurier (Berlin), December 31, 1949, "Ein ernstes Wort."

PART II

Materials in which Meinecke or Meinecke's intellectual milieu is the subject.

Anderson, Eugene N., "Meinecke's *Ideengeschichte* and the Crisis in Historical Thinking" in *Medieval and Historiographical Essays in Honor of James Westphal Thompson*, edited by James L. Cate and Eugene N. Anderson, Chicago, 1938, 361-396.

Anonymous, "Reason of State" (a review of *Machiavellism*, the English translation of *Die Idee der Staatsraeson*), *The Times Literary Supplement*, December 6, 1957.

Anonymous, "Das Testament Bismarcks," *Mitteilungen der deutschen Vaterlands-Partei*, February 20, 1918.

Antoni, Carlo, *Vom Historismus zur Soziologie* (translated from the Italian by Walter Goetz), Stuttgart, 1951.

Barraclough, Geoffrey, Comments on "Irrwege in unserer Geschichte?" *Der Monat*, no. 17, February, 1950, 535-538.

Beard, Charles A. and Vagts, Alfred, "Currents of Thought in Historiography," *American Historical Review,* vol. 42, 1936-1937, 460-483.

Becheyras, A., Review of *Die Entstehung des Historismus, Revue des Questions Historiques,* vol. 132, May-September, 1938, 162.

Beyerhaus, Gisbert, "Notwendigkeit und Freiheit in der deutschen Katastrophe: Gedanken zu Friedrich Meineckes juengstem Buch," *HZ,*[1] vol. 169, 1949, 73-87.

Bilger, Ferdinand, "Ein Beitrag zur Gelehrtengeschichte des spaeten 19. Jahrhunderts: Friedrich Meineckes *Erlebtes, 1862-1901.*" *HZ,* vol. 166, 1942, 99-107.

Cartellieri, A., Review of *Die Idee der Staatsraeson, Jahrbuecher fuer Nationaloekonomie und Statistik* (Jena), vol. 125, 1926, 370-374.

Coker, Francis W., Review of *Die Idee der Staatsraeson, American Historical Review,* vol. 26, 1925, 120-123.

Friedrich Meinecke zum 30. Oktober 1950 von seinem Colloquium (twenty-two typewritten essays by Meinecke's post-1945 students.)

Croce, Benedetto, *History as the Story of Liberty,* London, 1941.

Daniels, Emil and Ruehlmann, Paul (editors) *Am Webstuhl der Zeit,* eine Erinnerungsgabe Hans Delbrueck . . . dargebracht, Berlin, 1928.

Dehio, Ludwig, *Friedrich Meinecke: der Historiker in der Krise,* Berlin, 1952.

———, Review of Walther Hofer's *Geschichtschreibung und Weltanschauung, HZ,* vol. 170, 1950, 331-333.

———, "Ranke und der deutsche Imperialismus," *HZ,* vol. 170, 1950, 307-328.

———, "Gedanken ueber die deutsche Sendung 1900-1918," *HZ,* vol. 174, 1952, 479-502.

Delbrueck, Hans, Review of *Weltbuergertum und Nationalstaat, Preussische Jahrbuecher,* vol. 136, 1909, 433ff.

Diether, Otto, *Leopold von Ranke als Politiker,* Leipzig, 1910.

Elviken, Andreas, Review of *Die Entstehung des Historismus, Journal of Modern History,* vol. 9, 1937, 370-371.

Epstein, Fritz, "Friedrich Meinecke in seinem Verhaeltnis zum europaeischen Osten," *Jahrbuch fuer die Geschichte Mittel- und Ostdeutschlands,* vol. 3. Tuebingen, 1954.

Erdmann, Karl Dietrich, "Anmerkungen zu Friedrich Meineckes 'Irrwege in unserer Geschichte,' und *Die deutsche Katastrophe,*" *Geschichte in Wissenschaft und Unterricht,* vol. 2, 1951, 85-91.

Frank, Walter, "Zunft und Nation," *HZ,* vol. 153, 1936, 6-23.

[1] *Historische Zeitschrift.*

Friedlaender, Fritz, "Friedrich Meinecke—zum siebzigsten Geburts-tag des grossen Historikers," *Central-Verein Zeitung* (Organ des Central-Vereins deutscher Staatsbuerger juedischen Glaubens), December 1932.

Friedrich, Carl J., Review of *Die Idee der Staatsraeson, American Political Science Review*, vol. 25, 1931, 1064-1069.

———, "Die Staatsraison im Verfassungsstaat," *Politische Studien*, vol. 73, May, 1956, 1-15.

Fueter, Eduard, *Review of Erinnerungen, Erasmus*, vol. 5, January 25, 1952, 64-65.

Glockner, Hermann, Review of *Schiller und der Individualitaets-Gedanke, HZ*, vol. 160, 1939, 359-363.

Goetz, Walter, "*Friedrich Meinecke: Leben und Persoenlichkeit,*" *HZ*, vol. 174, 1952, 231-250.

Gooch, George P., "Some Conceptions of History," *The Sociological Review*, vol. 31, No. 3, 1939, 233-247.

———, Commentary on "Irrwege in unserer Geschichte?" *Der Monat*, No. 16, January, 1950, 445-448.

———, Review of *Die Entstehung des Historismus, English Historical Review*, vol. 52, 1937, 340-343.

Heuss, Theodor, Review of *Staat und Persoenlichkeit, Der deutsche Volkswirt* (literary supplement), December 23, 1932.

———, "Grusswort," *HZ*, vol. 174, 1952, 225-229.

Heussi, Karl, *Die Krise des Historismus*, Tuebingen, 1932.

Hintze, Otto, "Troeltsch und das Problem des Historismus," *HZ*, vol. 135, 1926-27, 188-239.

Hoelzle, Erwin, "Ein Meister der Geschichte—zum Ableben Fried-rich Meineckes." (Undated manuscript.)

Hofer, Walther, "Friedrich Meinecke: Eine Skizze," Europa Archiv, vol. 5, March 20, 1950, 2897-2904.

———, "Geschichte und Politik," *HZ*, vol. 174, 1952, 287-306.

———, *Geschichtschreibung und Weltanschauung: Betrachtungen zum Werk Friedrich Meineckes*, Munich, 1950.

———, *Geschichte zwischen Philosophie und Politik*, Basel, 1956.

———, Introduction to the fourth edition of *Die Idee der Staats-raeson*, Munich, 1957.

Holborn, Hajo, "Friedrich Meinecke—zum 70. Geburtstag des His-torikers," *Vossische Zeitung*, October 29, 1932.

———, "Verfassung und Verwaltung der deutschen Republik," *HZ*, vol. 147, 1932, 115-128.

———, Commentary on "Irrwege in unserer Geschichte?" *Der Monat*, no. 17, February 1950, 531-535.

BIBLIOGRAPHY

Holldack, Heinz, "Friedrich Meinecke; das Machtproblem in der neuesten deutschen Geschichte," *Hochland*, vol. 46, 1954, 437-451.

Kaehler, Siegfried, "Friedrich Meinecke: zum Gedaechtnis des Grossen Historikers," *Deutsche Universitaetszeitung*, vol. 9, April 5, 1954, 6-8.

Kessel, Eberhard, "Friedrich Meinecke," *Die Welt als Geschichte*, 1954, no. 1, 1-9.

Kogon, Eugen, Review of *Die deutsche Katastrophe*, *Frankfurter Hefte*, vol. 1, November 1946, 776-779.

Kohn, Hans (editor), *German History: Some New German Views*, Boston, 1954.

Kollman, Eric C., "Eine Diagnose der Weimarer Republik: Ernst Troeltschs politische Anschauungen," *HZ*, vol. 182, 1956, 291-319.

Krieck, Ernst, "Schoepferisches Epigonentum?" *Voelkischer Beobachter*, July 14, 1935, 5.

Latour, C. F., "Portrait of a German Historian: Friedrich Meinecke, 1862-1954," *The Historian*, vol. 27, 1955, 157-171.

Lorenz, Reinhold, Review of *Die Entstehung des Historismus*, *Mitteilungen des oesterreichischen Instituts fuer Geschichtsforschung*, vol. 52, 1937, 98-108.

Mannheim, Karl, "Historismus," *Archiv fuer Sozialwissenschaft und Sozialpolitik*, vol. 52, 1924, 1-60.

Marcuse, Herbert, Review of *Die Entstehung des Historismus*, *Zeitschrift fuer Sozialforschung*, 1937, no. 1.

Masur, Gerhard, "Friedrich Meinecke," *The American-German Review*, vol. 20, 1954, 8-12.

Menzel, Adolf, Review of *Die Idee der Staatsraeson*, *Zeitschrift fuer oeffentliches Recht*, vol. 5, 1926, 124-131.

von Mueller, Karl Alexander, *Zwoelf Historiker Profile*, Stuttgart and Berlin, 1935.

——, Review of *Vom geschichtlichen Sinn und vom Sinn der Geschichte*, *HZ*, vol. 162, 1940, 339-346.

Neumann, Sigmund, "Decision in Germany?" (Review of Friedrich Meinecke's *The German Catastrophe*), *The Yale Review*, vol. XXXIX, Summer, 1950, 735-738.

Oncken, Hermann, Review of *Weltbuergertum und Nationalstaat*, *Forschungen zur Brandenburgischen und Preussischen Geschichte*, vol. 22, 1909, 306-318.

——, Review of *Die Idee der Staatsraeson*, *Deutsche Literaturzeitung*, vol. 47, 1926, 1304-1315.

BIBLIOGRAPHY

———, "Zum siebzigsten Geburtstag von Friedrich Meinecke," *Forschungen und Fortschritte*, vol. 8, 1932, 403-404.

Ritter, Gerhard, Review of *Die Idee der Staatsraeson, Neue Jahrbuecher fuer Wissenschaft und Jugendbildung*, vol. 1, 1925, 101-114.

Rothfels, Hans, *Friedrich Meinecke: Ein Rueckblick auf sein wissenschaftliches Lebenswerk*, Berlin, 1954.

Schmitt, Carl, *Positionen und Begriffe*, Hamburg, 1940.

Schnabel, Franz, Review of *Die Idee der Statsraeson, Zeitschrift fuer Politik*, vol. 14, 1925, 461-464.

———, "Friedrich Meinecke und die deutsche Geschichtschreibung," *Hochland*, vol. 34, no. 2, 1937, 157-164.

Schwartze, E. Review of *Die Idee der Staatsraeson, Archiv fuer Politik und Geschichte*, vol. 6, 1926, 497-503.

Sée, Henri, Review of *Die Idee der Statsraeson, Revue Historique*, vol. 151, 1926, 104-106.

———, Review of *Weltbuergertum und Nationalstaat, ibid.*, vol. 163, 1930, 696-698.

Seeberg, Erich, "Zur Entstehung des Historismus: Gedanken zu Friedrich Meineckes juengstem Work," *HZ*, vol. 157, 1937, 241-266.

Snyder, Louis L., *German Nationalism: The Tragedy of a People*, Harrisburg, 1952.

Spranger, Eduard, "Gedenkworte fuer Friedrich Meinecke," *Bulletin des Presse- und Informationsamtes der Bundesregierung*, no. 102, June 3, 1954, 920-922.

von Srbik, Heinrich, Review of *Die Idee der Staatsraeson, Mitteilungen des oesterreichischen Instituts fuer Geschichtsforschung*, vol. 40, 1925, 356-362.

———, Review of Gerhard Schroeder's *Geschichtschreibung als politische Erziehungsmacht, HZ*, vol. 162, 1940, 335-339.

———, *Geist und Geschichte vom deutschen Humanismus bis zur Gegenwart*, vol. II, Salzburg, 1951.

Staritz, Ekkehart, "Friedrich Meinecke, Geschichte des deutsch-englischen Buendnisproblems von 1890-1901," *Die Buecherschale*, February 1928, 42-51.

Steding, Christoph, *Das Reich und die Krankheit der europaeischen Kultur*, Hamburg, 1938.

Thimme, Friedrich, Review of *Das Zeitalter der deutschen Erhebung, Forschungen zur Brandenburgischen und Preussischen Geschichte*, vol. 20, 1907, 578-581.

BIBLIOGRAPHY

Troeltsch, Ernst, "Das stoisch-christliche Naturrecht und das moderne profane Naturrecht," *HZ*, vol. 106, 1911, 237-267.

————, *Der Historismus und seine Ueberwindung*, Berlin, 1924.

————, *Der Historismus und seine Probleme, Gesammelte Schriften*, vol. III, Tuebingen, 1922.

Veritas, Justitia, Libertas, Festschrift zur 200-Jahrfeier der Columbia University, New York, ueberreicht von der Freien Universitaet Berlin und der Deutschen Hochschule fuer Politik, Berlin, 1954.

Ward, A. W., Review of *Weltbuergertum und Nationalstaat*, *English Historical Review*, vol. 25, 1910, 374-378.

Wentzcke, Paul (editor) *Deutscher Staat und deutsche Parteien*, Friedrich Meinecke zum 60. Geburtstag dargebracht. Munich and Berlin, 1922.

Wolfson, Philip J., *Friedrich Meinecke and the German Nation* (unpublished master's dissertation, University of Chicago, 1947).

————, "Friedrich Meinecke, 1862-1954," *Journal of the History of Ideas*, vol. 17, 1956, 511-525.

INDEX

INDEX

Printed in Great Britain
by Amazon